Antjie Krog and the Post-Apartheid Public Sphere

Antjie Krog and the Post-Apartheid Public Sphere

Speaking Poetry to Power

ANTHEA GARMAN

UNIVERSITY OF KwaZulu-Natal Press

Published in 2015 by University of KwaZulu-Natal Press
Private Bag X01
Scottsville, 3209
Pietermaritzburg
South Africa
Email: books@ukzn.ac.za
Website: www.ukznpress.co.za

ISBN: 978 1 86914 293 3

Managing editor: Sally Hines
Editor: Alison Lockhart
Proofreader: Karen Press
Typesetter: Patricia Comrie
Indexer: Ethné Clarke
Cover design: Nicolene van Loggerenberg, IdeaExchange
Cover photo: Die Burger/Yunus Mohammed/Gallo Images

Printed and bound in South Africa by Interpak Books, Pietermaritzburg

Contents

Acknowledgements

A great debt of thanks is owed to:

The Constitution of Public Intellectual Life research cluster and wider collegiate community at the University of the Witwatersrand: Carolyn Hamilton, David Attwell, Lesley Cowling, Rory Bester, Yvette Greslé, Litheko Modisane, Pascal Mwale, Windsor Leroke, Alan Finlay, Sue van Zyl, Xolela Mangcu, Jane Taylor, Deborah Posel and Leon de Kock.

My other indispensable interlocutors: Mark Sanders, Gillian Whitlock, Ivor Chipkin, Tim Huisamen, Louise Viljoen, Judith Lütge Coullie, Andries Visagie and Joan Hambidge.

The librarians and archivists: Eileen Shepherd, Anne Moon and Debbie Martindale at Rhodes University, Hester van den Bergh at the University of the Free State SA Media Archive, Ann Torlesse at the National English Literary Museum in Grahamstown, the Cory Library, Bernard Monyai at the SABC Sound Archives, the librarians at Times Media and Media24.

My research assistants: Annetjie van Wynegaard and Mia van der Merwe.

My editor: Alison Lockhart.

My family: Brian Garman and Gemma Garman.

The Sonnekus family (Neil, Hanke, Katie and Leo) who gave me a home in Johannesburg for two years in which to write.

My friends and colleagues: Janet Trisk, Linda Schwartz, Gillian Rennie, Theresa Edlmann, Tracy Witelson, Megan Knight, Angie Kapelianis, Rod Amner, Jeanne du Toit, Alette Schoon, Vanessa Malila and Herman Wasserman.

And to Antjie Krog.

Preface

This book has several moments of origin. The most obvious one is my doctoral thesis, which was part of a research project on the constitution of public intellectual life in South Africa at the University of the Witwatersrand (2004–8). But my interest was set in motion much earlier than that, possibly in my early meetings with Antjie Krog in the 1990s, when she was an SABC radio reporter. My first introduction to Krog was at a workshop that my friend Hannes Siebert from the Media Peace Centre set up in 1997 to discuss the challenges the Truth and Reconciliation Commission was posing to run-of-the-mill, everyday, objective news journalism. The second was an interview I did with Krog for *Rhodes Journalism Review* when *Country of My Skull* was published in 1999 to great acclaim from literary critics but quite a lot of dismay and controversy among fellow journalists. Like many other English-speaking white South Africans, I did not know of Krog as a well-established Afrikaans poet and literary luminary and my first encounters with her were in relation to journalism and politics.

Another more indefinable moment of genesis was in my own struggles as a journalist and then as an academic to understand the value of intelligent, thoughtful words put out into the public realm and the political and social power they could have – sometimes. This struggle is not separate from the simultaneous process that I was going through as a white English-speaking South African living through the late 1980s and 1990s, trying to make sense of the enormous shifts going on around me. As a journalist for *The Natal Witness* (1989–96), it felt as if I was at the centre of the political maelstrom of this country as Pietermaritzburg, in what is now the province of KwaZulu-Natal, was engulfed in what is best described as a civil war. But it was not journalism (despite the constant flow of information into our newsroom) that gave me insight and understanding into this very complex and shifting situation. It was the friendships I had made with academics at the university, the 'experts' we turned to for quotes, and the research they were conducting that enlightened in a way I felt that journalism did not.

I was drawn to study again (despite an unremarkable undergraduate degree) and the years of doing an Honour's and then a Master's degree sedimented my fascination with making big ideas and thoughts accessible, useful and understandable beyond the confines of the university. It was the beginning of what has become a very deep and abiding interest in what is now easily spoken of as 'public intellectualism'.

But it was not called that then. When it became clear that to know and understand the African National Congress (ANC) in exile would be a savvy move for the future, groups of 'intellectuals' (so called by news journalists) trekked across the border into once-forbidden Africa (Dakar, Lusaka) to meet with the liberation movement and in particular its 'intellectual' spokesperson Thabo Mbeki, who impressed every journalist with his *savoir faire*. Krog was in one of these groups and the appellation of 'intellectual' stuck, as it did for others in the groups that crossed the border to meet the future.

I suppose the other seminal experience of that turbulent time for me, and this goes further into the past, into the years I spent working with the Christian organisation African Enterprise, was how very powerful talk and conversation were in changing minds and actions schooled in apartheid fear and certitude. I had been part of the Mamelodi Encounters, organised by Dr Nico Smith in the township outside Pretoria, along with 200 other white South Africans at the height of the 1985 state of emergency. I had also been involved in many encounters 'across the colour bar' with teenagers, together with one of my colleagues, Dennis Bailey, and I was keenly aware of how listening to a fellow black South African speak her truth and life experience had rearranged my head and made me a different person, with different ideas about how I should live my life and direct my future.

*   *   *

In the early 2000s I was teaching journalism at Rhodes University in Grahamstown. Mbeki was president and Krog had published her second award-winning book in English about South Africa's transition, *A Change of Tongue*. The air was full of talk about the need for South African public intellectuals to help think the country into a new space. Most vociferous in this talk was Mbeki, who inspired the African Renaissance conference with its focus on the need for a new brand of public intellectual in South Africa and who widened the debate to Africa more generally at two conferences on the subject held in Dakar in 2003 and 2004.

Calls were made in the media for African intellectuals, revolutionary intellectuals, collective intellectuals, organic intellectuals, black and white intellectuals, native and Afrikaner intellectuals, women intellectuals, black women and gay intellectuals to get involved in the national debate.

There were calls to reclaim the intellectuals of the past – as in *African Intellectuals in 19th and Early 20th Century South Africa* by Mcebisi Ndletyana (2008) – and calls to self-proclaim as an intellectual – for example, journalist, academic and book author Xolela Mangcu (2008). Into the fray – and most often through the newspapers – came Max du Preez, Jonathan Jansen, Mathatha Tsedu, Judge Dennis Davis, Suzy Bell, Tim Cohen, AnnMarie Wolpe, John Kane-Berman, Steven Friedman, Fred Khumalo, Nithaya Chetty, Raymond Suttner, Sipho Seepe, Kader Asmal, Adam Habib, Thandika Mkandawire and Themba Sono (among many, many others). The language of 'thought leaders' became common parlance (and was enshrined in a dedicated website for columnists via the *Mail & Guardian* website) and debate intensified about who could consider themselves to have this appellation, who deserved to be listened to and what the actual topics of the national debate were supposed to be. Mbeki, in the weekly email newsletter *ANC Today* of 21 January 2005, was clear about what he thought:

> In South Africa the fight is really about who sets the national agenda. Should it be the African National Congress (ANC) or

should it be the white elite? On the one hand the black majority government believes that it has a mandate to set the country's priorities. On the other hand the white elite believes its role is to provide thought leadership to the black majority. However, this group's real interest is to protect its wealth and lifestyle. This tension manifests itself in many ways.[1]

Another difficult moment in this profusion of talk about public intellectuals occurred with the formation of the Native Club in 2006, announced and explained by former journalist Sandile Memela in an article titled 'Black Brainpower' in the *Mail & Guardian* (2006). He argued for a separate space for black intellectuals to think, debate and formulate ideas without feeling obliged to bow to the persistent white knowledge hegemony or to consider how white people might react to their ideas.

Against this debate, heightened with racial tensions and strongly clashing ideas, it seemed to me quite extraordinary that Krog, an Afrikaans-speaking white South African was acclaimed, given space, frequently asked to make public addresses and was the go-to South African overseas if you wanted insight into the new South Africa and its transition from a very traumatic past. It looked as if some fruitful answers about the country, the shape and health of its public sphere, who could speak and be heard, how literature, journalism and politics affected this and what this all meant could be discovered in a research project that investigated just how Krog had come to have such a powerful platform and speaking voice at this tumultuous juncture in the life of our nation. (And it was a particular time, now that I look back. Jacob Zuma's presidency has brought different questions and arguments to the fore and few people, with the exceptions of Mangcu, Du Preez and William Gumede, continue to talk in the same way about the value and importance of public intellectuals. Not that we have become a calm society in public; we still shout, argue and slander but we do not cast this activity in quite the same way as we did under Mbeki.)

And so in 2004 I undertook a study called 'Antjie Krog, Self and Society: The Making and Mediation of a Public Intellectual in South Africa' as part of the project on intellectual life at the University of the Witwatersrand directed by Professor Carolyn Hamilton. It was a heady moment to embark on such a study as the debate swirled about our heads.

We could arrive in the morning in our shared space in the South East Engineering building and see the debate unfold in the daily newspapers (often in the now defunct but very exciting newspaper *ThisDay*) and discuss its significance for our project as we had our first cup of coffee.

It is important to note that the debate was not only happening in South Africa. It echoed very similar deliberations in the United States, the United Kingdom and Australia about the role that intellectuals should be playing in a rapidly changing world with new, confusing and only partially understood demands. What was interesting about many of these debates was how often Edward Said (1994) and his frequently repeated 'speaking truth to power' was evoked. This was also echoed here in South Africa. Despite the forays into retrieving information about African roots for public intellectual performances, the conversation at the time was guided often by ideas circulating in the Western world and often resorted to Said as evidence for its arguments.

*   *   *

What follows here is my exploration of South Africa's public sphere and the debates about thought leadership in a fraught and intense historic moment through a close focus on one person – a poet, author, journalist and media personality, a white South African woman responding reflexively and with power, putting her ideas into the public realm, through publication or public appearances, interviews or other kinds of interventions (such as editorial pieces and occasional columns).

I want to make a few remarks about how I came to understand and shape the project I embarked upon. Firstly, following Nancy Fraser (1992), I was determined to assume nothing about how the public sphere in South Africa *ought to* or *should* work (and this included suspending judgement about journalism, in particular, which assumes a simple relationship between information made public and politics and ordinary people's ability to affect power with this information). I adopted her words 'actually existing' and sought to describe and understand current phenomena and then to ask questions without prior judgement as to their value.

Jürgen Habermas's (1991) very fine work on the public sphere in the eighteenth and nineteenth centuries in the United Kingdom and

Western Europe I treated, in the words of Craig Calhoun (1992: 41), as 'an indispensable point of theoretical departure'. Habermas's description of the nineteenth-century bourgeois public sphere has often been used as a yardstick for measuring the health of various national public spheres. This approach, used by many in the media normatively, simplifies and ignores context in a most cavalier way and brings into play the desire to prejudge. As a result, the relationship between Habermas's work as an ideal situation and the reality before us often leads us to dismiss his very interesting book as entirely irrelevant for today and for contexts other than Europe. I continue to find *The Structural Transformation of the Public Sphere* a very stimulating and inspiring study. I imagine myself back in the eighteenth and nineteenth centuries when it became possible to circulate ideas and information widely through the new newspapers and to discuss ideas in the salons and coffee shops (although how many of them would have been open to me as a woman is questionable!). The shift of social and political power into the hands of the thinking, writing, arguing and educated middle class is fascinating. As one of my PhD fellows, Rory Bester, pointed out, Habermas's study is a kind of 'ghost' behind my own work, the presence behind this inquiry.

Second, I decided not to do what others writing about public intellectuals have sought to do: draw up a list of required attributes (say, using the Said formulation of a public intellectual) and then judge the person and the performance in public against them. I took the advice of Australian literary theorist David Carter (2001) and American literary theorist Eleanor Townsley (2006) and treated any figure who stood out in public and made pronouncements as a proxy or 'trope', somebody who could embody for others the promises made by democracies to each one of us that we have voices and can speak meaningfully in our societies and that this matters to the health of the polity. I also used Pierre Bourdieu's wonderfully versatile field theory to deal with agency and to understand why some people seem to have so much of it. Using the idea of various types of capital and its accumulation, I was able to carefully unpick how someone like Krog comes to have power, attention and impact.

* * *

This book looks at how Krog's particular biography and trajectory as an Afrikaans female writer have contributed to a distinctive voice emerging in public, not only in South Africa but also internationally. I am curious about how, through poetry, news journalism, essays and her hybrid-genre books, Krog has developed a particular persona and subjectivity as a writer of testimony and witness, consciously addressing a divided South African public on issues of concern. I am interested in exploring how this speaking/writing has been mediated by journalists and publishers since its emergence in 1970, with Krog being both mediated and at times acting as mediator and agenda-setter herself. And I am interested in how, at this particular political moment in post-apartheid South Africa, the desire to deal decisively with the past has allowed for the emergence of a particular kind of voice that reaches across publics, audiences and communities and forges a way of speaking that has attracted national and international recognition.

Given the nature of the post-apartheid public domain in South Africa, how has Krog's particular public intellectual performance received such a resounding response? It is because in Krog's biography and trajectory there is a complex intertwining of the literary as a field and the creation of writer subjectivity, the political sphere as the necessary stimulating environment for her writings and activities and the workings of the media and its a/effects in the world. A concatenation of factors (with distinctive roots in each of these fields) has allowed Krog to construct a distinct subjectivity as a writer, which she has used to transcend the literary, engage the political, enter the media and finally, with accumulated symbolic capital and acclaim, to arrive at a position that, despite the complexity of the South African public space, continues to allow her both a platform and a voice in making an exemplary South African intellectual contribution.

Note
1. http://www.anc.org.za/docs/anctoday/2005/at03.htm#art2.

1

Who Speaks?
Public Intellectual Activity in Post-Apartheid South Africa

Kader Asmal: In the South African context, is a distinction to be
made between the native intellectual and a settler intellectual?
Adam Habib: It seems to me that the easy answer is to say, no,
no, no, everybody can speak. But I do think there is such a thing
as a settler public intellectual. And I'll tell you what I think it is.
And it's particularly quite dramatic in the context of postcolonial
societies where there is a layer of people who actually believe
and argue for, and articulate a discourse that talks about the re-
colonisation of the continent. There is a settler discourse, whose
views are articulated as the antithesis to the society that has been
constructed.[1]

In postcolonial, post-apartheid South Africa, in which the majority black
population now has access to power, the African National Congress
(ANC) has taken seriously the idea that as part of the functioning of
democracy this new nation needs a vibrant public space for the airing
of ideas and the formation of public opinion. The idea of the public
sphere, steeped in the Enlightenment and the earliest formations of
democracies in Western European countries, has been harnessed to the
ideal of an inclusive democracy, which represents the majority, upholds

their interests and promotes their activities as vocal citizens participating in the life of the nation. Thus a crucial dimension of the energy expended on the functioning of the public sphere in the early years of South Africa's democracy has been on widening the public domain, beyond the participation of the bourgeoisie, to facilitate the inclusion of the voices of the black majority.

In the same way that there are concerns expressed in other parts of the world about the decline of the public sphere and public intellectual activity, so too in the South African public domain and media the rhetoric about the parlous state of the public sphere, a strong concern with who populates it and what ideas they put into it is evident. A great many calls have been made for various types of intellectuals to take up a public position and contribute to the healthiness of public life. A lot of energy, from both government and various civil society bodies, has been put into encouraging and cultivating public intellectuals of all sorts. While all citizens are to be included (particularly in the ANC understanding of the public sphere), there have been calls, in particular, for the educated, the skilled and the thoughtful among black South Africans to emerge from different locations politically and socially as intellectuals. Calls have been made for revolutionary intellectuals, organic intellectuals, black intellectuals, native intellectuals, African intellectuals and the intelligentsia to come forward, join and direct debate. Often coupled with these calls are statements invoking Edward Said's concerns with public intellectual representation and his phrase 'speaking truth to power' (with multiple interpretations) has become familiar in South African public discourse.

But South Africa's public domain is shot through with anomalies. The exclusion and alienation that colonial and apartheid experiences generated live on in crises of authority, contestation over sources of legitimation and an ongoing suspicion of Western-informed knowledge practices. This suspicion was sharpened by the findings of the Truth and Reconciliation Commission (TRC) hearings, which opened up the past for scrutinising the atrocities committed by the apartheid government and heightened by global debates about the spread of human rights, the inclusion of the marginalised peoples of the world into proper nationhood and the struggles in many democratic states for full citizenship and recognition.

Redress and restitution and different types of representation are high on the global agenda and in South Africa.

The mode of rational-critical debate conducted by a 'free-floating', independent intellectual with roots in liberal democracy and the Enlightenment – both historically implicated in the politics of colonialism and apartheid – is therefore not embraced unequivocally in South Africa as the only useful means for engaging with the public or the only mode with power or for driving a programme of redress and reclamation of dignity and indigenous wisdom.[2] So while there are classic performances in which public intellectuals in South Africa 'speak truth to power' via debate and the generation of persuasive ideas, there is also a proliferation of other types of engagement, which root their authorisation not in the bourgeois public sphere ideal or in Western universalism but in other modes and traditions. This results in furious discussions about styles of engagement, suitable subject matter, sources of authority, vested interests and arguments about degrees of independence from government, the nation-building project and national and even continental projects (such as the African Renaissance). A notable feature of these debates is that discussions are often couched in the language of 'crisis', which points not to the overt dangers being espoused but another one entirely – a crisis about what constitutes authority to speak (and especially to speak on behalf of others) in such a postcolonial situation.

Australian literary theorist David Carter (2001) says that the 'ramping up of public discourse' about the state of the public sphere and the need for intellectuals in his country is evidence of some other, deeper, maybe invisible, social shift taking place. In a similar vein, in South Africa the multiplicity of public figures urged to come forward could be read as evidence of a deep anxiety about authority, legitimacy and knowledge foundations in a postcolonial state.

To understand more about this situation, I focus on one particular public figure in South Africa, Antjie Krog, the poet, journalist and book author, in order to unpick how the platform to speak in public is created and crafted. A focus on one seemingly anomalous public person, her biography, works, media coverage and trajectory illuminates the factors that constitute the making of such a public persona. Krog continues to speak into the post-apartheid South African public sphere when racial markers of identity, history and experience that attach to the person speaking remain powerfully in place in all spaces of dialogue, so that *who* talks *for whom* on *what issues* are very important but fraught factors.

'Public sphere' is a useful – but sometimes limiting – term for a shifting and liminal space in the world in which an abundant range of practices occur that are difficult to grasp in a comprehensive and detailed way. However, some recent work allows me to sketch some suggestive markers of the domain that give a sense of the major concerns, shape, spaces and guiding practices of the post-apartheid (yet still transitional) public sphere.

Deborah Posel (2008) is helpful when she points to the provisions of the new South African Constitution as a guide to understanding the shift in post-apartheid notions of public and citizenship. She says that the TRC hearings are the 'first vector' of the reconstitution of new South African nationhood. Posel points out in a National Arts Festival lecture that at the heart of the new Constitution is the provision for freedom of expression for every South African citizen but this is linked intrinsically to the shedding of a terrible past and implies that all South Africans have shared humanity (ubuntu) and are 'in it together'. Ubuntu is therefore the 'ethical bedrock' of the new nation. Posel quotes Constitutional Court judge Albie Sachs as saying that ubuntu is 'a new analytical framework' for South Africa. There are three critically important ideas intertwined here: the right to speak, the recognition of shared humanity and the impulse to speak out about the horrors of a past that has scarred every South African. The result is a public domain filled with confessional practices: there is an 'outing' of the past and an airing of damage and trauma, as well as a plethora of personal stories in multiple forums and media. According to Posel: 'Post-apartheid is about new forms of speaking: a politics of speaking out, predicated on new-found democratic freedoms, and revelling in the eradication of apartheid censorship and prohibitions.' At the same time, there is also 'virulent argument' about what gets said and the powerful impetus to speak is accompanied by active silencing. Posel comments that there are still 'long-standing [and] powerful, cultural and political impulses to silence and secrecy', most particularly seen in conversations about the AIDS epidemic and sexual practices.

While Posel focuses on particular, very powerful animating ideas that give talk its political, social and constitutional power, Carolyn Hamilton (2008: 4) says features of the post-apartheid South African public sphere are:

> the state as committed to participatory democracy; the way in which a capitalist market economy, with significant global links, forms its basis; the widespread availability of broadcast media and a limitation of most other forms of media access in the hands of a small educated minority; the presence of an old, established white elite, the emergence of a new black bourgeoisie, the impact of a small but significant organised working class and a number of small social movements, and the existence of a large mass of unemployed or informally employed.

Hamilton also emphasises that the maintenance of the public sphere is understood to be an explicit part of the government's mandate and that 'active public citizenship' is considered more important than 'mere voter participation' (2008: 3). Lesley Cowling and Hamilton (2008: 6) note that there are 'historical legacies that valorise deliberation'. These include

> a celebrated tradition of public engagement by African intellectuals that dates back to the middle of the nineteenth century; concern about the long exclusion under colonialism and apartheid of the majority from the concept of the public itself and acknowledgement of a need for redress; and a commitment to face-to-face, spoken consultation symbolised by the valorised procedures of the traditional lekhotla/imbizo/volksvergadering/indaba; the drafting of the Freedom Charter celebrated as a process of collective deliberation; and ideals of community articulated in the struggle against apartheid.

The result, they say, is that spoken consultation is 'institutionalised in a variety of instruments, organisations, and policies designed to promote public comment on government initiatives and legislation, and public engagement more generally' (Cowling and Hamilton 2008: 6).

But there is also evidence of 'silencing, self-silencing and the evasion rather than the confrontation of the fetters' in what Hamilton calls 'the convened public sphere' (2008: 7). This 'convening' is seen, most notably, in the state's – and particularly in Thabo Mbeki's – interventions in the public domain. An interesting vehicle for former president Mbeki and his presidency staff to intervene in public was the weekly email newsletter *ANC Today*, which was sent to anyone who subscribed electronically. In an attempt to forcibly direct public discussions, after a number of severe criticisms of government by important political figures, a series called 'The Sociology of the Public Discourse in Democratic South Africa' was published in *ANC Today*.

In the 21 January 2005 edition, the debate is set out as follows: 'In South Africa the fight is really about who sets the national agenda. Should it be the African National Congress (ANC) or should it be the white elite?'[3] The newsletter makes the points that the intellectual battle going on in public is between the 'white elite' and the ANC 'black majority government'. The ANC believes it 'has a mandate to set the country's priorities'. In contrast, the white elite's 'interest is to protect its wealth and lifestyle'. The white elite 'believes its role is to provide thought leadership to an African population that is intellectually at zero'. While the newsletter asserts the importance of robust public debate and the value of hearing opinions from all quarters, the 'white elite' is characterised as wanting to confine this debate in both tone and space.

This racialising of the power to control the direction of public debate provokes the concern – expressed best by Thandika Mkandawire (2005) and reiterated by Raymond Suttner (2005) – that the demand by African governments that intellectual activity be in line with the state's definition of national reconstruction is very problematic. In an article for the *Mail & Guardian* in 2005, Suttner, a research fellow in the Department of History at the University of South Africa (UNISA), who was a political prisoner and a member of both the ANC and South African Communist Party

(SACP) leadership, focused on white South Africans who were involved in the liberation struggle and articulated their anxiety about their place in the present dispensation:

> A striking feature of the post-1994 period is the retreat from politics or emigration of large numbers of people from the white community who were part of the active resistance to apartheid. Some have decided to focus on personal issues, such as rebuilding family relationships, for which there was little time during the struggle. Yet others have become despondent. Democratic South Africa has fallen short of their hopes, and there is a sense of not identifying wholeheartedly with the new order. Some believe that their contributions have been insufficiently recognised; they feel that whites have been 'marginalised' (Suttner 2005).

Anton Harber, a founding editor of the anti-government *Weekly Mail* during the 1980s, now a professor of journalism at the University of the Witwatersrand, commented in the fourth Harold Wolpe Memorial Lecture:

> I have been asked to talk about the market and journalism. This is a discussion about the public sphere and the nature and quality of debate within it. In South Africa, we have an awful irony – that much of the journalism and the public debate (even when it had to be conducted secretly) was richer under the repressive conditions of apartheid than it is in a free South Africa (Harber 2002).

Reflecting on the inventiveness that inspired anti-apartheid activity, Harber said: 'It is harder now to see the same depth of public debate, imagination and intellectual innovation' (2002). In his assessment, journalism in the post-apartheid era is divided into two crude camps: watchdog of government power and assisting government in nation-building. 'Both are inadequate positions; both put their adherents into political corners where they tend to produce predictable and shallow journalism' and 'caution and conformism' are rife in not only newsrooms but also 'sweeping our polity'.

However, this situation of retreat and uncertainty needs to be overlaid with a generalised feeling of the right to a voice that also exists in the public domain: there is no shortage of people expressing opinions through radio and television talk shows – as Posel (2008) points out – and through newspapers' letter columns and, as online forums have burgeoned, so has the proliferation of commentators. But, as previously mentioned, the racial markers of identity, history and experience that attach to the person speaking in public remain powerfully in place in all these spaces of dialogue. It is also important to note that while freedom of expression is entrenched as a constitutional right, South Africans are often careful *what* they say *to whom* and in *which* public spaces.

It is against this complex context, where the public debate about who has authority to speak often falls into racial polarisation or pro- or anti-ANC government positions, that a focus on Krog enables an elucidation of the many hidden factors that make voice possible. That a white female voice continues to speak means attention must be given to subjectivity and identity – the use of self, body, the experiential, the confessional – and to larger, issue-based connections with wider global processes that impact on the South Africa public sphere and, therefore, on speaking individuals in public domains.

As part of seeking to understand what is going on in the public domain of post-apartheid South Africa, I focus on this one individual who, over a period of nearly five decades, has continued to find means of expression, despite the shifts and complexities – and constraints – of our public discourse and spaces. This focus on the *figure* of the public intellectual, as the embodiment of the provisions of the public sphere, reveals the mechanisms through which a speaking position can be found and used and tells us a great deal about democracy in post-repressive spaces in which healing and reconciliation are still fundamental issues.

My focus on this writer is a deliberate attempt to understand why certain public figures with speaking powers play a key role in society. This enables me to answer questions that are larger and more difficult to assess, such as: what is the relationship of democracy to the imagined national public sphere and the interplay of ideas in public domains? What is the influence of the literary? Why are so many who are considered intellectuals also writers? How is a platform to speak with authority in public crafted? By what means does a person come to have the capacity to take on such a role? What role does the news media play? How is a public generated for a speaker's words? By what authority does a public intellectual gain a sympathetic hearing that weighs and takes account of her statements? And finally, in a country that has undergone enormous political and social upheavals, how does such a person traverse dramatically changing situations and continue to speak into the public space with authority?

Notes

1. 'Defining the Role of Intellectuals', *Sunday Times*, 2 December 2007: 34. The panel included Kader Asmal, Jeremy Cronin, Raenette Taljaard, Adam Habib, Frederik van Zyl Slabbert and Xolela Mangcu, with Mohau Pheko as moderator.
2. 'Free-floating' is Xolela Mangcu's term (*Business Day*, 21 February 2008).
3. See http://www.anc.org.za/docs/anctoday/2005/at03.htm#art2.

2

Writing at a 'White Heat'

Antjie Krog, a white Afrikaans woman born in 1952 in Kroonstad in the former Orange Free State province into the heart of Afrikaner privilege, burst into the Afrikaans literary world in 1970, with a set of poems in her high school magazine. The sexual and political content caused a furore among the parents at the school, which drew the attention of an Afrikaans Sunday newspaper (the now defunct *Die Beeld*) and then the English-language papers. Through the Afrikaans paper and subsequently the publisher Human & Rousseau, two major Afrikaans poets (Etienne van Heerden and D.J. Opperman) were brought into the fracas. Both commented approvingly on the standard of the poetry and this resulted in Krog's first volume of poems (*Dogter van Jefta*) being published in 1970 when she was only seventeen years old.

At university Krog continued to produce three more volumes in quick succession: *Januarie-Suite* (1972), which won the Eugène Marais Prize, and in 1975 *Mannin* and *Beminde Antarktika*, for which two volumes she won the Reina Prinsen-Geerlig Prize for Literature in 1977. By 1975 she was married with a child, living in Cape Town and studying at Stellenbosch University with Opperman, who had become her mentor. By this time the Afrikaans press had her firmly on their radar and Krog was set on a trajectory to become a career poet. Over the next seven years she divorced, remarried (to her high school sweetheart John Samuel), had two more children, moved to Pretoria and continued to write poetry that grabbed reader and media attention. *Otters in Bronslaai* was published in 1981 and showed a distinctive use of colloquial language, with an emphasis on experiences of sexuality and the body. By this time literary academics were taking note and beginning to study Krog's work. In the Afrikaans newspapers every shift in her personal life and her progress poetically was recorded in detail in news reports and reviews of her work and in interviews about her life, family and career.

In 1980 the Samuel family moved back to Kroonstad. In the coming years Krog enrolled for a Master's degree through the University of Pretoria, focusing on Opperman's poetry. She also started teaching at the Mphohadi Technical College in Maokeng, a township, since she was unable to work in a white school as a teacher because she was technically unqualified. Her stature as a poet grew (in 1985 she produced the prize-winning *Jerusalemgangers*, which was awarded the 1987 Rapport Prize) and she started receiving invitations to speak publicly about poetry and literature. From her stance of increasing opposition to the National Party regime, she began to use these events – and the resulting media attention – to denounce Afrikaans cultural institutions' collusion with apartheid.

Until this point, media attention had been mostly confined to the Afrikaans press. But Dene Smuts, editor of *Fair Lady* magazine, invited Krog – whom she had interviewed for *Beeld* in 1975 – to join other invited authors at the magazine's book week in 1986. Krog was introduced to English-speaking and black South African authors and photographers and was disarmingly honest in public about her ignorance of the new names in South African literature and their work. She marked this week in an essay for *Die Suid-Afrikaan*, saying it had provoked her into crossing the 'boundaries of language, genre and politics' (Krog 1987: 43).[1]

In the final years of the 1980s Krog's dissidence deepened; she became more involved with township activists (through her involvement in the lives of the pupils she was teaching, now at the Coloured Brent Park High School) and she became even more outspoken in public about the devastating impact of apartheid on culture and literature. She became a member of the Congress of South African Writers (COSAW) and joined Miriam Tlali and Nadine Gordimer in Soweto for a Women Speak event in November 1988. In 1989 she marched with her township pupils in demonstrations against the government, joined a group of Afrikaner intellectuals and authors who crossed the border into Zimbabwe to meet an ANC delegation and produced *Lady Anne*, the volume of poetry that was to win her Afrikaans literature's most prestigious award, the Hertzog Prize.

In October of the same year, Ahmed Kathrada, a Rivonia treason trialist jailed for life on Robben Island in 1962, was released. At a reception rally before a crowd of 80 000 in Soweto, he read a fragment of one of Krog's poems from the school magazine of 1970. The poem, which had never been published (not even in her first volume of poetry), caused a media storm with journalists scuttling to find out how the poem had reached Kathrada in jail, why it had never been published and, for the English press, just who Krog was. Krog's name was all over the papers in 1989: not only did she visit the ANC in July at Victoria Falls but she was also part of a second delegation in November to Paris to further the talks that endorsed the cultural boycott against South Africa. And the contents of *Lady Anne* (which was blatantly postmodern in structure and shockingly included her own menstrual chart) were being debated furiously by poets and critics in the Afrikaans media.

As soon as the ANC was unbanned in 1990, Krog joined the liberation movement. She also resigned from the white branch of the Dutch Reformed Church and began attending the Sendingkerk. Despite winning the Hertzog Prize, for which she was acclaimed as having arrived as a poet and as demonstrating her independence and maturity (particularly from Opperman) and even though she was now considered one of the Afrikaans literary establishment's leading lights, Krog kept up the barrage of accusations against Afrikaans cultural institutions for their hold over writers and the language. In the same year she was interviewed by Pippa Green for *Leadership SA* magazine and the story of Krog's early start as a poet, her activism in Kroonstad and her encounters with the ANC were all relayed to the magazine's influential, English-speaking, business readership (Green 1990).

In 1992, in the violent run-up to the first democratic elections, Krog's involvement with the Kroonstad township comrades was to become complex and dangerous. A local gang leader was murdered by ANC activists, who then turned up at Krog's house, asking her to drive them back to the township. They hid a gun and a bloodied T-shirt on her premises and she became embroiled in their subsequent murder trial as a state witness. She began to receive threatening calls from the town's militant right wing. When, in 1993, as the trial was proceeding, she was offered a job in Cape Town as editor of Die Suid-Afrikaan, she accepted with alacrity. While teaching in Kroonstad, she had continued to keep up a strenuous programme of writing poetry, speaking in public, attending an international poetry festival in Rotterdam and reviewing and writing about literature for the Afrikaans press. She continued to be a favoured contributor to the mainstream press but also had a regular column in the alternative Vrye Weekblad.

In 1994, as the country made its transition through elections to majority rule, Krog became involved in Institute for a Democratic Alternative for South Africa (IDASA) conferences and meetings about the need for national reconciliation. Her speech, 'Focus on Healing' (Krog 1994a), to the Truth and Reconciliation conference was excerpted and commented on in a number of publications around the country, both English and Afrikaans. Despite saying she was too busy with the details of running a magazine to write poetry, Krog produced Gedigte: 1989–1995 and an account of her involvement in the murder of the gang leader in Kroonstad, Relaas van 'n Moord (both published in 1995). Through the autobiographical details in the latter book, it was clear that Krog had been on the receiving end of aggressive and frightening right-wing attention in her last years in Kroonstad.

In January of 1995, tired of the arduous work of keeping a magazine solvent, Krog took a job offered by the new editor of radio news for the SABC, Pippa Green, and joined the reconstructed parliamentary journalistic team as its Afrikaans reporter. As soon as the new government passed a law making a commission of inquiry into the atrocities of the past a reality, Green and the head of radio, Franz Krüger, put together a reporting team to focus solely on the commission and offered Krog leadership of the team.

As the TRC undertook its first hearings in East London in April of 1996, Krog was there. By May the horror of the details surfaced by the hearings started to affect the journalists covering them. When Anton Harber, then editor of the Mail & Guardian, asked various authors to 'celebrate the second birthday of our democracy and explore the nuances of a changing society' in a series called 'Two Years of Transition', Krog, one of those invited to write, blurted out the toll for her personally of covering the TRC:

> Voice after voice; account after account – the four weeks of the truth commission hearings were like travelling on a rainy night behind a huge truck – images of devastation breaking wave upon wave on the window. And one can't overtake, because one can't see; and one can't lessen speed or stop, because then one will never progress (Krog 1996b: 30).

The essay touched a chord with both the editor and readers and Krog was invited to write more in this vein about the experience of being an implicated witness to the hearings (see, for example, Krog 1996a, 1996c, 1997b, 1997c). These articles won Krog the Foreign Correspondents' Award for 1997 (shared with Justice Malala, a senior writer for the *Financial Mail*) and the SABC radio reporting team won the South African Union of Journalists' Pringle Award for its determined coverage of every hearing. The *Mail & Guardian* articles had also caught the eye of Stephen Johnson, then managing director of the South African branch of Random House, and he approached Krog to turn the writing and experiences into a book, which resulted in *Country of My Skull*, published in 1998.

The book's blend of journalistic reportage, verbatim testimony, poetry and other literary material made it a work that reviewers found difficult to categorise. Literary theorist Mark Sanders called it 'a hybrid work, written at the edges of reportage, memoir and metafiction' (2000: 16) and Krog's fellow Afrikaans author Rian Malan (author of *My Traitor's Heart*) called it 'a great impressionistic splurge of blood and guts and vivid imagery, leavened with swathes of post-modern literary discourse and fragments of brilliant poetry' (1998: 36). The book propelled Krog into the international arena as an authority on the South African transition. It won the *Sunday Times*'s Alan Paton Award (shared with Stephen Clingman for *Bram Fischer: Afrikaner Revolutionary*); the BookData/South African Booksellers' Book of the Year; the Hiroshima Foundation for Peace and Culture Award (shared with actor John Kani); the Olive Schreiner Award for the best work of prose published between 1998 and 2000; and received an honourable mention in the 1999 Noma Awards for Publishing in Africa. It also appears as one of 'Africa's 100 best books of the twentieth century' and in 2005 was adapted by screenwriter Linda Peacock into a film, *In My Country*, directed by John Boorman and starring Samuel Jackson and Juliette Binoche.[2]

Country of My Skull made Krog a nationally and internationally recognised public figure whose opinions and ideas were sought for a variety of forums on the subjects of dealing with the past, transition, healing and change. As a result she has received offers from various governments, universities and international agencies to visit, read and speak as a representative writer and witness of the South African transition to democracy. To give a sense of the attention that was focused on her because of this book: Krog gave the keynote speech at the World Bank's conference on 'Women and Violence' in Washington, DC in 1998. A year later, she gave the keynote speech, 'Women to the Fore', at the Zimbabwe Book Fair. Her play *Waarom Is Dié Wat Voor Toyi-Toyi Altyd So Vet?* (Why Are Those Who Toyi-Toyi in Front Always So Fat?) was performed at arts festivals in South Africa in 1999 and 2000. Also in 2000, Krog appeared in a three-part television series called *Landscape of Memory*, a documentary series about truth and reconciliation in southern Africa, which aired on SABC and in June of that year she led the English session at a conference on Writing As a Duty of Memory, held in Rwanda.

As a result of this enhanced stature as a literary figure, Krog started to receive renewed attention from the academic world. In the years after the publication of *Country of My Skull*, many international universities invited her to talk about witnessing the TRC hearings and to give her thoughts and opinions on reconciliation. Krog has had invitations from the University of London; the University of Glasgow; the universities of Essen and Dortmund in Germany; the University of Utrecht, Tilburg University and the Netherlands Institute for Southern Africa in Holland; the universities of Bishops, Concordia, McGill, Carleton and Toronto in Canada; and New York University, Brandeis University and Bard College in the United States; as well as the Central European University in Hungary. *Country of My Skull* is widely prescribed at universities in Europe and the United States as essential reading for students studying South African history or issues of dealing with the past. At Ohio University it is prescribed in History 342B/542B for the course 'South Africa since 1899'. It is the only book for the section 'The Transition and the New South Africa 1989–2000'. At Brandeis University Krog lectured and her work was read as part of the course 'Mass Violence and Literature: An International Perspective'.

Krog continues to speak both locally and internationally on the topic of reconciliation more than ten years after the TRC and more than twenty years into the South African transition. She was a speaker at the racism conference in South Africa in 2000 and in November 2001 she spoke at the Chile/South Africa conference on globalisation and South/South co-operation held in Santiago.[3] In 2003, she talked about 'Facing Up to the Past' at the University of the Witwatersrand. Her lecture on 'Forgiveness in the South African TRC' in 2005 was followed by a panel discussion with local inhabitants in Sarajevo and in Cologne she gave a paper on 'Wholeness As Part of Forgiveness in the TRC Process'; in The Hague in the same year she participated in a panel on language, addressing Queen Beatrix at her palace. She was part of a delegation briefing the newly appointed Liberia Truth Commission in 2006; co-ordinated and chaired a panel on art and the media in October of the same year for the TRC's tenth anniversary review conference organised by the Institute for Justice and Reconciliation, the Foundation for Human Rights and the Desmond Tutu Peace Centre; with Kopano Ratele and Nosisi Mpolweni-Zantsi she presented 'Ndabetha Lilitya: Language and Culture in the Testimony of One Person before the TRC' at the Memory, Narrative and Forgiveness conference at the University of Cape Town; and in New York she spoke on 'Interconnectedness, Memory and Wholeness' to the Congregation B'nai Jeshurun and participated in a panel discussion about memory in a seminar organised by the Lower Manhattan Cultural Council. She gave the keynote talk in 2007 for the International Society for African Philosophy and Studies at Rhodes University and was an invited speaker at the International Association for Analytical Psychology Congress XVII in Cape Town. In September 2008 Krog and Urvashi Butalia spoke on a panel about 'Division and Memory: Writing on Partition and the TRC' at the Indian-South Africa Shared Histories Festival at the University of the Witwatersrand Origins Centre. She participated in the University of Cape Town's Dialogue in December 2009, 'Beyond Reconciliation: Dealing with the Aftermath of Mass Trauma and Political Violence'; in 2010 she was interviewed on Canadian Radio One and on the BBC about the South African TRC and published 'This Thing Called Reconciliation' in *In the Balance: South Africans Debate Reconciliation*, edited by Fanie du Toit and Erik Doxtader (Krog 2010a). Krog spoke at the Kingston Writers' Festival in Jamaica about 'Shame, Truth and Reconciliation' and at Rhodes College on 'Truth versus Revenge' in 2011. Most recently Columbia University academic Rosalind Morris, editor of The Africa List for Seagull Books, has compiled Krog's TRC-inspired writings into a book called *Conditional Tense: Memory and Vocabulary after the South African Truth and Reconciliation Commission* (Krog 2013b).

After writing *Country of My Skull*, Krog returned to parliament as editor of the SABC radio journalists in 1999, but she left journalism soon afterwards. Her literary output since the publication of *Country of My Skull* has not only intensified but has also been singled out for further awards and praise. For Random House in 2003 she published a second non-fiction book about the South African transformation called *A Change of Tongue*, which won the 2004 Booksellers' Choice Award (published in Afrikaans in 2005 as '*n Ander Tongval*) and a third in 2009, *Begging to Be Black*, in which again, she used a mix of writing genres (reportage, autobiography, letters and philosophical reflection) to ask questions about the possibilities of rootedness and connection in South Africa. Also in 2009, *There Was This Goat* (with Kopano Ratele and Nosisi Mpolweni), which investigates the TRC testimony of Notrose Nobomvu Konile, was published by University of KwaZulu-Natal Press and Krog contributed 'Two "Useless" Recipes from My Mother and an Unsent Letter' to *uMama: Recollections of South African Mothers and Grandmothers* (edited by Marion Keim).

While Krog has travelled the world reading and speaking, perhaps the most interesting recent development of her renown has been the attention of editors and publishers in the United States, with a compilation of her poetry in a special edition for the North American market, *Skinned*, launched in New York in April 2013. In South Africa, Krog's output as a poet has been prolific. Her poetry publications after 1999 include *Kleur Kom Nooit Alleen Nie* (Krog 2000b), which received the RAU Prize in 2001; *Down to My Last Skin* (2000a), which received the FNB Vita Poetry Award in 2001; the re-release of *Eerste Gedigte* (2004a); *Body Bereft* and *Verweerskrif* (released at the same time in both English and Afrikaans, 2006), which was awarded the Protea Prize in 2007; a book of poems for children (of all ages), *Fynbosfeetjies* and *Fynbos Fairies* (in both English and Afrikaans, 2007); 'Marital Psalm' in *Open: Erotic Stories from South African Women Writers*, edited by Karin Schimke (2008); and – again in both English and Afrikaans versions – *Synapse* and *Mede-Wete* (2014b, 2014a).

Krog was invited by the Malian minister of culture to be one of ten poets on La Caravane de la Poésie, which retraced the slave route from Gorée Island back to Timbuktu in 1999 (chronicled in *A Change of Tongue*). She participated in the Barcelona Poetry Festival in 2001 and was the keynote speaker at Winternachten Literature Festival in The Hague in 2004. Krog has also been the keynote speaker in defence of poetry at the Poetry International Festival in Rotterdam and at the Berlin Literature Festival. She was invited by the Rockefeller Foundation to be resident in writing at Bellagio in Italy and in 2005 she participated in a poetry festival in Indonesia as part of a former Dutch colonial group visiting Djakarta, Bandung and Lampung, performing with local poets. She spoke at the Time of the Writer Festival at the University of KwaZulu-Natal, opened a poetry festival in Colombia and did readings in Bogotá, Medellín and Kali; she read poetry at the Nigerian Arts Festival in Lagos and shared a panel with Nigerian journalist Christina Anyanwu; she attended the poetry festival in Saint-Nazaire Acte Sud in France and did a travelling poetry show with Tom Lanoye in Belgium and the Netherlands. In 2006 she participated in a literary festival in Vienna, the poetry festival HAIFA in Harare and did a writer's retreat at Civitella, Umbertide in Italy. In 2008 she had a writing sabbatical in Berlin and spoke at the Akademie der Künste during a poetry festival. She has also participated locally in the Klein Karoo Nasionale Kunstefees, the Cape Town Book Fair, the Suidoosterfees, the Franschhoek Literary Festival, the *Mail & Guardian*

Literary Festival and the University of Stellenbosch's Woordfees; and internationally in the Poetry Festival on the Suffolk coast in the United Kingdom, Huis van de Poëzie in Utrecht, the annual Marathon des Mots in Toulouse and the Frankfurt Book Fair.

But also, since 2000, Krog has focused her energy on the reclamation of poetry in indigenous languages and the translation of poetry and important literary works into Afrikaans. She translated Nelson Mandela's *Long Walk to Freedom* into Afrikaans (Mandela 2001) and in *Met Woorde Soos met Kerse* (Krog 2002), which won the South African Institute of Translators' Prize, she translated indigenous language pieces into Afrikaans. *The Stars Say 'Tsau'* was selected and adapted by Krog from the Bleek-Lloyd collection of |Xam and !Xun documents and drawings and published in both English and Afrikaans in 2004. She also co-edited two collections of creative writing – *Nuwe Stemme 3* (poetry) with Alfred Schaffer (2005) and *This Is My Land* (youth writing) with Sindiwe Magona and Meg van der Merwe (2012).

She also occupies the newly coined position of 'curator' of poetry (as the word appears in the publicity material for these events): in 2004 she curated the Tradewinds Poetry Festival in Cape Town and since 2006 she has directed the Spier Arts Summer Season Open-Air Poetry Festival, also in the Western Cape. Her international exposure and connections are recognised and valued here, as she brings to these festivals a host of voices from other parts of the world. Krog also has a formidable yearly calendar appearing at international literary and poetry festivals and at many of these events she uses her literary stature to talk about politics and poetry or the complexities of reconciliation. In 2014 she and Njabulo Ndebele were invited to the Edinburgh World Writers' Conference to speak on 'Should Power Listen to Poetry?' (in the end this had to happen via a video link-up because the Icelandic volcano eruption prevented the two South Africans from travelling to the United Kingdom).

While Krog's literary output has always been the topic of attention for literary study, after the publication of *Country of My Skull* the academy began to treat her differently, not only as the author of a literary corpus but also as a producer of knowledge in her own right. This has often taken the form of conferring of honorary doctorate status (she has four, from the University of the Free State, Stellenbosch University, Nelson Mandela Metropolitan University and Tavistock Clinic of the University of East London in the United Kingdom), her inclusion as a keynote speaker among academics at major conferences and more importantly in a post created especially for her as an extraordinary professor attached to the Faculty of Arts at the University of the Western Cape. Her status is also the serious subject of academic inquiry with, for instance, a special edition in 2007 of the journal *Current Writing* devoted to Krog as a 'mediator of South African culture'.[4] The University of the Western Cape acknowledges her as one of their foremost women academics (primarily for her work with fellow writer Sindiwe Magona on a writing programme called UWC Creates). But she has also been recognised by the National Institute of Humanities and Social Sciences for her pioneering work on South Africa's indigenous languages (Sitas and Mosoetsa 2013: 5).

Other indications that Krog has attained a position of great public renown are the features of celebrity and popularity now attached to her public persona – particularly in and by the media. In December of 1997 she was named by the *Mail & Guardian* one of the 'next hot one hundred South Africans . . . the people who are set to influence (and are influenced by) the way we live and the issues which we debate'; in December 1999 the women's magazine *Femina* put her at number 39 on their list of the 'top 100 women who shook South Africa' (Koz, Mageza and Streek 1999) and in 2004 she was named 75th by public participants voting in the SABC's poll of the '100 greatest South Africans of all time'.[5]

When Krog was accused of plagiarism by fellow poet Stephen Watson (2005), the media coverage was intense and sustained, showing clearly the media and literary worlds' anxiety about a figure of such stature being accused of a practice that can undermine personal status and has impacts on the field: the consecration of such a person is called into question and therefore the field's methods of recognition (for a discussion of Pierre Bourdieu's terms 'field' and 'consecration', see Chapter 3).[6] Krog emerged from these damaging allegations with barely a scratch on her reputation as a writer. In fact, she was subsequently paid an extraordinary token of support by J.M. Coetzee in *Diary of a Bad Year*, in which his fictional Australian author J.C. writes of her:

15. On Antjie Krog

Over the airwaves yesterday, poems by Antjie Krog read in English translation by the author herself. Her first exposure, if I am not mistaken, to the Australian public. Her theme is a large one: historical experience in the South Africa of her lifetime. Her capacities as a poet have grown in response to the challenge, refusing to be dwarfed. Utter sincerity backed with an acute, feminine intelligence, and a body of heart-rending experience to draw upon. Her answer to the terrible cruelties she has witnessed, to the anguish and despair they evoke: turn to the children, to the human future, to ever-self-renewing life.

No one in Australia writes at a comparable white heat. The phenomenon of Antjie Krog strikes me as quite Russian. In South Africa, as in Russia, life may be wretched; but how the brave spirit leaps to respond (Coetzee 2007: 199).

Of this attention, *Sunday Independent* book editor Maureen Isaacson remarked: 'Antjie Krog is bestowed with laurels by J.M. Coetzee through his 72-year-old protagonist of his new novel' (2007: 17).

In the same year highly respected public figure Jakes Gerwel, previously vice chancellor of the University of the Western Cape and a presidential adviser to Nelson Mandela, who was preoccupied with questions about the health of public debate in South Africa, remarked in *Rapport*:

If I have to find among Afrikaans thinkers *one* who I would call an 'African intellectual', it is her. I have been so formed as a 'Western' intellectual; that it is Antjie Krog who, every time I read her, challenges me to acknowledge the restrictions of that formation and to address them. Few other Afrikaans thinkers dig so deeply and insistently about Africa and the moral and intellectual challenges of our continent and land (2007: 20).

And, as has become a hallmark in Krog's relationship with the media, she is not only the object of media attention but also continues to be a commentator and opinion writer who weighs into national debates on occasion. For example, in 2000 she made a plea for 'white action' at the Human Rights Commission Racism Conference and then followed this up in the *Cape Times* of 8 September (Jaffer 2000: 6) by calling for whites to 'make one single fateful gesture'. And in 2006 when former apartheid minister of law and order Adriaan Vlok symbolically washed the feet of ANC activist Frank Chikane, causing an outraged public reaction, Krog appealed for a 'space for the disgraced' in the *Mail & Guardian* (Krog 2006b). When Bok de Blerk's popular Afrikaans song calling for Boer War hero General de la Rey to come and lead his people sparked controversy, Krog weighed into the debate, writing 'De la Rey: Afrikaner Absolution' for the *Mail & Guardian* (2007a: 23).[7]

To this public recognition is added the attention of politicians who recognise her value for the national reconstruction project. This is demonstrated by more than simply the quoting of her work publicly. In June of 2003 Krog was selected as part of a panel of eminent South Africans to advise President Mbeki on appointments to the Commission for the Promotion and Protection of the Rights of Cultural, Religious, and Linguistic Communities. Krog has often been positioned and used as the voice of ethical response in the context of the nation-building and democratising project post-1994.

Since her appointment at the University of the Western Cape in 2004, Krog has added to her ferocious output as a poet, translator, convenor of poetry events and keynote speaking across the world an academic career that involves research, conference presentation and peer-reviewed publication.[8] She was recently acclaimed by her university as one of its eminent 'women in research'.[9] She continues to be the subject of academic investigations.[10] The experiences of the TRC and the preoccupation with the failure to achieve a realised democracy for all have provoked her to speak and write about this publicly and she is consulted again and again for her opinion, showing that interest in her direct involvement in the making of the new South African nation has not waned.[11]

*   *   *

Over the years that I have been tracking Krog's activities, writings, thoughts and ideas, media exposure and academic career, I have noticed an interesting development in the documents that the various search engines produce. In the early years there is little evidence of her activity beyond her poetry and reviews in the newspapers; then, from about 1989–90, her media profile blooms but still remains somewhat confined to the Afrikaans press and radio stations. Media coverage of Krog spikes with the reports and reviews of *Country of My Skull* in both the Afrikaans and the English press and is then sustained at a high level. The reports reach a new peak over the various plagiarism allegations against her in 2005 and a new level of interest is maintained and persists to the date of writing this book. But there is another interesting development; in the last few years (since about 2010) any search for Krog uncovers an enormous amount of material that fundamentally has little to do with her thoughts, writings and activities but is unearthed in association with other writers and public figures who are compared with or linked to her in some way. This change in the documentation (noted by my research assistant as 'Krog mentioned' over and over again) puzzled me for a while until I started to realise that Krog has entered the general media and public consciousness in such a deep and enduring way that she has become a reference point in multiple spheres, against which other people's writings, thoughts and actions are constantly being measured.[12] This goes further, with journalists and commentators who are responding to the often perplexing and depressing political and social situation in South Africa invoking Krog and her attitudes and actions as a touchstone – 'an appropriate role model' (as the *Mail & Guardian* called her in an editorial in 2006) and a 'new parent of the nation' (Thamm 2011: 5). This new role as reference point and touchstone is fascinating as an evolution of Krog's public persona, as it implies that her way of being, her ideas and commitments have now been woven into the weft and warp of our lives and conversations as South Africans.

Notes

1. The article, 'Skrywers Gee Rekenskap', published in *Die Suid-Afrikaan* (January 1987: 43) was reprinted in English in the *Fair Lady* of 4 February.
2. 'Africa's 100 Best Books of the Twentieth Century': http://africanhistory.about. com/library/weekly/aa100BestBooks.htm. See http://www.columbia.edu/cu/lweb/ indiv/africa/cuvl/Afbks.html#list for the list.
3. *The Sunday Independent* carried an edited version of her talk 'Healing Stream Petered out Too Soon' (Krog 2001: 6).
4. This phrase comes from the call for papers by editors Andries Visagie and Judith Lütge Coullie for the 2007 special edition of *Current Writing* 19 (2) devoted to Krog and her work.
5. 'The Next Hot One Hundred', *Mail & Guardian*, 23 December 1997. The '100 greatest South Africans' list can be found at http://en.wikipedia.org/wiki/SABC3's_Great_ South_Africans#The_list.
6. Krog has been accused of plagiarism a number of times other than by Watson – by Robert Kirby (2005) for plagiarising Ted Hughes in *Country of My Skull* and then by Tony Harding, the author of *Lekgowa*, regarding the definition of 'lekgowa' in *Begging to Be Black* that he claims is his. See also Krog (2006c), Jacobson (2006), Morris (2006), Philp (2010) and Verstraete (2006).
7. She also wrote about the death of Eugene Terre'Blanche for the *Sunday Times* (25 April 2010: 11) and the meaning of Mandela for Afrikaners for both *The Argus* and *Cape Times* (Krog 2013a, 2013d).
8. See, for example, Krog (2005, 2009b); Ratele, Mpolweni-Zantsi and Krog (2007); Krog and Mpolweni (2009) and Brown and Krog (2011).
9. See http://mg.co.za/article/2011-02-18-women-in-research.
10. See, for example, *Current Writing* 19 (2) 2007, a special edition on Krog, edited by Judith Lütge Coullie and Andries Visagie, Van Vuuren (2011) and Coullie and Visagie (2014).
11. See, for example, http://bookslive.co.za/blog/2009/04/08/antjie-krog-opens-up-on-south-africas-future/ and the University of Cape Town's Dialogue in December 2009 at which Krog, Mamphela Ramphele and Jonathan Jansen spoke on 'Reconciliation in South Africa: Are Things Falling Apart?' In 2010 Krog and Rian Malan got into a very public spat at the Franschhoek Literary Festival about the appropriate attitude for whites to speak in public about South Africa.
12. She is often invoked in relation to other poets and writers. For example, Joan Hambidge (2011) reviewed Mongane Serote's novel *Revelations* in *Rapport*, saying it should be read alongside *Country of My Skull* and in Judith February's 2011 article in the *Cape Times* about the 'shocking' appointment of Mogoeng Mogoeng as chief justice, she cites Krog for a 'new way of seeing'.

3

'Digter, Christen, Afrikaner'
Krog's Poet Subjectivity

In 2003 Antjie Krog released her second book in English, *A Change of Tongue*. At the time, she was already a highly acclaimed writer and public figure. In this book about change, metamorphosis, identity, belonging and journeys, Krog also tells a fascinating autobiographical story in the third person about her own beginnings as a poet and public figure. Reaching back into the apartheid South Africa of 1970, she recounts the story of a small-town Afrikaans girl who wrote a poem, shocked a town and came to the attention of the ANC in exile. This story is woven through the first part of *A Change of Tongue* and is distinguished from the present-day account by chapter headings in lower case and italics. The book's first part 'Town' consists of accounts in which Krog, who has returned to her childhood home on a farm in Kroonstad to sequester herself to write, employs journalistic-style investigation by conducting interviews about the present-day challenges of post-apartheid life. Making a living on a farm, running a municipality, processing sewage, managing schools, perceptions of security and shifts in personal relationships are among the topics she covers. She also weaves into this account her discussions and involvements with her own family and their voices and opinions and her ongoing preoccupation with writing and its usefulness in the South African situation of political and social change.

In this narrative, she has returned to the very rondavel on the farm her own mother (Dot Serfontein) used while trying to escape her children to write.[1] In this story Krog's computer crashes, destroying writing she has been working on for years and she suffers a mild stroke, making it necessary for her husband to drive from Cape Town to take her home. There is a confluence of narrative events that is significant: while investigating how people she knows and who formed part of her formative years are giving up the familiar and adapting to change, she reacts to the loss of digital words encoded by the computer's hard drive:

> There are things in one's life one simply cannot lose. Dare not lose . . . I have lost more on a computer than everything the Old and New South Africa, plus the Receiver of Revenue, plus old age, plus illness was able to plunder from me . . . I am without memory, my life has been taken from me (Krog 2003: 91–2).

That same night she suffers the stroke. It is into this textual situation of cataclysm and loss of words that she injects the climax of the story of the precocious seventeen-year-old poet she once was.

By this point in the book we have already encountered the whimsical, idiosyncratic but clever and richly imaginative teenage girl who aspires to be a writer and to feel and experience life powerfully and deeply. She is in the throes of first love, using words to evoke more meaningful experiences of life than life itself. Writing about rereading her own work of that time, Krog says: 'The words have not lost their power. The words have kept their content like bottled fruit, and every time she reads them she will experience her grandmother's funeral again' (Krog 2003: 60).

The young girl is experimenting with the sensual (making a god out of mud on the riverbank to worship, letting the ants crawl over her naked body) and battling her mother – over the length of a hem but more importantly as a writer. After a trip the two take to Lesotho, she sneaks a look at her mother's account of the journey: 'In the morning, when her mother takes a walk, she quietly goes to read at the typewriter . . . She sits in wonderment. That her mother is so good. When she tears up her own attempt, she realises that she is fiercely jealous' (Krog 2003: 102).

Into this context of teenage self-absorption comes the shock of the town's reception of her poem 'My Mooi Land', which was published in the school magazine in the year of her matriculation (1969). As Krog relates in A *Change of Tongue*: 'She puts together several protest stanzas, in which she experiments more freely with rhyme, and calls the poem "My Beautiful Land".

"look, I build myself a land
where skin colour doesn't count
only the inner brand

of self; where no goatface in parliament
can keep things permanently verkrampt

where I can love you,
can lie beside you in the grass
without saying 'I do'

where black and white hand in hand
can bring peace and love
to my beautiful land"' (Krog 2003: 124).

The details Krog tells in this story are that her mother receives a telephone call from the editor of *Die Beeld* newspaper, Schalk Pienaar, who tells her that the adverse reaction in the town to the publication of the poem in the Kroonstad High School magazine is going to be reported in his paper; the reactions have come from a Frank Boswell, two ministers and a Mrs Spies. The report in the Sunday paper, headlined 'Town Buzzes over Poems in School Magazine', includes commentary from Dr Ernst van Heerden, a poet and head of the Department of Afrikaans and Nederlands at the University of the Witwatersrand. That afternoon two reporters from the *Sunday Times* arrive at Krog's house and speak to her mother. Subsequently a story appears under the name 'Fairbairn Pringle', headlined 'Poems Cause Furore in OFS Town'. Telegrams and letters arrive for Krog at the school. Pienaar sends her mother a cartoon by Bob

Connolly from an English newspaper on the matter.[2] Her mother takes a call from a publisher who asks if Krog has written enough poems for a volume and says that respected poet D.J. Opperman wants to see the poems. Later Krog receives a letter from a Saul Radunsky congratulating her 'on her brave stance'. Her letters in response to the many people who write to her are intercepted and her parents are angry that unwittingly she has been in touch with 'an underground communist cell'. Her father is summoned by the local branch of the Broederbond to explain. There is also a newspaper article headlined 'Schoolgirl's Poem Is Used against Our Country' lying on her father's desk. Her mother is asked by her own publishers (Human & Rousseau) whether her daughter has accumulated enough material for a volume of poetry. Antjie puts together a manuscript; a telegram arrives announcing that Opperman recommends publication of her poetry. And it is with this announcement that the story ends in *A Change of Tongue*.

From newspaper archive fragments I have reconstructed the events that took place at this time in Krog's life as an emerging writer. These fragments tell a story that both confirms and diverges from Krog's in *A Change of Tongue*. The archival story starts with a report in a now defunct newspaper called *Die Beeld*, edited by Schalk Pienaar, on Sunday 16 August 1970. Reporter Franz Kemp is the author of the story headlined 'Dorp Gons oor Gedigte in Skoolblad' (Town Buzzes over Poems in School Magazine). Surprisingly for a Sunday newspaper, whose lifeblood is sensation and for whom the backwardness of small towns is always a staple, the story opens:

> *Een van ons voorste digters reken haar werk is verbasend goed. Sy lewe kuns, sê haar skoolhoof, en baie mense kan haar werk nie na behore waardeer nie. Maar Kroonstad gons oor die sewentienjarige Antjie Krog, Matriekleerling aan die hoërskool.*
>
> One of our foremost poets reckons her work is surprisingly good. She produces art, her headmaster says, and many people cannot adequately appreciate her work. But Kroonstad is buzzing over the seventeen-year-old Antjie Krog, matric pupil at the high school (Kemp 1970: 5).[3]

The main article then relates the story of the 'shock' with which her poetry has been received. It tells of Krog getting an A for poetry, reports that she is the daughter of established writer Dot Serfontein and then names several members of the Kroonstad community – all past pupils of the school – whose reactions have been negative: church elder Frank Boswell, an unnamed parent and businessman in the town, Mrs E.J. Spies, a Mr Laubscher and an anonymous mother who wants this brought to the attention of the Department of Education. Serfontein is quoted extensively, explaining that she and her daughter have discussed that this work should not have been published in the school magazine. Serfontein's opinion is that the work is 'beyond matric standard' and of the genre of 'modern poetry' (which she 'understands very well') and it is, therefore, better suited for a published collection. The headmaster insisted on publication in the school magazine, she implies, against her better judgement.

An inset story quotes Dr Ernst van Heerden, poet and head of the Department of Afrikaans and Nederlands at the University of the Witwatersrand, who is of the opinion that this is surprising work for someone so young. He also comments that young writers usually follow the pattern laid down by others but Krog does not. He advises readers to read the poetry of established poets Breyten Breytenbach and D.J. Opperman to hear echoes of Krog's themes. Interestingly the poetry actually printed on this page does not focus solely on the poem 'My Mooi Land'. The inset starts with a sexually suggestive piece of prose in which Krog graphically describes the serpent moving over her (Eve's) body in the garden. Nowhere in this article is 'My Mooi Land' singled out as particularly shocking, with its suggestion of love 'across the colour bar'. The objection seems to have been generally aimed at all the poetry by Krog printed in the school magazine. The poem appears in the paper as below:

My Mooi Land

Kyk, ek bou vir my 'n land
waar 'n vel niks tel nie, net jou verstand.
Waar geen bokgesig in 'n parlement
kan spook om dinge permanent
verkramp te hou nie

Waar ek jou lief kan hê
langs jou in die gras kan lê
sonder in 'n kerk 'ja' te sê

Waar ons snags met kitare sing
en vir mekaar wit jasmyne bring

Waar ek jou nie gif hoef te voer
as 'n vreemde duif in my hare koer

Waar geen skeihof
my kinders se oë sal verdof

Waar swart en wit hand aan hand
vrede en liefde kan bring in my mooi land (Kemp 1970: 5).

Notably the *Rand Daily Mail*, an English-language newspaper based in Johannesburg, carried a story about the incident and this poem the next day. Headlining the story 'Verse by Girl Pupil "Shocking"', the paper repeats the details carried in *Die Beeld*.[4] The only new information is from an interview with the headmaster, Mr D.J. Scheepers, who is quoted as being bitterly disappointed by the reaction because he considers Krog's work a 'masterpiece': 'She is an outstanding pupil who lives for poetry and art. I am proud of her.' The paper printed a translation of the poem, with the title 'Where Skin Means Nothing':

Look, I am building myself a land
Where skin means nothing,
just your understanding.
Where no goat face in Parliament shouts to keep verkramp
    things permanent.
Where I can love you
And lie next to you in the grass without saying 'yes' in church.
Where we can play the guitar at night and sing
And bring Jasmines for each other.

Where I don't have to feed you poison if a strange dove calls in
   my ear.
Where no divorce court can dim my children's eyes.
Where White and Black, hand in hand,
Will bring peace and love to my beautiful land.[5]

The next appearance of Krog in the Afrikaans newspapers is in a story called 'Antjie Se Eerste Digbundel' (Antjie's First Volume of Poetry) in *Die Beeld* of 6 September 1970.[6] This article introduces Krog by reminding readers that she is the Kroonstad matric pupil whose poetry has caused an outcry. It is reported that Human & Rousseau (her mother's publisher) is to publish a selection of her poetry and that Professor Dirk Opperman of Stellenbosch University has approved publication. Opperman says that he does not want to say that this indicates a new high point in Afrikaans poetry but he is impressed with her freshness and spontaneity as a writer. He picks out one particular poem for attention: 'Albatros Gough-Eiland'. 'My Mooi Land' is not mentioned at all. As Stephen Johnson, the managing director of Krog's publisher Random House, has remarked, it is notable that 'My Mooi Land' was not selected to appear in Krog's first volume *Dogter van Jefta* and it does not appear again in a poetry collection under her name until after the publication of *Country of My Skull* in English, when he and Krog decided to publish it in English (translated by Krog) and included it as the first poem in a selection of her work for English readers called *Down to My Last Skin* (Krog 2000a).[7]

Then *Die Beeld* ceased publication and Naspers and Perskor, the rival Afrikaans publishing companies, launched a new Sunday paper called *Rapport*. In January 1971 *Rapport* carried a major half-page story about censorship and whether poets 'get away with murder'.[8] This seemed to have been planned as a result of an outcry in the letters pages of the newspaper in response to a poem by Opperman, published in a December edition of the paper, which characterised the three wise men of Christian lore as '*drie outas in die haai Karoo / die ster gesien en die engel geglo*' (three old Coloured men in the barren Karoo / saw the star and believed the angel).[9] Ernst van Heerden is again consulted for his opinion and he refers to the '*onlangse geval van die skooldigteres Antjie Krog*' (recent incident involving the school poetess Antjie Krog). The article ranges across the opinions of many people about whether poets should have the freedom to push the boundaries of religion and sexuality.

In the same month, the ANC publication *Sechaba*, based in London, published a translated version of 'My Mooi Land'. The poem was introduced as follows: 'Antjie Krog, a 17-year-old Afrikaans schoolgirl has stunned her backveld Kroonstad community with this poem. Where there is so much hatred a germ of love she grows.' It was accompanied by her school magazine photo, which had also been used again and again in the South African newspaper reports.

My Beautiful Land
Look, I am building myself a
land where skin means nothing,
just your understanding.
Where no goatface in Parliament
shouts to keep verkramp
things permanent
Where I can love you
and lie next to you in the grass
without saying 'yes' in church.
Where we can play the guitar
at night and sing
And bring jasmines for each other.
Where I don't have to feed you
poison if a strange dove calls
in my ear.
Where no divorce court can
dim my children's eyes,
Where White and Black, hand in hand
Will bring peace and love to
my beautiful land (Krog 1971: 16).

In *Sechaba*, as in the other newspapers, this poem was singled out from the other poems in the school magazine. But here it was set on a different journey, for a different purpose and for a different audience. It had jumped the boundaries of this isolated country, come to the attention of someone in exile in the ANC, was translated into English and found its way into a publication banned by the National Party government and probably never to be seen legally in this country until after 1990, when members of the liberation movements returned with their archives.[10] And until very recently the actual translator of the poem remained secret until Ronnie Kasrils confessed to Krog that it was he who had translated it into English.[11]

But it took a while before news of this use of the poem came home. Only in March of 1971 did the London correspondent of *Rapport* discover the translation and write a piece under the headline 'Antjie Se Gedig Misbruik teen Ons Land' (Antjie's Poem Misused against Our Land).[12] With a tone of high indignation, the unnamed writer declared:

> *Een van die omstrede gedigte van die sewentienjarige skoolmeisie van Kroonstad, Antjie Krog, word nou deur Suid-Afrika se vyande in die buiteland misbruik. Die African National Congress het haar gedig My Mooi Land in Engels vertaal en in 'n pamflet afgedruk. Die pamflet word nou oor die hele wêreld teen Suid-Afrika versprei.*
>
> One of the controversial poems of the seventeen-year-old schoolgirl from Kroonstad, Antjie Krog, is now being misused by South Africa's enemies outside the country. The African National Congress has translated her poem My Mooi Land into English and published it in a pamphlet. The pamphlet is now being distributed across the whole world against South Africa.[13]

The report went on to speculate how this situation arose. The caption under the now-standard photograph of Krog said:

> *Die gedig is blykbaar in Tanzanië deur een van die nie-blanke Afrikaans-sprekende omroepers van Radio Dar-es-Salaam in Engels vertaal. Die radio saai daagliks in Afrikaans uit. Op die oomblik word die gedig in*

Londen versprei. Antjie het destyds groot lof van kenners gekry toe haar gedigte in die skooljaarblad verskyn het, maar ander mense het gesê hulle is geskok oor die seksuele ondertone van die verse.

The poem was evidently translated into English in Tanzania by one of the non-white Afrikaans-speaking announcers from Radio Dar-es-Salaam. This station broadcasts daily in Afrikaans. At the moment the poem is being disseminated in London. At the time Antjie received great praise from experts when her poems appeared in the school magazine, but other people have said they are shocked by the sexual undertones of the verses.[14]

The report also presented within the body of the story both the Afrikaans version of the poem (the same version as in *Die Beeld*) and the English version copied from *Sechaba*. However, the name of the ANC publication is not given. The report ends by telling readers how the ANC 'pamphlet' introduced the poem and translates the English words into Afrikaans: '*Antjie Krog, sewentienjarige Afrikaanse skoolmeisie die mense van die agterlike Kroonstad met die gedig geskok het. Waar daar so baie haat is, is daar tog 'n juweel van liefde*' (Antjie Krog, seventeen-year-old Afrikaans schoolgirl shocked the people of backward Kroonstad with the poem. Where there is so much hate, there is yet a gem of love).[15]

The next news event in the life of this new poet occurred the very next Sunday (4 April) when *Rapport* approached Krog's mother to put into context this latest furore surrounding 'My Mooi Land'.[16] The poem was reprinted again, in the centre of the page, and Serfontein was given an entire page in a broadsheet newspaper (minus the advertising space and one short story on the side, which also dealt with a poetry controversy) to '*verduidelik*' (explain/clarify) the situation. The introductory note (not written by Serfontein but by someone at the newspaper) sets the scene by telling readers: '*Nou is dit selfs in die buiteland in Engels vertaal as 'n propagandaset*' (Now it is being used overseas as a piece of propaganda translated into English). Serfontein begins:

Verlede jaar toe die 'herrie' losgebars het oor ons kind se gedigte, het 'n verteenwoordiger van Die Beeld my gevra om kommentaar daarop te lewer. Kommentaar was juis wat ons probeer vermy het. So iets leef jy net af. Nou het die goeie ou Sondagkoerant weer die sakie opgerakel en ek voel dat 'n tydige stukkie volwasse sprake in hierdie stadium dalk nie onvanpas sal wees nie.

Last year when 'all hell' broke loose over our child's poems, a representative from *Die Beeld* asked me to comment on it. Commentary was exactly what we tried to avoid. Such a thing you just live through. Now the good old Sunday paper has resurrected the little affair again and I feel that a timely little bit of adult talk in this instance perhaps will not be amiss.[17]

Serfontein reveals that the poem was written in the last half of 1969 when she and her husband were registering voters at the National Party local office. They attempted to find young people to help them and only two came forward, their daughter Antjie being one of them. Their task entailed going from door to door in the town, being at the mercy of the irritation and anger of those who did not want to be told about the 'new' National Party. She also explains her lapse of judgement in not giving Antjie advice about what poetry to publish by saying that at the time she was embroiled in responding to requests to write about the psychological motivation of a Maria Groesbeek who had murdered her husband (the reference to doves cooing about poisoning one's spouse in Krog's poem relates to this event). She says, however, that she does not believe that the poem showed a sinister slide towards liberalism and accuses adult propagandists involved in electioneering of making public unflattering depictions of the leader of the Herstigte Nasionale Party (a reference to the 'goatface' of the poem). She puts forward her view that young people all over the world are dealing with the kinds of issues raised by the poem and that facing these issues with the support of adults is important. On the issue of poetry itself, she opines that poets are people hypersensitive to influences. She also tells readers that her advice to Antjie has been to put her poetry into a volume for publication so that she can put herself forward in public as '*digter, as Christen en as Afrikaner*' (as poet, as Christian and as Afrikaner). It is clear, though, from this piece, that Serfontein is responding to the publication of the poem by *Sechaba*. On this issue she says: '*Ek is bevrees dat dit nog op baie ander plekke tot nadeel van ons land gebruik kan word*' (I am afraid that it might still be used to disadvantage against our land in many more places). The secondary headline on the page roots the causes of the furore around the poem in '*die politiek en Groesbeek*' (politics and Groesbeek) – in other words, the climate of electioneering inspiring reactionary behaviour from voters and sensationalist reporting of murder by newspapers – and the mother's own preoccupation, which meant she did not have her mind focused on the 'naive' poem that was to unleash such a fuss.

A month later, the story found its way into the English press with a report by Colin Legum, which appeared in the *Daily Dispatch* in East London on 17 May 1971. The report is marked 'OFNS' at the end, indicating that it came to this newspaper via *The Observer*'s Foreign News Service. It is interesting to note how this information from London came to be published in East London in South Africa and nowhere else. Legum had left South Africa in 1949 (a year after the National Party came to power) and was living in London in exile and writing for *The Observer* newspaper. As a journalist he had developed close relationships with Africa's emerging new political leadership.[18] In the 1970s Legum was sympathetic to the ANC position on South Africa and in touch with the *Daily Dispatch* editor, Donald Woods, who would later become a friend of Steve Biko and flee into exile with his family after Biko's death at the hands of security police.[19] Legum's story reads:

> A poem by a 16-year-old South African schoolgirl has made her an internationally famous controversial figure. Antjie Krog's poem was first published in her school magazine last year. It started a tremendous row in South Africa and now the controversy has become wider because of the decision of the exiled African National Congress – which spearheads a guerrilla struggle from its headquarters in Tanzania – to reproduce her poem for international distribution (Legum 1971).

The translated version of the poem from *Sechaba* was reprinted, although again the name of the ANC publication is tellingly omitted. Legum had obviously seen the *Rapport* article by Serfontein as he includes her arguments in defence of her daughter. He ends the article by commenting:

Antjie Krog is a new phenomenon among younger Afrikaners who, in increasing numbers, are beginning to react against the established racial attitudes and morality of South Africa. Although still relatively few in number, they are the harbingers of changed ideas among the younger Afrikaners. These changes, when they do occur, do so mainly at universities – especially in recent years at Stellenbosch University, traditionally the nursery of Afrikaner nationalism. What is unusual about Antjie Krog is that she has broken from the conventional thinking while still at high school, not in the sophisticated urban setting, but in the heart of the platteland, the rural outback of the apartheid Republic (Legum 1971).

The tone of this report is remarkable in its contrast to the tone of the *Rapport* article on the poem's '*misbruik*' (misuse). It is clear that Legum's commentary comes from a quite different ideological position.

At this point the archival trail goes cold. The poem disappeared from view for eighteen years only to reappear in 1989 in the most unexpected way and in a different but equally politically charged context (the subject of the next chapter). But in the intervening period Krog charted a predominantly literary course, which although it always had a political dimension, was to remain within the Afrikaans literary sphere and confined to Afrikaans vehicles of public discussion.

Telling an autobiographical story as a claiming of authority

I turn now to the significance of Krog's accumulation of literary field capital and her autobiographical work, which was to become a distinction of her voice as a poet. I employ Pierre Bourdieu's field theory to examine the emergence of Krog as a public figure in South Africa and consider the development of her public persona by looking at the complex intertwining of the literary as a field and the creation of writer subjectivity, the political sphere as a necessary stimulating environment and context and the workings of the media and its a/effects in the world. I want to draw attention to the enabling and constraining features of the literary field, the development of Krog's adaptive subjectivity as a writer, her accumulation of literary symbolic capital and the actions and interventions of powerful field consecrators who generated critical consecratory or transitional moments in her trajectory.

I deliberately began this chapter with an autobiographical moment in a text in which an author of great renown and symbolic capital (at the point of publication of *Change of Tongue*) reached back in time to tell an originary story about her own entry into the literary field (and also into the alternative political field). I did this for several methodological reasons: the first is to make a point about the place of the analysis of texts in a project determining the development of a particular person's writer subjectivity. As Helen Malson says:

> Texts are analysed, not as a means of revealing the 'truth' about the speaker or writer (their attitudes, cognitions, traits or whatever) or about the events or experiences they describe. Rather, texts are analysed in order to explicate the culturally specific discursive resources that have been drawn upon in order to produce a *particular* account of 'reality' . . . with the interactions and dilemmas that may be created for the speaker in taking up particular constructions of themselves or others . . . or with the functions or effects (whether intended or not) of the particular discursive resources used and the power relations embedded therein (2000: 153).

The second reason for beginning the chapter in this way is that in field theory, as explicated by Bourdieu, a critical moment of shift in both an individual's life, and in the greater relations of an already existing field, is the critical moment of entry of a new and important actor. This moment in 1969 is the beginning of Krog's *trajectory* as a public figure and a public intellectual. By engaging with Krog's texts and the media texts generated about her, I find within the autobiographical and biographical information clues to the project of writer *subjectivity* (or more narrowly poet subjectivity), which connect with what Bourdieu calls the 'duty to emerge' in a field as an actor of distinctive production. If I take seriously Paul de Man's insight that 'we assume that life *produces* the autobiography as an act produces its consequences, but can we not suggest, with equal justice, that the autobiographical project may itself produce and determine the life' (Eakin 1985: 185), this telling of a particular story of self by Krog in *A Change of Tongue* is a significant statement about her credentials as a writer, one that interestingly spans 33 years and is being performed to the new public that Krog is now addressing in English after the major success of *Country of My Skull*. Krog is telling an originary story to a new audience, who may not have travelled with her as the readers of her poetry in Afrikaans have over the years. She is gathering them in to participate in her story of justification and legitimation as a witness and writer of change, which depends on an extraordinary originary story. But more than that, for the purposes of this inquiry, this story and particularly its appearance in archival and media fragments enables me to go back to Krog's moment of entry into *public* life and so begin to unravel the beginning of her trajectory towards public recognition and her stature as a representative South African.

To return to the moment at which the young Krog became a poet and walked out onto a public stage, Bourdieu emphasises that moments of *entry* and *emergence* are critically important to an individual's successful negotiation of a field in which, like the literary field, autonomy is high and a grasp of the immanent logic of the field is vital. Bourdieu calls this 'the right to enter and the duty to emerge' (2005: 46). Rodney Benson underlines this point: 'In field theory, changes in the structure of fields are produced from two basic sources. Since to exist in a field is "to differ", a "dialectic of distinction" ensures the constant production of change as new actors attempt to enter and make their mark in the field' (1998: 487-8).

Krog's achievement of a published volume of poetry at the age of seventeen is a remarkable story about how journalistic news values, framing and agenda-setting provoked her entry into the literary field.[20] In the sequence of media events outlined at the beginning of this chapter, there is a very clear indication of a controversy or sensation attracting the attention of journalists and galvanising them into the production of 'news', stimulated also by the newspaper editors operating according to the explicit economic imperatives of journalism. But we also see an act of media power across fields and society that facilitates Krog's entry, not only into the Afrikaans literary field in South Africa but also into the alternative political field as a young dissident. This is a classic case of agenda-setting, signifying to the public at large that this person is noteworthy and has interest beyond the field of literature. To explore the significance of the story of Krog's writing life and growing capital across fields, I use two main thematic devices to chart these developments: *trajectory* (which shows her movement through a field and her acquisition of its capital) and *subjectivity* (which shows her work on the self). These two components, I believe, are key to understanding her unique situation in the public domain today.

Trajectory: Entry and emergence as a poet in the Afrikaans literary field

It is evident that Kemp's story in *Die Beeld* applied the news values of surprise, conflict or sensation to his assessment of the newsworthiness of the reaction of some people to Krog's high school poems. He produced a fairly standard, sensational Sunday paper story, using the frame of shocking events in small towns causing an outcry among their unsophisticated inhabitants. But, interestingly, Kemp also contacted Van Heerden as an expert to give his opinion on the poetry and allowed Serfontein to express her views. The news value of controversy attracted the paper's attention, the story was framed in a particular way for Sunday paper reader consumption and, by seeking out an expert to comment on the poetry, Krog herself was also framed – as precocious, brilliant, dissident and associated with Afrikaans literature's most esteemed poets. It is important to note that seeking out expert opinions is one of the routine ways in which journalism enhances its authority as the communication of 'truth' in public but it coincidentally also involves drawing a field 'consecrator' (a very helpful term from Bourdieu for people with power and authority in a field) into a public realm (outside the literary field) in which pronouncements can be made that are seen as having worth and legitimacy. As a result Krog was marked as a newsworthy person and placed firmly on the Afrikaans press's news agenda. This agenda-setting had an immediate effect in the reaction of publishers Human & Rousseau who sought to publish her work and who consulted highly esteemed Afrikaans poet and academic Professor D.J. Opperman (another consecrator) at Stellenbosch University on its worth.

Die Beeld's agenda-setting had another unexpected effect in the publication of the poem in English in *Sechaba*. Here one sees another set of journalists, with a different set of news values and agendas, framing Krog for their purposes as a young dissident voice of promise and hope from within the bastion of apartheid. This contradictory framing and agenda-setting by a banned publication provoked outrage back home but facilitated Krog's entry into another field – the alternative space of political dissidence. It also provoked a renewed attempt to recapture and frame Krog back into a well-behaved, but brilliant Afrikaner girl, with Serfontein clarifying the situation and assuring *Rapport*'s readers that Krog was a good Christian and National Party supporter. The framing battle continued with Legum's story, which sought to reaffirm Krog as a voice of promise and hope from within the Afrikaans laager.

The actions of the reporter, the mother, the two literary field consecrators and the established publisher ushered Krog decisively into the literary field. And simultaneously the attention of the ANC and Legum ushered her into the alternative political field of South Africa in the 1970s. This entry into the alternative political field was to frame and set Krog on as important a trajectory as her entry into the literary field. And in terms of media agenda-setting, Krog had been 'snagged' in the news net (Reese 2007: 150).

Krog was to make good use of her decisive entry into the literary field by producing another three volumes of poetry while at university, *Januarie-Suite*, *Mannin* and *Beminde Antarktika*. She benefited from the alliance with Opperman who became her mentor for years, first as editor of her poetry, then as teacher during her Honour's degree in his 'poetry laboratory' at the University of Stellenbosch.[21] As Bourdieu points out, successful negotiation through a field in order to accumulate the field's capital and accolades is greatly enhanced by an alliance with a field consecrator.[22] But also, having been caught in the news net of the Afrikaans press, Krog became a standard newsmaker to keep tabs on. Each volume of poetry was reviewed, each prize acclaimed and every change in her personal life (divorce, remarriage, births of children, moving cities, changes in jobs) captured through a combination of news reports, literary reviews and highly personalised interviews and photographs of her at home with her family.[23]

Subjectivity: 'The cartography of the self', the production of distinction

As Krog started to produce poetry prolifically after *Dogter van Jefta*, Afrikaans literary critics and canonisers began to categorise her as a poet of the 'domestic' – J.C. Kannemeyer's term for her subject matter was *'huislike gedigte'* (1983: 504). This was not only a pigeonholing of her choice of subjects and preoccupations, it was also an acknowledgement of the fact that Krog had set out to create an individuality of poetic voice – or idiolect – via *'die kartering van die self'* (the cartography of the self), Tom Gouws's term (1998: 550), by capturing the intellectual and physical experiences of being lover, wife and mother.

Literary critic Louise Viljoen remarks that Krog's poetry 'can be read as an autobiographical record' (2007: 188) and that autobiography and poetry have both played an important role in 'empowering women writers' and, quoting Celeste Schenk, in allowing women 'a way of coming *to* writing'.[24] Viljoen continues: 'Reading Krog's poetry one becomes aware that she did indeed use the lyric poem as a space in which to establish her female subjectivity, but also as a space in which to constantly revise and reform it.' Krog's refining of the use of autobiographical material connected to a distinctiveness of expression over many years of writing poetry came to mark her voice and characteristic methods of expression, not only in poetry and in the literary field but also over time in other genres and public expressions. The individuality of this voice in itself acquired capital and value.

In her examination of Krog's translation in the volume of indigenous poetry *Met Woorde Soos met Kerse*, Viljoen remarks that Krog has a 'Romanticist poetics' (2006: 38) in which 'language and especially sound' is the 'dominant feature of poetry'.[25] In addition, Krog's particular poetics is centred on performance and the social uses – or even the social relevance – of poetry. Viljoen notes: 'Krog's poetics is also known for the way in which it transgresses limits with regard to subject matter, poetic technique, language and genre' (39). She also suggests that the transgressive in Krog's poetics is closely allied with a strong feminist voice and in some cases a display of 'utter passion'. She is attracted, says Viljoen, to fury and violence (40). Finally, one detects in Krog's poetry-making an ongoing preoccupation with 'the conflict between aesthetics and politics'.

In his review of *Kleur Kom Nooit Alleen Nie* and *Down to My Last Skin*, Leon de Kock (2000: 9) characterises Krog as

> an extraordinary, versatile, provocative and messy poet. She messes with proprieties both sexual and political, she shoves shit and semen, and much besides, in your face, she refuses to give up trying to speak the voices of the land, she risks sentimentality everywhere, and she continues to be both publicly personal (right down to details about her husband's member) and very personally public.

Within a very short time Krog became known to Afrikaans readers as a poet who uses slang and swear words, who picks up street language, throws in English words and does not shy away from graphic descriptions of the sexual and the body. As each new volume of her poetry appeared, it was scanned for these hallmarks and reviewers and journalists documented each of these shocking details and the debates about them in the literary world. This was against the backdrop of the National Party-Broederbond project of crafting a sophisticated and controlled body of literature to enhance the status and legitimacy of the Afrikaans language vis-à-vis other world languages. Krog's poetics seamlessly combined a transgression of conventional language and poetic craft and her discomfort and dissension with Afrikaans cultural institutions' relationship to the apartheid state, a poetics that continued drawing media attention and making of Krog a newsmaker and agenda-setter.

Some examples from the early volumes of poetry will give a sense of the singularity of Krog's voice and its shock value in South Africa in the 1970s. *Januarie-Suite*, written while Krog was doing her undergraduate degree at the University of the Orange Free State, contains a poem called 'Sonnet', which begins '*vanaand weet ek / dat ek jou nooit weer lief sal hê nie*' (tonight I know / that I will never love you again) and ends '*omdat ek moeg is / vir jou nat snoet in my lies'* (because I am tired / of your wet snout in my groin) (1972: 44). There is also the poem ''n Bundel Bedoel vir Aborsie' (A Volume Intended for Abortion), which begins *'ek moes hom laat doodmaak het'* (I should have allowed him to be killed) (19).

Beminde Antarktika contains the poem 'Ekshibisionis' (literally 'Exhibitionist' but more accurately 'Flasher'), an excerpt of which reads:

> *en die Slamse man wat straat af kom*
> *hy had 'n mus en donkerbril*
> *sy mond bewende so soel sy vel*
> *dat ek verwonderd na hom staar*
> *sy hand af na sy gulp*
> *en skielik*
> *tussen sy vingers steier nat*
> *'n donkerblou peul in aar.*
> and the *Slamse* man coming down the street[26]
> he had a cap and dark glasses
> his mouth trembling so swarthy his skin
> that I stare at him in wonder
> slide down to his fly
> and suddenly
> between his fingers wet scaffold
> a dark pod in vein (1975a: 15).

Mannin (Virago) contains the poem 'Speelmaats' (Playmates):

> *my liefling het 'n skilpad*
> *groen gemaak van lap*
> *wat met sy doekvoet-pote*
> *snags oor my gewete stap*
>
> *my liefling het 'n houtpop*
> *Pinokkio is sy naam*
> *en oral waar my liefling woon*
> *kan jy sweer woon langneus saam*
> *die twee heers ewe opgewek*

al jare oor my lief se bed
maar sedert ék by hom kom speel
maak hul berekend vir my plek
my sweetheart made a tortoise
green from rags
whose stealthy muffled paws
walk across my conscience at night
my sweetheart has a wooden doll
Pinocchio is his name
and everywhere my sweetheart lives
you can swear longnose lives too
the two have reigned cheerfully
for years over my love's bed
but since *I* have come to play with him
they make calculations for my place (1975b: 8).

Krog's fifth volume of poetry *Otters in Bronslaai* (published in 1981) was shocking in subject matter – it touched on the theme of homosexuality and set off rumours of her discovery that her first husband was homosexual, which had led to his abandoning her – and acclaimed for its vitality. The poetry was called 'boisterous' and 'angry' (see De Wet 1981; Bertyn 1981; Le Roux 1981; Pretorius 1981; Kruger 1981; Olivier 1981; Viljoen 1982).[27] The SABC refused to allow Joan Hambidge to read the poem 'Die Skryfproses, As Sonnet' (The Writing Process As Sonnet) on the programme *Digterkeuse*.[28] The poem reads as follows:

hoe bang het ek geword om poëties baldadig te dink,
om my geliefde rymloos en vormloos te laat uitrank
hoe sku het ek geword om in lote onbevange vers
sy penis onverantwoordelik ysterklaar by die naam te noem

die krimp en los van sy balle by daglig waar te neem
die sagte kurk van sy tepels tot harde stukkies bas
om brutale stuifmeel oor blare to vlek
en argloos sy anus aan my pen te laat bot

maar totaal geïnhibeer deur laboratoriumtoetse en handleidings
bedink ek elke derde nag netjiese stellasies vers, noukeurig
en dimensioneel opgelei, verrassend berym en kosmies met titels bemes

en uiteindelik: ryp gekwatryn, onpersoonlik met kenners
oor gekweel, word die hele seksdaad nou
'n slim-slim slimmer ritueel.
how fearful I have become to think poetically exuberantly,
to allow my loved one to ramble free and formless
how shy I have become in writhing open verse
to call by name his penis irresponsible ironready

to take in the shrivel and slack of his balls by daylight
the soft cork of his nipples to hard bits of bark
to smear brutal pollen over leaves
and artlessly allow his anus on my pen to bloom

but totally inhibited by laboratory tests and textbooks
every third night I contrive neat scaffolds of verse, carefully
and dimensionally trained, startlingly rhymed and cosmically
        fertilised with titles

and at last: ripely quatrained, impersonally warbled
with expert ear, the whole sex act is now
a clever-clever cleverer ritual.

The important point to note in terms of field theory is that Krog was not only emerging as a poet of distinctive voice but she was also conforming strongly to the logic of the literary field, which requires that the boundaries of what is allowable in expression be tested and that language itself be manipulated. This became one of the hallmarks of her work and resulted in the following conversation on SABC radio between Krog and the writer Celine Celliers:

Celine Cilliers: *Jy gebruik vreeslik baie Engels, is dit jou persoonlike skryfstyl?*

You use an awful lot of English, is this your personal writing style?
Krog: *Ons praat almal so.*
We all speak like this.[29]

As Krog grew in stature as a poet, she began a public, mediated battle against the stifling control that Afrikaans cultural institutions exercised over the language and culture, thus furthering her status and trajectory as a young dissident in the alternative political field. She began to use the platforms she was afforded by her cultural capital and, in full knowledge that it would be reported, to declare her stance. Some examples: in July of 1984 she told the Afrikaans Olympiad in Bloemfontein that the Afrikaans language could look after itself without the interference of the cultural institutions.[30] She told the Afrikaanse Letterkundevereniging at the University of Port Elizabeth in 1985, that '*die Afrikaanse letterkunde van vandag is feitlik een groot neurose*' (the Afrikaans literature of today is actually one great neurosis).[31] In 1987 when she was elected onto the executive of the Afrikaanse Skrywersgilde, she made use of the position to take a stand against the prevailing anxiety about 'alternative and worker Afrikaans'.[32] At the Nasionale Leeskring seminar in 1988, she said apartheid had come between writer and reader (Van Zyl 1988) and told the annual meeting of the board of the Skrywersgilde that Afrikaans needed to be set free of that very institution.[33] When in 1989 IDASA and the Skrywersgilde held a Writers' Indaba, Krog told the gathering that Afrikaans 'had failed this country' and would need to reflect a broader reality to survive (Scheffer 1990: 10).

Krog had for many years been in the vanguard of using 'street Afrikaans' as a poet but this practice is perhaps best described as representing a political force for change by Max du Preez, founding editor of *Vrye Weekblad* (to which Krog was a regular contributor in the 1980s):

And then there was our use of the *Taal* . . . I didn't make a conscious decision before the launch of *Vrye Weekblad* to promote the use of 'liberated' Afrikaans. It started happening organically; it was the natural, creative way to write. But when we were criticised right from the early days for not sticking to 'civilised standard

Afrikaans', I explained in an interview: 'There was a gap between
the Afrikaans being used by the speakers of the language and the
Afrikaans being used in newspapers. The gap was unnaturally big
and not in the interests of Afrikaans. So from the start we said:
This is not our Afrikaans. We didn't say that it wasn't a good
thing to have a proper knowledge of Afrikaans, on the contrary,
but we said: Who are these little men who make the rules for
our language? For all the years middle-aged Broederbond-types
with grey shoes, appointed by some Academy dictated to us how
to spell, how to speak and how to write. And the next year they
publish a new book of words and spelling rules, and we all have
to follow like sheep.

   This did not only bring a huge schism between writers and
users of the language, it also brought resistance. The only criterion
is what feels good and right. Each person is an interpreter of the
language on the tongue of the people. What do you do not to
sound like a *dominee* or a magistrate? You close your eyes and think
how you would have said it to someone on the street. It is what
will save Afrikaans. Get down from the pedestal and the pulpit,
move away from the academic rostrum and speak the language
as it grows and as it lies warmly on the tongue' (2004: 204–5).[34]

What one sees is that Krog's early production of distinction was not only
about how she wrote her poetry but also about the position within the
field she was taking up (aligning herself with dissident writers such as
André Brink and Breyten Breytenbach). It is also clear that Krog's literary
and political trajectories were converging in her focus on the cultural
institutions' handmaid relationship to the apartheid regime. But it is also
noticeable that Krog had come to a particular realisation about media
power: moments of media attention are focused on particular events and
people and because of her growing cultural capital as a literary figure,
she had become one of those people – an agenda-setter – who could then
insert certain topics onto the media agenda and hence into the public
arena. In an interview in 1987 with André le Roux of *Die Burger*, after
winning the Rapport Prize for *Jerusalemgangers*, Krog said something very

revealing about this strategy: '*Ek was eintlik bang ek wen nie, anders sou ek nie die kans kry om die "statement" te maak nie*' (I was scared actually I wouldn't win, otherwise I would not get the chance to make the 'statement') (Le Roux 1987: 13).[35] It is remarkable that in this growing relationship with and reliance on the media to convey her dissident stance, Krog was confident that the media would frame her and her words as she intended. By this time, the way she is framed can be captured most succinctly by two repeated appellations: the use of her first name in headlines, 'Antjie' – the diminutive indicating familiarity and endearment (see Fowler 1991: 110) – and the use of the adjective '*gekroonde*' (crowned/anointed), signalling her literary status and hence weight and worth.

*   *   *

The originary story Krog told in *A Change of Tongue* at the height of her power and prestige as a public figure and the supporting media texts show that an extraordinary confluence of events, including the intervention of the news media, ushered her into both the literary field and the alternative political field at the age of seventeen. Krog was also firmly captured as a newsmaker for the years to come. Various people acted as consecrators in interesting and important ways, most notably her mother, an already established writer with connections to magazines and a publisher, and Opperman who became her mentor and editor, which was important to get her beyond the first flush of young poetry-making. The acclaim bestowed on her by anti-apartheid activists, which was then to lie dormant for many years, nevertheless brought her to the attention of significant political figures, which was to have interesting consequences in the future. Krog's embrace in these years of the position and identity of poet worked not only to produce work of distinction in the literary field but also for the creation of a unique and larger subjectivity, one that responded powerfully to the political context of South Africa in the 1970s and 1980s. And as Krog continued to write and produce poetry, we see the crafting of a facility with language that, while in the early years dealt with self, home and family and was mostly autobiographical, was also being used to deal with the visceral, the body (especially the female body) and commanding the space, poetically, of passion and the affective. With each successive volume, Krog was authoritatively taking up the position of the poet with an affinity for the affective.

Her public, at this time, was bounded by the reach of the Afrikaans language. But for a poet, her work sold well and continues to do so, with even her earliest poetry still available. Krog was also steadily attracting the attention of the gatekeepers of the literary field – the anthologisers and the canonisers, such as Kannemeyer – and her work was becoming a topic of study for literary critics and their students.[36] Literary critics such as Hambidge and Viljoen started paying attention to Krog in these years and have continued to chart her writing ever since.

Notes

1. Dot Serfontein is also a prolific writer. For many years she wrote short stories and sketches as well as serialised pieces for the women's magazine *Sarie*. She is the author of *Tiendes van Anys* (published in 1962); *So Min Blomme* (published in 1966); *Onder Skewe Sterre* (published in 1967); *Ek Is Maar Ene* (published in 1972); *Sonder Klein Trou* (published in 1974); *Rang in Der Staten Rij* (published in 1979); *Sy Stap onder die Juk* and *Die Laaste Jagtog* (both published in 1982); *Serfontein-Atlas* (published in 1984); *Galery van Reenmakers* (published in 1986); *Keurskrif vir Kroonstad* (published in 1990); *Deurloop* (co-authored with Krog, published in 1992); *Vertel! Vertel!* (published in 1995); *Vis en Tjips* and *Huis van Papier* (both published in 1997); *Amper My Mense* and, in her eighties, a book of memoirs, *Vrypas* (both published in 2009).

2. The obviously made-up name is intriguing. Thomas Pringle and John Fairbairn published South Africa's first independent newspaper the *South African Commercial Advertiser* and the first magazine the *South African Journal* (see Draisma 1999). No searching by librarians in the newspaper group's archives could unearth an article in the *Sunday Times* by 'Fairbairn Pringle' or any information about Krog or her poem. It has also proved impossible to find the cartoon by Bob Connolly. And the Kroonstad High School documentation from the 1970s was destroyed when the school was merged with two others after South Africa's transition to democracy. In *A Change of Tongue* (2003: 64), Krog relates how she cut out a picture of John Fairbairn ('utterly handsome . . . fighter for freedom of the press') from her high school history textbook. Later, her mother says: 'The journalist even claimed that his name was Fairbairn Pringle – as if I would believe a name like that' (132). It is possible that Krog has made up this name as part of her 'creative non-fiction' project, perhaps partly as a joke, perhaps partly to make a (coded) point about freedom of expression, perhaps partly as a (coded) expression of her own belief in freedom of the press. My thanks to Alison Lockhart for pointing this out.

3. Unless noted otherwise, the translations from Afrikaans into English in this book are mine.
4. 'Verse by Girl Pupil "Shocking"', *Rand Daily Mail*, 17 August 1970: 3, 8.
5. It is worth noting that each appearance of the poem in translation is slightly different, in choice of words and line breaks and even in how stanzas are arranged. It is also often titled differently. This shows that the poem was being used as a vehicle politically to remark on the significance of a young Afrikaner girl breaking ranks with the Afrikaner establishment, rather than as a literary work. It is interesting to contrast this rather cavalier set of translations of that moment against how careful Krog is now about her work being translated and her own attention to translation for the purposes of publication.
6. 'Antjie Se Eerste Digbundel', *Die Beeld*, 6 September 1970: 10.
7. Personal communication from Stephen Johnson, 19 August 2004.
8. 'Ons Digters Kan Moor sonder Skoor: Poësie Is Veel Vryer As Prosa', *Rapport*, 17 January 1971: 6.
9. 'Lesers Onstoke . . . en Vol Lof', *Rapport*, 3 January 1971: 10.
10. Liberation movement archives are now housed at the Mayibuye Centre at the University of the Western Cape and the ANC archives at the University of Fort Hare in the Eastern Cape. Also see http://www.disa.nu.ac.za, the digital archive that has collected the once-banned publications of the liberation movements online.
11. See http://podcasts.ox.ac.uk/peter-d-mcdonald-conversation-antjie-krog-audio.
12. 'Antjie Se Gedig Misbruik teen Ons Land', *Rapport*, 28 March 1971: 3.
13. Referring to *Sechaba* as a *'pamflet'* (pamphlet) creates associations with political propaganda that the words 'magazine' or 'journal' do not have.
14. 'Antjie Se Gedig Misbruik teen Ons Land', *Rapport*, 28 March 1971: 3.
15. The word in *Sechaba* is 'germ' not 'gem'.
16. 'Antjie Se Skoolgedig Verduidelik: Dot Skryf oor Haar Dogter', *Rapport*, 4 April 1971: 9.
17. Ibid.
18. http://www.theguardian.com/world/2003/jun/15/theobserver1.
19. In 1964 Colin Legum and his wife Margaret wrote *South Africa: Crisis for the West*, in which they argued for economic sanctions against the South African government in order to bring down the apartheid system.
20. For further exploration on the mediation of Krog, see Garman (2014a).
21. Krog went on to write her Master's thesis on his poetry (Krog 1983).
22. Bourdieu and Nice explain that the more powerful the consecrator is, the more the work is strongly consecrated and that the consecrator 'invests his prestige in the author's cause' (1980: 283).
23. For example, see Slabber (1987), a broadsheet page article in *Rapport*, with a photograph of the Samuel family on the veranda of their home in Kroonstad.
24. I am quoting here from Louise Viljoen (2007: 188). The reference there for Schenk is: Celeste Schenk, 'All of a Piece: Women's Poetry and Autobiography', in *Life/Lines: Theorising Women's Autobiography*, ed. Bella Brodzki and Celeste Schenk, 281–305. Ithaca: Cornell University Press, 1988.

25. Viljoen (2006: 38) defines poetics as consisting of 'two components: one is an inventory of literary devices, genres, motifs, prototypical characters and situations, and symbols; the other a concept of what the role of literature is, or shold be, in the social system as a whole (Lefevere 1992: 26)'. The reference for Lefevere is André Lefevere, *Translation, Rewriting and the Manipulation of Literary Fame*. London and New York: Routledge, 1992.

26. '*Slamse*' is Cape Afrikaans slang for a Muslim of Malay descent.

27. See also 'Antjie Krog, Gewildste SA Digteres: Werklikheid met Eerlikheid Verwoord', *Die Burger*, 9 September 1981; 'Nuwe Krog-Bundel Dalk Nog 'n Kultusroering', *Die Volksblad*, 27 October 1981: 10; 'Antjie Krog: Baldadigste Poësie in Afrikaans', *Die Suidwester*, 1 February 1982: 2.

28. *Rapport*, 16 October 1988: 12 reported the banning and said the poem was a 'description of her husband from head to toe'. The writer 'Nelia', commented: '*Is ons dan almal nog naive kleuters?*' (Are we then all naive toddlers?).

29. 'Leeskring oor die Lug', 17 February 1983, SABC Sound Archives, T83/61–62 (Ruda Landman and Nic Swanepoel talking to Celine and Rika Cilliers and Dot Serfontein and Antjie Krog).

30. 'Taal Kan vir Homself Sorg – Antjie Krog', *Die Volksblad*, 18 July 1984: 13.

31. 'Antjie Krog Raak Betrokke', *Oosterlig*, 16 August 1985: 10.

32. 'Die Onderdrukte Moet 'n Stem Kry', *Die Vaderland*, 4 July 1987: 9.

33. '"Bevry Afrikaans van die Gilde!"' *Rapport*, 14 October 1989: 41. Krog was quoted as saying: '[die gilde] *laat die skrywers nie uit hul hokke kom nie*' ([the guild] does not let writers come out of their cages).

34. Another term for 'street Afrikaans' is '*loslitafrikaans*', 'hair-down Afrikaans' (Van Coller and Odendaal 2007: 114, note 2).

35. In a personal communication (5 November 2005) Krog said how carefully she plans the launches of books and speaking tours with her publishers so as to focus media attention on what she considers important.

36. Kannemeyer's *Geskiedenis van die Afrikaanse Literatuur II* (1983) has a chapter on Krog.

4

Self-Othering

Or Living Honourably in an 'Era of Horror'

On Sunday 29 October 1989, Ahmed Kathrada, one of the Rivonia treason trialists who had been jailed for life by the apartheid regime, who had just been released from Robben Island as one of the first of the unbanned ANC leadership, was given a reception at Soccer City Stadium in Soweto. Before a crowd of 80 000 people he read a part of Antjie Krog's teenage poem, 'My Mooi Land', translated into English. The extraordinariness of this situation is that Kathrada had been in jail since 1964 and the poem had seen publication only a few times in newspapers in 1970 before disappearing entirely. Schalk le Roux (1989: 1) from *Beeld* was there and reported that Kathrada read the following lines:

> Build me a land where skin colour does not count
> where no goatface in parliament
> can keep things permanently verkrampt
> where black and white hand in hand
> can bring peace and love in my land.

The report stated that Kathrada said to the crowd:

> *Baie jare gelede op Robbeneiland het ek 'n gediggie van Antjie Krog*
> *gelees. Sy was toe 'n sewentien jaar oud meisie wie met haar matriek op*

Kroonstad besig was. Die gedig het my baie geimponeer. En ek het dit neergeskryf.

Many years ago on Robben Island I read a poem by Antjie Krog. She was then a seventeen-year-old girl who was busy with her matric in Kroonstad. The poem impressed me a great deal. And I wrote it down (Le Roux 1989: 1).

Kathrada also told Le Roux that after reading the poem he heard that Krog was working for *Die Burger* (this would have been 1974) and then a while later that she was becoming highly thought of as a poet. Then just a few months before his release he heard – '*tot my groot vreugde*' (to my great joy) – that Krog had joined the delegation of writers to meet with the ANC in exile (Le Roux 1989: 1). Kathrada told Le Roux that he felt Krog was part of a 'growing group of Afrikaners who are prepared to talk to the ANC and to return to report to their people'. The report ended with the interjection of another writer, Eugene Gunning, who had interviewed Krog about this occurrence. He reported that she was surprised to hear the news of the poem's revival, commenting: '*Ek voel ontroerd en ook diep hartseer. Dit is 20 jaar gelede geskryf en nog steeds het dit nie 'n werklikheid geword nie*' (I feel moved and also very heartsore. It was written twenty years ago and it still has not become a reality).

A while later the *Weekly Mail* carried a report on the same incident by Hans Pienaar (1989: 18). This report includes the few lines of the poem Kathrada read but Pienaar adds a piece of information that sheds light on the textual travels and translations of 'My Mooi Land': 'The poem was published in her school's annual which mysteriously made it to the small library on Robben Island, where Kathrada read it'.[1] The *Sunday Times* report of 5 November 1989 adds more details:

A young Afrikaans poet, whose poem 'Jammer' was quoted to 70 000 people at the Freedom Rally in Soweto last week, said she wrote it 17 years ago when she was a Standard 9 schoolgirl.[2] And until it was read by Rivonia trialist Mr Ahmed Kathrada, Antjie Krog believed the poem had been 'lost'. The poem expresses the hope that one day in South Africa 'black and white' will 'hand in hand' bring peace to this 'beautiful land'. The poem was published in a school yearbook, says the poet, and has never been included in any of her eight published volumes of verse.

Mr Kathrada said he first read the poem over 10 years ago when he was imprisoned on Robben Island. It was written in Afrikaans but had been translated into English for him by a fellow prisoner. He said he believed it may have been in one of the few magazines political prisoners were allowed to read. 'The poem moved me then and I am still moved by it,' he said. 'I decided to read it at last week's rally because to me it shows an encouraging sign that the monolith of apartheid is also being cracked by Afrikaans youth from within the establishment. The old values are being overturned and replaced with new. And it's an encouraging sign for the shared future of our country. The poem appealed to me as well because it is so anti-racist' (Holtzhausen 1989: 15).

Accompanying the report are the lines from the poem Kathrada read. What is notable – and this is in contrast to the Afrikaans journalists' and readers' familiarity and knowledge of Krog the poet – is that the English papers have to assume that they must give their readers background and history since they will not necessarily know of Krog, her much-reported exploits or her work.

In 2005 when Sahm Venter edited and published *Ahmed Kathrada's Notebook from Robben Island*, the poem appeared like this:

Build me a land where skin (colour) does not count
Only your understanding
Where no goat-face in a parliament can haunt
And keep things permanently verkramp
When I can love you
Lie next to you on the grass without the churches blessing.
Where at night with guitars we can sing together with gifts of
    flowers.
When I am not willed to feed you with poison
As a strange bird in my nest

When no divorce court
Will blind our children's eyes
When Black & white hand in hand
Can bring peace & love
In my land.
– Antjie Krog (17) Kroonstad Std 10
(*Huisgenoot* – translation).[3]

In his *Memoirs* Kathrada gives some background to his discovery of this poem while on Robben Island:

> Towards the end of 1968 the rigid regulations on reading matter were relaxed slightly, and we were allowed to subscribe to approved magazines such as *Reader's Digest*, *Panorama*, *Farmer's Weekly*, *Lantern* and *Huisgenoot*. We were also given some free publications – *Fiat Lux*, *Alpha*, *Tswelopele* and other deeply boring government-funded journals targeted at specific ethnic groups (2004: 234).
>
> More than anything else, books helped to keep our minds occupied . . . I also kept secret notebooks, filling about seven over the years with favourite quotations and extracts that struck a chord in me (236).
>
> There was another poem, also by a young girl in her matric year, that made a great impact on me when I chanced upon it in a weekly magazine in 1967 or 1968 . . . I was greatly moved by this poem and copied it into my secret notebook. It spoke to me of the ability, especially of youth, to transcend their upbringing, to shake off the blinkers of racism and stereotyping that school and society reinforced at every opportunity, every day. It was written by a seventeen-year-old Afrikaans schoolgirl from the Free State town of Kroonstad. Her name was Antjie Krog (230–1).[4]

Trajectory: The attention of important political field consecrators
Consecration by Kathrada
On Sunday 29 October 1989 when Krog's 'lost' poem re-emerged at that highly charged moment of major political transition from someone with

impeccable anti-apartheid credentials, Kathrada was not only reminiscing about his need for comforting words in jail, he was performatively using the words at an event marking a major political change in the life of a nation to proclaim a different future for all South Africans and in the process conferring political legitimacy on Krog the poet. Krog, who was not present, was sought out by journalists to explain the genesis of the poem and asked for her reaction to Kathrada's speech. For the first time the *Weekly Mail* – a paper of high journalistic and political legitimacy in 1989 – paid attention to Krog. The resulting story had to fill in the years in which English-speaking readers had more than likely missed out on her work, her activism and her growing status as a literary figure. What had Kathrada done? He had consecrated Krog publicly as the type of Afrikaner who was welcome in the struggle for a new and different South Africa. But he had also anointed her as a voice in that struggle by using her words to mark an event of heightened significance at a time of great political volatility. Kathrada's consecration of Krog at the time that South Africa embarked on a five-year period of major political upheaval and transition (1989–94) was only one of a series of important sanctifications, which altered Krog's trajectory and moved her from operating primarily as a poet with views on the political via the cultural into the political world proper. They also reinforced each other, giving her symbolic capital of the most extraordinary sort as a writer and an Afrikaans voice.

But before Kathrada as a key member of the internal ANC leadership in jail drew the national media's attention to Krog the poet, two other processes of political consecration were firmly underway in Krog's life: the visits to meet with the ANC leadership in exile (as a result of Krog's association with the Afrikaans intellectual elite) and the approval of township comrades in Kroonstad.

Consecration by the ANC in exile
As the political impasse and the violence in South Africa deepened in the mid-1980s, several organisations and business leaders felt that extraordinary efforts had to be made to talk to the ANC in exile.[5] One of these organisations was the newly formed IDASA, which had been set up in 1987 by former leader of the Progressive Federal Party, Frederik van

Zyl Slabbert, and Dr Alex Boraine, also a former member of parliament. In July of 1987 IDASA had instigated, with the help of writer Breyten Breytenbach (a member of the ANC living in exile in France) and the president of Senegal, Abdou Diouf, a meeting in Dakar between 16 ANC members and 61 Afrikaans opinion-formers. The success of the meeting led to further trips to familiarise important South Africans from a range of positions with the ideas, aims and personages of the ANC. In July of 1989 IDASA again set up a meeting, this time with Afrikaans writers and members of the ANC involved in cultural production, to talk about the cultural boycott at Victoria Falls in Zimbabwe. Krog was invited to be part of the delegation with fellow writers André Brink and Etienne van Heerden. They met Marius Schoon who told Krog he and Bram Fischer had read her poetry in jail. Among the ANC delegation were Breyten Breytenbach, Jeremy Cronin, Vernon February, Mongane Wally Serote, Albie Sachs, Keorapetse Kgositsile, Barbara Kgositsile and Barbara Masekela. In December Krog wrote of this encounter for *Die Suid-Afrikaan*. She admitted that her motive for accepting the invitation was '*totale onbeheerbare nuuskierigheid*' (totally irrepressible curiosity) (1989c: 6) and went on to describe at some length an emotionally laden encounter. The mostly Afrikaans delegation of writers and academics from within South Africa found to their delight that the ANC members were fluent in Afrikaans and eager to speak it, were nostalgic about the country and longing to return. They enjoyed Afrikaans literature and culture and were eager to share their own writings. Readings of poetry took place but the main task was to discuss the cultural boycott and to get the South African delegation to formally agree to take a position on it, which they did. They issued a communiqué which, in part, read:

> As writers together, from both inside and outside South Africa, intensely aware of our shared concerns and deploring the way in which our culture is impoverished by our enforced separation, we commit ourselves to work for:
> * the unbanning of the ANC and all other political organisations
> * the lifting of the state of emergency
> * the release of all political prisoners

- the removal of troops from the townships
- the abrogation of all legislation that illegalises legitimate political activity.

Entering the struggle is the means of beginning to be a South African. It is not heroic to oppose apartheid – it is normal (Scheffer 1989: 4).

Of course, this caused a strong reaction back in South Africa, which forced Krog to explain her association with the ANC and this endorsement.[6] She told readers of *Die Volksblad* that her choice was 'boycott over violence'. Her stance drew the public ire of her mother (a situation then remarked on in the press) and a powerful reaction from other writers, which was then fed into Skrywersgilde meetings and discussed further.[7] In December Krog was again part of an IDASA delegation to meet with the ANC, this time in Paris. *Rapport* carried Krog's 'Los van die Afrikanerlaer' (Loose from the Afrikaner Laager), an excerpt from her piece in the collection *Afrikaners tussen die Tye*, edited by Bernard Lategan and Hans Müller, in which she claimed ''n gans ander wêreld het vir my oopgestaan' (a whole other world opened up for me) (Krog 1991: 1).

As Kathrada noted in his interview with *Beeld* (Le Roux 1989), Krog the young voice of hope from within the Afrikaner laager, first noted in 1970, had over the intervening years become aligned with the faction of dissident Afrikaans writers who could then be drawn upon to build a bridge with the ANC. In the 1980s Krog's outspokenness in the Afrikaans literary world about the cultural institutions, her alignment with *Vrye Weekblad*, her friendship with Brink, her association via her poetic style and themes with Breytenbach, all worked to mark her as the type of enlightened Afrikaner who could represent those seeking a political resolution beyond racism and apartheid. When she was included in the 1989 delegations by IDASA and Breytenbach, it was still with consciousness that she was located within the literary field and so could represent and speak from that literary-aesthetic platform. But the introduction to the ANC members in exile was a significant moment of consecration with future import, in that most of these exiles would return to become rulers and take up significant positions of political influence. Krog again was made known to another group of important political players – just as she was in 1970 with the publication of her poem in *Sechaba*. This introduction and knowledge of Krog among exile members of the ANC was to be reinforced by the Kathrada consecration. But another – and in the South Africa of the late 1980s perhaps the most important – third form of consecration was to take place in the classrooms and streets of Kroonstad's townships.

Consecration by the comrades

> If I look back I had a hunger to belong somewhere and I felt rejection from the group I was supposed to belong to. It was exhilarating to live an anti-apartheid life – the languages, the people, the feelings on the ground. The links were tough: I had several unspeakable experiences, but it always sparked off critical thinking.[8]

Krog's desire to live an anti-apartheid life took shape in the townships of Kroonstad in about 1985 when, unable to obtain a teaching position in a white school, she found work at the Mphohadi Technical College and then at Brent Park High School in the Coloured area in the late 1980s. Writing for *Leadership SA* Pippa Green quotes Krog's *Lady Anne* editor and friend Gerrit Olivier: 'There's a lot of easy talk about the struggle in Afrikaans literary circles at the moment, but very few people expose themselves to their immediate environment as Antjie does' (Green 1990: 44). Green continues: 'In a country where unity is still only a rallying call, Krog is slowly trying to build a "oneness" (a word she uses often) on her home ground.' In this extensive interview with Krog (after she had won the Hertzog Prize for *Lady Anne*) Green probed Krog's involvement in her students' lives. Krog said when she first started teaching she was full of curiosity, asking questions such as 'What do you eat? Where do you live? Where do you come from?' She told Green: 'The township is 10 kilometres away from me and I didn't know anything about the people who lived there' (48). It was Krog's interactions with her students – many of them seasoned activists – and her membership in the local branch of COSAW that drew her into their activism, often assisting in mundane tasks such as writing pamphlets and organising meetings. Very often 'Comrade Antjie' spent a lot of time in her car, driving activists to and from meetings. She had made a decision about whose side of the apartheid divide she was on and the localness of her political commitment. So when the invitation came from IDASA to join other Afrikaans writers on a journey beyond South Africa's borders to meet the ANC at Victoria Falls in late 1989, she decided – in the spirit of true grassroots struggle accountability – not to go if the local comrades were unhappy that they had not been consulted (by IDASA) about the decision:

> They said I already had all the privileges and here they were, they had devoted their lives to the struggle and they weren't invited. So I said I wouldn't go. I told them, to me the most important contact is with you. The ANC is not going to do anything important to my life here. You are (Green 1990: 49).

Eventually the comrades relented – with some outside pressure – and decided that as she was a 'comrade in good standing' she should go on their behalf, Krog said.

But Krog's involvement with township activists also included her work as a poet. A collaboration with Sesotho oral poet Thami Phaliso from Kroonstad resulted in Krog putting her poetry at the service of the struggle. She had met Phaliso at the 'Women Speak' COSAW rally in Soweto when she realised they both came from Kroonstad. He invited her to join the local branch of COSAW. Krog talked on radio with Joan Hambidge about a singular experience she had with Phaliso at a rally in Bloemfontein in 1990 when 30 000 people gathered to welcome Nelson Mandela who had just been released from jail. Both of them recited poetry to a resounding response from the audience. Reflecting on this particular interregnum political moment when poets were called on to serve the struggle, Krog said she was

> working with COSAW and being commanded to read at rallies. This is poetry not from the inside, you are commanded to address 5 000 people with a microphone and small, useless sound

equipment. You have to ask what phrases will connect with black people, how will they believe what you say (especially because you are a woman). It's a wonderful challenge.[9]

In the next four years Krog's township involvement was to become as complex as the country's transition out of apartheid and the interwoven strands of grassroots activism and criminality were to enmesh her deeply. Upon F.W. de Klerk's announcement of the unbanning of the liberation organisations, she was interviewed by *Rapport* about her reaction. Journalist Coenie Slabber (1990b: 2), calls her one of the 'most active fighters against apartheid' and quotes her as saying she is very pleased about De Klerk's announcement. Krog got deeply involved in the local celebrations to welcome the freed Mandela and in various marches in the townships. These activities drew the attention of Kroonstad's conservative Afrikaners and Krog came out of her house one day to find the letters 'ANC' painted on the side of her car with enamel paint.[10] Dennis Bloem of the Maokeng Democratic Crisis Committee told *Beeld* that this was not the first time Krog had been intimidated and that she was also receiving threatening telephone calls.[11]

Things were to get much worse. On 25 February 1992 a local criminal, the leader of the Three Million Gang, George Ramasimong ('Diwiti') was murdered. Bloem was arrested and Krog was investigated but not charged. The three men implicated in the murder (Bloem, Roland Petrus and Cassius Ntlokosi) were all known to Krog and the gun used had been hidden at her house (unbeknown to her). Eventually she testified for the state, thus provoking headlines in the English press such as 'The Rebel Poet, the Activist . . . and the Dead Gang Leader' (Gevisser 1992: 7) and 'It's ANC Facing ANC in This Trial' (Collinge 1993: 6). The *Weekly Mail* quoted Bloem as saying of Krog's turning state witness: 'The community still loves Antjie. She's done so much good work here. She's been an activist here since she was 12. She's our sister. She's my sister and, whatever happens, I will not hold it against her' (Gevisser 1992: 7) Gevisser called Krog 'Afrikanerdom's renegade poet, an elegant wordsmith and eloquent conscience, one of only two white ANC members in town'.

The trial resumed in April of 1993 but in the same month *Beeld* reported that Krog had taken up the job of editor of the soon to be relaunched *Die Suid-Afrikaan* and was moving to Cape Town.[12] Local politics had become too difficult for Krog to negotiate any longer. While press interest waned in the trial – and it is hard to find archival material giving the conclusion to the saga – Krog turned the events into fiction, releasing *Relaas van 'n Moord* (*Account of a Murder*) published by Human & Rousseau in 1995.[13] Strictly speaking, this work of non-fiction predates *Country of My Skull* as Krog's first foray into this literary territory. The book is a typical Krog retelling of events that have factual references but she employs literary devices to destabilise a strictly referential reading of the story of the murder and her involvement.

*   *   *

The extraordinariness of these three mutually reinforcing consecrations by those working against the apartheid regime is that few white South Africans traversed these boundaries in the alternative political field of the time in quite this way. Krog's situation in the literary field and as an award-winning poet was useful to all three of these groups and their common struggle, as is evident. But these experiences – with a jailed ANC stalwart, with the ANC leadership in exile and with comrades in the townships – were to mark Krog as a different kind of Afrikaner, as a person firmly on the side of the struggle against apartheid and as a speaking voice, giving words to that struggle.

Trajectory: Achieving the literary heights with the Hertzog Prize

''n rym wat 1 minuut neem om te lees (sonder die sitaat)'
'Na ontvangs van die prys stap
u na die kateder en spreek 'n kort
dankwoord van nie langer as
een minuut nie. U samewerking in die
verband sal waardeer word.'[14]
Die boodskap is loud and clear: ons beplan,

ons diagram, ons protokol
óns sê op watter stoel sit watter pol

óns prys, óns betaal
van ons sal jy jou bek afhaal
baaskraties ja, en outakraties
maar die akademie is nie my baby nie
nie my baby nie
nie my baby nie
so lank sy in sulke tjalietjies lê
lyk sy nie na my nie

(wees nie ongemaklik nie dames en here, maar prakties –
die akademie is mos (l)eerbaar en demokra(k)ties)

volgens opdrag sê ek vinnig baie dankie
(10 sekondes is reeds nie meer)
die Hertzogprys bly onontvlugbaar 'n eer
(wat my hopelik nie sal dryf na drama, prosa of drank nie!)

die eer word herverdeel
onder my backupsystem fisies, geestelik, finansieel
onder kamerade, Degenaar, Anna Mofokeng
familie, vriende, kyse wat my kinders tem
oupas, oumas wat verwytloos aanvaar
kleinkinders wat soms sonder hul name verjaar
my John se instaan, uitstaan, opstaan en bakstaan
so bontstaan om demokragties my te laat oorstaan
       'had hom lief ja dit stry ek nie
       anders sou ek hom nie wou gevry het nie'
ook met Taurus wil ek herverdeel
defiantly oopgevou staan hul sambreel
oor waarhede, wanhopige, en dwarse skrywers
en laat ons nie vergeet o akademie
hoe tot die dood toe dinge was en nie wou ruimte gee nie

die geld van Afrikanerreputasie
word plesierig herverdeel na konsultasie
60% vir boeke in Afrikaans
uitgegee by Buchu, Genadendal, die balans
by Kasselsvlei, Ravanpress, St. Helenabaai en Taurus
(laasgenoemde twee kry die grootste advance)
40% om Afrikaanse kinderboeke te koop
waarin swart en wit kinders as matertjies loop
Daan R., H en R, T.berg, Taurus voorsien aan die nood
wat geskenk word aan COSAW biblioteke volgens akkoord

tenslotte 3 sekondes se rymende koeplet:
geld by uitgewers wat demokraties let, boeke by mense
vir wie'k alles feil het, in die taal wat my dié winternag
                                            moersverdaan beethet.
Ek dank u.[15]
'A rhyme that takes 1 minute to read (without the citation)'
'after receiving the prize you walk
to the lectern and deliver a brief
word of thanks no longer than
one minute. Your co-operation herein
will be appreciated.'
The message is loud and clear: we plan,
we diagram, we protocol
we say on which chair which tuft will sit[16]

our prize, *we* pay
you will shut your trap about us
baascratic yes, and outacratic[17]
but the academy is not my baby
not my baby
not my baby
while she's covered in that shawl
she does not look like me[18]

(do not be uncomfortable ladies and gentlemen, but practical –
the academy is after all receptive to knowledge and democra(c)tic)[19]

according to instructions I briefly say thank you very much
(10 seconds have already gone)
the Hertzog Prize remains an inescapable honour
(that will hopefully not drive me to drama, prose or drink!)

the honour is redivided
amongst my backupsystem physical, spiritual, financial
amongst comrades, Degenaar, Anna Mofokeng
family, friends, dates who tame my children
grandpas, grandmas who accept without reproach
grandchildren who at times celebrate nameless birthdays
my John's standing in, standing out, standing up, standing
ever ready to powerfully let me be[20]
      'loved him yes that I do not dispute
        else I would not have wanted to make love to him'[21]
with Taurus too I want to redivide
defiantly, vulnerable, their umbrella
shelters truths, despairing, and otherwise writers
and let us not forget O academe
how moribund things were and oppressive

the money of Afrikaner reputation
is happily redivided after consultation
60% for books in Afrikaans
published by Buchu, Genadendal, the balance
at Kasselsvlei, Ravanpress, St. Helenabaai and Taurus
(the latter two receive the largest advance)
40% to buy Afrikaans children's books
in which black and white children are buddies
Daan R., H en R, T.berg, Taurus address the need
donated to COSAW libraries as agreed

in conclusion three words of rhyming couplet:
money to publishers democratically alert, books for people
to whom I owe all, in the language that locks me this winter's night
in her fucking exhausting grip.[22]
I thank you (translated by Leonore Mackenzie).[23]

A fourth very significant consecration in this period was to come from the establishment in the literary field who crowned Krog with Afrikaans literature's highest award, the Hertzog Prize. In April of 1990 came the announcement from the Akademie vir Wetenskap en Kuns (Academy for Science and Arts) that the prize was being awarded for her latest volume of poetry *Lady Anne* (Krog 1989b). Previous winners included N.P. van Wyk Louw, D.J. Opperman, Elisabeth Eybers, Uys Krige and Ernst van Heerden. Because in 1984 Breyten Breytenbach had famously refused to accept the prize tainted by the Academy's association with the apartheid regime, questions were raised in the Afrikaans press as to whether Krog would accept it. Krog told *Rapport*, '*sy is die soort mens "wat alles aanvaar wat na jou kant toe kom – van smeerbriewe tot die Hertzogprys"*' (she is the sort of person 'who accepts anything that comes to you – from smear letters to the Hertzog Prize') (Slabber 1990a: 6).

Vrye Weekblad reported that Krog would use part of the prize money to buy Afrikaans children's books for the COSAW library (Prinsloo 1990: 15). In her acceptance speech – for which she was allocated a single minute – she recited the sharply worded poem above in which, in trademark Krog-style, she mingled English and Afrikaans, made reference to her sex life and included the mocking refrain, '*die akademie is nie my baby nie / nie my baby nie / nie my baby nie*' (the academy is not my baby / not my baby / not my baby). There was such great interest in her acceptance of the prize and the controversial speech that *Beeld* printed it in full.

In 1994 when she was interviewed by Marinda Claassen for 'Woman's World', Krog said she was cynical about these kinds of prizes: 'It's all about who the judges are, what their hidden agendas are, who they're trying to please, who they want to work out.'[24] Krog felt she had become awfully respectable, lost her youth and joined the establishment after winning the prize. Two months later she told Joan Hambidge on radio:

The recognition comes afterwards, it is never in your mind while you are writing. There is suspicion surrounding the *akademie*, you recognise that they are trying to say something by awarding these prizes. Winning this prize puts you in a different league. I find it terrifying and disgusting; it gives you an establishedness which I resent.[25]

Krog's increasing salience for the news media

At this point in Krog's biography we see a person with a rising profile in two fields – political and literary. Various forms of consecration have given her a very unusual position in the alternative political field for a white Afrikaans-speaking poet and she has reached the heights of the Afrikaans literary establishment. It is tempting to ask, having reached this point in the literary field, what further accolade could she aspire to? In the third field that concerns this book – the news media – there are two things to take note of here. The first is that during the politically volatile second half of the 1980s, Krog was regularly writing for the mainstream Afrikaans press (*Volksblad, Beeld*) and for the alternative weekly *Vrye Weekblad*. However, except for the columns for *Vrye Weekblad* in which she freely proclaimed her opinions and political stance, she confined her writing to commentary on books and poetry. The second thing to note is the news media's attention to Krog. Using James Dearing and Everett Rogers's insight (1996: 18) that agenda-setting, which signals 'salience' to the public, is very much about the repetitive appearance of a newsmaker, we see that Krog's every controversial move and statement was being captured with assidiousness by journalists, both Afrikaans and English. In the next chapter we see Krog taking a much more decisive and interesting turn into journalism and the news media world with further extraordinary consecrations in that field and very interesting shifts in both trajectory and subjectivity.

At this moment, located as we are at this hinge of South African history – 1989–94 – in this chapter, it is now opportune to examine Krog's ongoing experimentations in subjectivity via her poetry writing and important to engage with the text that preoccupied her at this time – *Lady Anne*.

Subjectivity: Self-othering using Lady Anne Barnard as a guide
Maart '86
Kroonstad
Liewe S.
P.S. I found several names: Augusta de Mist, Mrs Koopmans de Wet
& Lady Anne Lindsay (Barnard). Will look into them (1989b: 15).

'Lady Anne As Guide'
I wanted to live a second life through you
Lady Anne Barnard – show it is possible
to hone the truth by pen
to live an honourable life in an era of horror

but from your letters you emerge
hand on the hip talented but a frivolous fool, pen
in sly ink, snob, naive liberal
being spoilt from your principles by your useless husband
you never had real pluck
      now that your whole frivolous life has arrived
      on my desk, I go beserk: as a metaphor, my Lady,
          you're not worth a fuck (2000a: 73).[26]

In 1986, after a period of literary dearth, Krog began work on the volume
that is often considered her greatest poetic work by literary critics.[27] True
to the form she had been taught by Opperman, she crafted the volume
around a theme through which various ideas and thoughts were worked
out but this time she went in search of a *person* to hold the poetry, a
'guide'.[28] The volume itself shows that she toyed with several names –
'Augusta de Mist, Mrs Koopmans de Wet & Lady Anne Lindsay (Barnard).
Will look into them' – and then settled on Lady Anne as her poetic
interlocutor.[29] It seems from the commonalities in this list that Krog was
deliberately seeking out a woman, a historical person from the early days
of settlement in South Africa, from the early days of colonialism and
first encounters with the indigenous peoples and a writing woman (both
De Mist and Barnard produced 'travel' accounts) or at least an educated,
aware, thinking, conversing, assessing woman, as in De Wet. Her reasons

for choosing Lady Anne seem – on the surface – to have been technical and personal, as well as literary. She told Rina Thom in an interview on SABC radio that she had wanted to write an epic and that Lady Anne 'lent herself' to this task.[30] Lady Anne was a prolific chronicler of her own life and – towards the end of her life – engaged in adding her own life's story to her nephew's project of putting the Lindsay family on paper from the 1300s![31] But from the poetry itself comes Krog's declaration that she sought a guide to help her navigate the 'era of horror', which was the South Africa of the late 1980s under P.W. Botha's successive states of emergency.[32] In an early poem in the first part of the volume she says:

> ek is op soek na 'n vrou met taal en transparante see
> wat kan droogdok op papier;
> ek dink nie voorts in verse nie
> maar bundels en die snode ys daarvandaan;
> is my liggaam so stort ek oorbord
> spoor ek haar nie in my biografiese Woord (1989b: 15).
> I am searching for a woman with language and transparent sea[33]
> who can drydock on paper;
> I am thinking from now on not in verses but collections
> and the heinous ice that comes from them;
> if that's what my body is like I'll fall overboard;
> I won't find a trace of her in my biographical Word.

Having settled on the Scottish aristocrat (who came to the Cape in 1797, accompanying her husband who was Cape Colony secretary under the newly established British imperial power), Krog then travelled to Scotland to do research on Lady Anne's original letters, diaries and drawings.[34] The resulting volume appeared shortly after Krog was included in the writers' delegation that travelled to Victoria Falls in July to meet the ANC to discuss the cultural boycott and just before the newly released Kathrada stood up at the Soweto rally and read her 'lost' poem 'My Mooi Land'. Because its publication was at the pivotal moment in South Africa's history in which apartheid began to visibly unwind and because it marks the shift that Krog makes from Afrikaans poet of the domestic subject to South African writer of the national situation, from literary Afrikaans audience to national (and eventually international) English-speaking and not necessarily literary audience, *Lady Anne* is worth some scrutiny. It is my contention that Krog's self-fashioning as both a poet and an ethical South African, with political conscience and consciousness, is to be found in the ongoing construction of her distinctive voice and in her embrace of particular concerns first worked out in *Lady Anne*.

Krog's experimentation with an interlocutor was to become an important literary device of experimenting with subject positions, which she would develop from an engagement with a single, historical female character into a wider listening to and hosting of hundreds of present-day voices in her work on the South African TRC. Krog's poetic reworking of the life and writings of others goes back to 1975 when, in *Beminde Antarktika*, she wrote a poem about the German settler Selma Paasch whose family lived on a farm called Okankasewa in the Grootfontein district near Otavi. The family travelled to Okavango in Angola where they were attacked and their two children captured by Bushmen, after which Paasch returned to Germany. Then in 1981 in the volume *Otters in Bronslaai* she created a poem about the trekker Susanna Smit, which was reconstructed from this woman's diary in Dutch of the years 1799–1863. Smit is the legendary woman who confronted British commissioner Henry Cloete in Pietermaritzburg, telling him that even though the all-male Volksraad had decided to submit to British rule of Natal, the trekker women would cross the Drakensberg mountains barefoot rather than submit to this loss of liberty (Giliomee 2003: 169). In Lady Anne Barnard, Krog was to extend this work by using this particular character and her experiences to engender an entire volume of poetry.

Anne Barnard

Lady Anne Lindsay was born on 8 December to the aged Earl of Balcarres and his much younger wife Anne Dalrymple, the first of eleven children. Through her maternal grandmother Lady Dalrymple, who lived in Edinburgh, she was to meet some of the brightest minds of the day – David Hume, Adam Smith and Samuel Johnson.[35] After the death of her father in 1768, Lady Anne, aged 23, moved to Edinburgh where she already had a circle of friends. She was considered charming, clever and elegant and it seems that it was during this time that she met and made a lifelong friend of Henry Dundas, a Scottish lawyer who had been appointed solicitor-general for Scotland and who was to become secretary for war and the colonies under King George III.[36] It was also at this time that she composed the ballad 'Auld Robin Gray', which was to become extremely famous as a poem although she kept her authorship secret for many years. In 1772 Lady Anne moved to London to live with her widowed sister. Madeleine Masson says of this time:

> By the time Anne arrived at her sister's house in London, Margaret had already formed the core of the famous coterie, which would carry abroad the fame of the Lindsay sisters. Allied to most of the great families of England and Scotland, the two young women had little difficulty in becoming integrated into London's smartest and most exclusive circles . . . the sisters soon realised that the salon of a great lady would be the seed-bed for most political manoeuvres which would later come to fruition in the House of Lords or the House of Commons. The influence of women was tremendous and subtle (Masson 1948: 43).

Dundas helped Lady Anne with introductions to his friends in London and it was not long before she became intimate with the Prince of Wales (who drew her into his romantic intrigues), with William Pitt, the prime minister, and William Windham. As Dundas rose in government, he made increasing use of Lady Anne as a confidante, often visiting her house to discuss issues of the day.

Working from a number of contemporary sources, in particular the many letters that passed between Lady Anne and her interlocutors, Masson constructs a picture of a highly intelligent, well-connected woman living in the last half of the eighteenth century and making full use of all the privileges of her situation. Lady Anne attended the salons and gatherings of the privileged class, furthered her education through her own reading and her contacts with the thinkers frequenting London. She travelled and was a perspicacious observer of and prolific writer on the events going on around her. For a woman she also had a high degree of control over her own financial circumstances – even at one point taking up the renovation and selling of houses in London in order to make extra money with her widowed sister. It was her eventual marriage to a younger man, Andrew Barnard, when she was in her forties, which was to precipitate her coming to South Africa.

On 31 October 1793 when she married Barnard, she was 43 and he was 32. She used her relationship with Dundas to get Barnard a post in the colonial system. England was worried that a war with France might lead to the French seizing the Cape Colony (then under the control of the Dutch) and thus damaging England's ability to reach the East and India. The government decided to take the colony pre-emptively in June of 1795. Lord Macartney was sent out as governor, with Barnard as his secretary. As was the case with many other colonial administrators, Macartney's wife remained in England. But Lady Anne went with her husband as she had her own purpose in travelling to the Cape – an unofficial commission from Dundas to be his informant.

When they arrived at the Cape, Macartney let the Barnards live in the Castle, the quarters traditionally reserved for the highest colonial authority, while he took up a smaller residence in the Company Gardens. Lady Anne took upon herself the duties of a governor's wife. Masson records that this did not go smoothly as Lady Anne had to deal with numbers of colonists who did not immediately bow to her authority and respond to her invitations and she found herself travelling out into the colony to meet and make friends with Dutch burghers and those often estranged from the new English power and suspicious of her intentions. It is evident from reading her letters that she threw herself into representing the compassionate face of the new colonial regime and learning as much as she could about the colony so that she could be an accurate and knowledgeable correspondent for Dundas. In the process she made many friends among the Dutch burghers and travelled beyond the boundaries of the town to visit outlying areas such as Stellenbosch and Swellendam.[37]

Towards the end of their five years in the Cape, Macartney became ill and returned to England and General Francis Dundas (Henry's nephew) took over as acting governor. This was to usher in a period of disagreement over Barnard's responsibilities as secretary and his and Lady

Anne's occupation of the governor's quarters in the Castle. Dundas was succeeded by Sir George Yonge, whose niece, a Mrs Blake, then acted as hostess for the governor. Lady Anne continued to entertain but on a lesser scale and her unrevised letters from this time show the strained relations with the governor and the jealousy she felt directed towards herself and her husband, who was seen as enjoying high status only because of his marriage to her. Yonge became a profligate governor, spending government money unwisely and drawing the disapproval of both the Barnards and General Dundas and it was Lady Anne's letters to Henry Dundas that persuaded the colonial regime to remove him from his office in the Cape.

At this time Anne began to petition Dundas to recall them to London. Eventually this happened when the Cape Colony was ceded to the Dutch following the Peace of Amiens. She returned on 9 January 1802, leaving her husband to see the government satisfactorily handed over to the new Batavian commissioner (Commissioner-General de Mist, Julie Augusta Uitenhage de Mist's father). When he returned to England, they settled in Wimbledon and waited anxiously for a new appointment. When Britain again took occupation of the Cape in January 1806 – after war broke out again against the French – her friend Windham, now secretary for war and the colonies, sent Barnard on a six-month return commission to the Cape in May 1807. He was ill on the boat going out and in October became very ill while on a journey inland and died. His grave is in a cemetery in Somerset West and bears the words written by his wife: 'Colonists – he sought the welfare of your country and loved its inhabitants' (Robinson 1973: 296).

Lady Anne lived at her sister Margaret's house in Berkeley Square for the next five years. Dundas died in 1811 and Windham in 1812. As she grew older Lady Anne withdrew from London society and from her role as confidante to the politicians of the day. She spent the last years of her life revising her diaries and letters for the publication of the great family history of the Lindsays. But before she died on 6 May 1825, she allowed Sir Walter Scott, who had become a great friend in her old age, to put the persistent speculation to rest and to reveal that it was she, a woman, who was the author of 'Auld Robin Gray'.

Barnard the writer

It is interesting to note that in picking Lady Anne as her guide, Krog chose – from the height of the Enlightenment – a woman who was engaged in many of the practices that this historical period was to usher in as features of the public sphere of the modern world. In his seminal work, *The Structural Transformation of the Public Sphere*, Jürgen Habermas (1991) points to the rise of a particular dimension of public life that involved circulating information through letters and gatherings in private places, most notably in the homes – salons – of various educated women who acted as hosts. In his investigation of the power of the literary during the Enlightenment, Robert Darnton (2000) notes the great flourishing of diaries, journals and letters and the publishing and disseminating of information that burgeoned during the last half of the eighteenth century. Lady Anne's commitment to documenting her own life and the lives of those around her was part of this opening up of literary activities to private persons and particularly women. In both Edinburgh and London (and fleetingly in Paris) she was at the centre of such activities, participating in the circulation of information and hosting discussions in her London home, thus forming this 'third' space between private, domestic life and state-public life, in which important and critical issues could be aired. When she came to the Cape, Lady Anne brought to this outpost of Europe a taste of the practices of the public sphere of London and Edinburgh.

Lady Anne is also located at a moment that feminist theorists call the 'First Wave' of feminism, a time in which women such as Mary Wollstonecraft were taking issue with the social roles allocated to women. As Masson claims, Lady Anne was no 'bluestocking'; she used her aristocratic lineage and political connections to participate fully in society with the power given her by those connections.[38] It is noteworthy that while she was happy to be known as the author of the letters and diaries, she concealed her authorship of her poem for many decades – it was seemly enough at the time to be a female author of the feminine genres of diaries and letters but not of the masculine genre of poetry. Notably, this moment is also the time at which the movement for the abolition of slavery was gathering momentum and so engaging with the issue of treating various colonial Others as commodities was also being placed on the public agenda. There is no question that Lady Anne was aware of – and even sympathetic to – the activities of campaigners such as William Wilberforce. Her letters from the Cape show her interest in the treatment of slaves and her desire to collect information from this outpost to inform the abolitionists' agenda.

Lady Anne's writing has been divided into two strands for analysis: the letters to Dundas when she was operating as his informant and the journals in which she was casting herself not only as a diarist and chronicler of events but also as a travel writer – particularly in her *Journal of a Tour into the Interior* – in the mould of the Victorian explorers and the writing of the day, which was scientifically driven to produce great volumes of knowledge about lands new and as yet undiscovered (for Europeans).[39] Intertwined with these two outputs is her position as a woman, which gives her a particular vantage point and style, which though unofficial, was not without power and durability.

During her time at the Cape, Lady Anne wrote screeds of letters, not only to Dundas. She also wrote to Windham, Marquis Wellesley (the governor-general of India who spent time at the Cape en route to the East in 1798), Lord Macartney once he had returned to England and various others. W.H. Wilkins, the first compiler of some of Lady Anne's letters, notes:

> They are not merely the letters of a clever woman to her intimate friend, but those of the wife of the first Secretary of the Cape Colony to the Secretary of State at home. Lord Melville was the Minister chiefly responsible for the annexation of the Cape Colony by the English. Almost alone among British statesmen, he early recognised the importance of our keeping the Cape, not only because of its value as a station on the road to India, but because of the internal resources of the Colony and the great possibilities of development. He called the Cape his 'favourite child,' he watched over it with unflagging zeal, and he resigned office rather than be a party to its cession to the Dutch (1913: v).

The topic of slavery is perhaps one of the most interesting to focus on when assessing the attitudes of colonial writers. At the time Lady Anne was in the Cape, a significant movement campaigning for the abolition of slavery was being mounted in London. A.M. Lewin Robinson and Margaret Lenta comment that at the Cape Colony this was a 'very touchy issue' (Robinson, Lenta and Driver 1994: xviii). The Dutch had traded in slaves and imported slaves to South Africa and while the British continued the practice, they were more alert to the growing resistance back home to this form of labour in their colonies. Robinson and Lenta point out that like other settlers the Barnards were slave owners and in her writing Lady Anne shows herself to be in agreement with the general British assumption at the time that their treatment of slaves at the Cape was relatively humane. She also showed an interest in the state of the Khoikhoi, who mostly worked on farms in a kind of serfdom and records with regret that the terms on which the Cape was ceded to the British by the Dutch in 1795 forbade changes in laws of slavery and oppression of Khoikhoi.

Lady Anne, the Other in Africa

In her reading of Lady Anne's journals, Dorothy Driver (1995) is at pains to release this example of early white South African literary production from the category of 'racist stereotypical writing'. She deplores the easy activation of the pejorative categories of 'self' and 'Other' used by critics of colonial writing (and applied to contemporary writers such as John Barrow) and returns to Lady Anne's journals to investigate more thoroughly how she observes and records the situation in the Cape from 1797 to 1801:

> Barnard's *Cape Journals* modify current readings of Cape colonial discourse: rather than simply reproducing established categories of gender, race and class, the journals show ideology *in construction* in eighteenth-century South Africa as Barnard self-consciously deals with the discourses at her disposal. Besides the interlocutory nature of much of Barnard's writing, which stems from its address to various members of an external audience and which often brings with it a certain self-consciousness regarding the writing subject

and the discourse being deployed, the *Cape Journals* are often intralocutory: her writing presents different facets of the self, as if the different speaking positions that constitute her subjectivity are engaged in negotiation (or contestation) with one another, the self engaged in dialogue with an 'otherness' within. I call the process 'self-othering'. Moreover, gender, race and class reveal themselves at their points of intersection (rather than as discrete categories), thus disturbing the binary oppositions of 'self' and 'other' which have formed the basis of much colonial theory (Driver 1995: 46).

For my purposes in assessing Lady Anne as a guide for Krog and her work of self-fashioning through poetry, there are four useful and transferable points Driver makes about the various subject positions Lady Anne adopts in her writing. She points out firstly that Lady Anne's texts call 'attention to the different discursive positions that make the writer "Anne Barnard"' (1995: 47) and quotes Lady Anne: 'He was mistaken if he supposed I was *one* woman, that I was one, two, or three different ones, and capable of being *more*, exactly as the Circumstances I was placed in required' (Robinson, Lenta and Driver 1994: 164). Driver continues:

> Similarly, Barnard does not merely show a consciousness of her various roles (naturalist, travel writer, artist, earl's daughter, working wife, first lady, and so on), but adopts in her writing one or other of the roles at her disposal, one or other of the generic voices appropriate to and productive of these different roles, thus enabling her to enunciate a set of different perspectives on herself and the world . . . Multiple roles and multiple voices make up a complex subjectivity, defined not by a static and passive discursive position but by a series of shifts (1995: 47–8).

Second, says Driver, Lady Anne also exhibits a consciousness of her own position often as the Other to the Dutch burghers or the 'Hottentots' or the 'natives'. She often records experiences of being *looked at* for her difference or not being seen at all – as in the 'Hottentot' congregation's reaction to her during a visit to the Genadendal Moravian Mission of

10 May 1798 (Robinson, Lenta and Driver 1994: 331). Driver comments: 'Barnard's momentary recognition of the defining context, which introduces the notion of relative value into these scenes, sometimes expands to give a more complete, if still fleeting, dislocation to her sense of her status as superior in this unknown land. Looked upon by others, she thus looks upon herself' (1995: 48).

Third, Lady Anne shows evidence of inhabiting the position of the Other. Driver cites many examples but probably the most interesting is Lady Anne's observation of slaves about to be sold. She watches the slaves watching her and notes that she cannot know their situation because she looks through 'free-born eyes' (Robinson, Lenta and Driver 1994: 157). Driver comments: 'This is substantially if subtly different from feeling "sorry for" slaves, for it is slavery's perspective on her as "free born" that has informed her gaze' (1995: 48).

Driver's fourth point is about being female. She says Lady Anne's shifts in position are notably enabled by way of gender: 'That is, through the writer's awareness of the social construction of self which comes through an awareness of her social construction as "woman"' (1995: 49). Lady Anne's training and practice as an artist was also to give her the facility to take up varying points of view and although she was writing primarily in an unofficial capacity, many of her letters were directed at a very senior member of the colonial power and therefore occupied the uncertain and ambiguous space between official and unofficial, private and public. But throughout, Driver finds that Lady Anne demonstrates a self-conscious taking up of positions in her writing.

At the time of Lady Anne's writing from the Cape, a major social shift was taking place in European society in relation to the role of women. The 1790s was to become marked by radical writings by women such as Wollstonecraft (who produced A Vindication of the Rights of Woman). These stood in contrast to the prevailing discourse of the day, which, by means of a strict philosophical dualism, aligned women and their weak bodies with 'nature', while men and their intelligence were aligned with 'culture'. The two competing philosophies were to result in a lived contradiction for late eighteenth-century women, with a 'habitual self-depreciation' being coupled with 'a sense of potential equality with men' (Driver 1995: 52).

This contradiction is evident in Lady Anne's self-positioning through her writings. Driver says:

> In an attempt to construct a way of speaking which was both socially and psychologically feasible, women's voices shifted between the available subject-positions, often taking on self-conscious stances towards *whichever* subject-position was adopted from the range of positions between the polarities of 'masculinity' and 'femininity', and the qualities or states associated with them: 'intellect' and 'emotion', for instance, or 'culture' and 'nature' . . . Her strategy is necessarily to observe one subject-position from the position of the other, the writer observing the distressed and timid woman, the woman observing the intrepid writer, the ethnographer conscious of the literary woman, and vice versa. These moments of self-othering constitute moments of interrogation and self-irony: the discursive positions are simultaneously recognised and questioned (1995: 53).

Lady Anne: Krog's interlocutor

While Lady Anne was living at the height of Enlightenment optimism in the flush of confidence in British imperialism, Krog was living in the dying days of a decrepit, racist regime. Krog says through her poetry that she sought a guide for direction on how 'to live an honourable life in an era of horror' (2000a: 73) but it is an important question to explore why she should feel that this woman of late eighteenth-century London and Cape Town could speak to her in the South African situation of the late 1980s. In one interview Krog said that in doing research on Lady Anne's writings in Scotland she came across the lines: 'Every page is a page of struggle. I write to destroy the borders of unbearable pain' (Le Grange 1990: 21). While Krog must have been drawn to Lady Anne Barnard, the keen observer, the prolific writer, the courageous woman and the outsider (she was Scottish among the English, British among the Dutch, colonial among the colonised), it is surely not a simple matter of comparing similar life experiences and finding a kindred writing spirit.[40] Lady Anne's sojourn in Africa, her encounter with colonialism's Others and her literary manipulation of subjectivity, notably through the position of woman and her use of both interlocution and intralocution, therefore offer an analytical route into understanding her usefulness as a guide – not only as the subject for Krog's poetry but also for the purposes of investigating Krog's altering writer subjectivity.

What was the 'era of horror' Krog refers to? By 1989 South Africa had suffered successive waves of states of emergency declared by President Botha. He had had a stroke in January of that year and was obviously impaired as a leader but refused to step down from the executive position he had created for himself although he resigned as party leader (thus creating a political crisis because of this unprecedented situation of dual power). Not only were the liberation movements banned but internal peaceful attempts to dislodge apartheid were being received with unbelievable viciousness and force from police, the security apparatus and the army. Nevertheless the outspokenness against and denunciations of apartheid were fierce and unsilenced despite the repression. The campaign to isolate South Africa internationally was gathering momentum and in many arenas (such as sport, the arts and travel) was extremely effective. In his review of *Lady Anne* for *Vrye Weekblad*, André Brink points to the concatenation of circumstances the poet was dealing with:

> *Hierdie vertelsituasie is eerstens dié van 'n vrouedigter wat haar in die Suid-Afrika van vandag besin op noodstoestande . . . terwyl geweld om haar woed . . . en terwyl die konkrete, essensiële land om haar sy gang gaan, terwyl haar private vroulike lotgevalle deurentyd in jukstaposisie staan met die groter geskiedenis wat hom voorwoed, probeer sy – móét sy – skryf* (Brink 1989: 13).

> This narrative situation is firstly that of a woman poet who reflects on emergency situations in the South Africa of today . . . while violence rages around her . . . and while the concrete, essential land surrounding her carries on regardless, while her personal female circumstances stand in continual juxtaposition with the greater history forging ahead, she tries to – she *must* – write.

As mentioned previously, at this time Krog was working as a teacher, first at the Mphohadi Technical College in the black area of Maokeng and then at the Coloured high school in Brent Park. As the National Party stranglehold on South Africa tightened, she was increasingly engaging with her students and their struggle against apartheid. What we see here is the same kind of Lady Anne Barnard forthrightness in engaging with the Other.[41] This time it is apartheid's Other – in many ways just as unknown, hidden and geographically demarcated as the colonial Other for a white British woman.

And in the years in which she was crafting the pieces for the *Lady Anne* volume (1986–9), Krog was actively taking issue in public with the control of writers and the language exercised by the Afrikaans literary laager. Through her friendship with Dene Smuts, who became editor of the magazine *Fair Lady*, she was invited to the magazine's book week and as her subsequent articles for *Die Suid-Afrikaan* (Krog 1987) and *Fair Lady* show, Krog had a startling encounter with her literary Others – English-speaking and black.

Lady Anne: The text

In the very first poem of *Lady Anne*, Krog puts into the mouth of Lady Anne Barnard the crass and irritable (and Afrikaans) words, '*Wie is dit wat my bleddiewil afwaarts stuur / na vreemde bodems?*' (Who is it that bloody-well sends me downwards / to strange depths?). She knows, and we know, that it is Lady Anne herself – with her ceaseless petitioning of Dundas – who has sent her to the Cape. And it is Krog who has put them both (Anne and Antjie) in this particular literary boat. In the next 100 or so pages, Krog undertakes the most complex literary task: to discover dignity and honour as a South African living under apartheid through the medium of a dense, highly metaphorically layered, literary text, manipulating a historical subject who, in her own right, is a woman with her own mind, writings and history. The project is fraught from the start with the possibilities that the Anne-Antjie fit will not always work, especially when one reads the invocation (in the first section but which comes after eight poems):

Wees gegroet Lady Anne Barnard!
U lewe wil ek besing en akkoorde
daaruit haal vir die wysie van ons Afrika kwart.

Ek knieval, buig en soen u hand:
wees u my gids, ek – u benarde bard (Krog 1989b: 16).
Be greeted Lady Anne Barnard!
Your life I want to sing and take chords
out of it for the tune of our quarter of Africa.
I kneefall, bow and kiss your hand:
be you my guide, I – your awkward bard.

This textual abasement and adoption of a grovelling pose at the feet of
Lady Anne with these dual and conflicting motives (one noble: sing of
Africa; one perhaps somewhat suspect: use another writer's words to
unclog one's own writer's block) is excessive and alerts the reader that
this relationship (bard to Barnard) cannot hold for long.

From previous work it is evident that Krog looks for women, often
in history, whom she can use as mirrors and counterpoints to herself.
In this case, Anne has a similar name. Anne is also Scottish, rather than
English, and Krog is attracted to those who know what it is to be Other
to the British/English. The subject of Boer-British animosity since the
South African Wars is something she is very conscious of in Afrikaner
history and has returned to often – see, for example, Krog (1994b: 19).
Another powerful connection is Lady Anne's one and only poem (as
far as we know) and the time of its writing. In section 2 of *Lady Anne*
Krog repeats the 'Auld Robin Gray' poem (in Afrikaans) and then dates
it 'Balcarres 1768'. In many of the editions dealing with Lady Anne's
writing no date is given and there are only the remarks that she wrote
it when still young.[42] But in her text Krog makes Barnard seventeen or
eighteen at the time of writing – the same age at which she herself became
a published writer. This detail is important: Krog is making a personal
connection with someone who (like herself) has been a precocious writer
and someone who primarily negotiates living through writing. But also
at this point, Lady Anne gives Krog – the mother raising four children
'without words' – her writing to manipulate and use and play against.[43]

Lady Anne is a thoroughly postmodern volume, full of fragments from
a multiplicity of sources: newspaper reports about the political situation,
quotes, opinions and comments, fragments from Krog's reading – the

acknowledgements show that she has been reading a political text and a book on feminism at the time – an advertisement, a political poster, aphorisms, a menstrual chart and drawings of the 'tongvis' (sole, literally 'tongue fish'), as well as some scattered information on this fish.[44] *Lady Anne* also ranges across time non-chronologically, dipping in and out of the time of writing, the time of research into Lady Anne's writings and the period of her life and winds together Krog the writer with Lady Anne the interlocutor, sometimes in a poem-inspired transcription very closely aligned to Lady Anne's actual words from a diary entry or letter. The volume is structured as follows: sections 1, 2, 5, 4 and 3 and it ends with two conclusions, 'slot' and 'slot'.

But it is not these overt experimentations with intertextuality that make this an obviously postmodern work. More importantly, Krog, the writer with writer's block, is using already written writing to work on writing, bending it, shaping it and sometimes breaking it, to her particular task of new poetry. In a radio interview Krog told Rina Thom that *Lady Anne* was constructed as a 'collage'.[45] She said she was preoccupied at the time with the relationship between 'writer and object, the role of the poet and how the poet looks out and reacts to the object and what the poet brings of her own texts and situation to the poem'. From this comment it would seem that the text would be better described as a 'narcissistic' text, as in the work of Linda Hutcheon who says this is writing that is 'textually self-conscious' (1980: xi) or 'in some dominant and constitutive way, self-referring or auto-representational: it provides, within itself, a commentary on its own status as fiction and as language, and also on its processes of production and reception' (xii).[46] Texts of this type show an interest in *how* art is created (8). Hutcheon outlines the development of such texts:

> Texts became interiorised, immanent to the work itself, as the narrator or point of view character reflected on the meaning of his creative experience. This phenomenon of the nineteenth century may well, as Foucault has suggested, be a result of a change in the conception of the relationship between words and things, idea and object (1980: 12).

In her evocation of Lady Anne, Krog says: 'I wanted to live a second life through you / Lady Anne Barnard – show it is possible / to hone the truth by pen' (2000a: 73). While it is certainly a truism that in periods of social horror writers feel compelled to bend the work of the pen to the service of the 'truth' (often politically defined and certainly in South Africa of the late 1980s, the refrain 'culture is a weapon of struggle' was a loud and persuasive cry permeating all dimensions of aesthetic production), Krog's particular engagement with the 'truth' has many facets. It is primarily a literary preoccupation.

in die begin was die WOORD
sal my volgende gedig sê:
enkele duisterlike woord
wat in hom sal dra   geen verledes net voorspellings
                    geen gidse net genade
                    alles ook
wat blinde blysinnige bloed is
in hierdie destruktiewe suidoostewind in Bo-Meulstraat
wil die digter 'n gedig skryf
verby die drag geraamtes
van almal wat mank en Afrikaans is
maar die tong sal anders moet lê:
bevry die allerwoordste woord deur vers
wat wil klapwiek namekaar en nuut
die gedig sal wys hoe
woord in hierdie landskap waar word
om woordsontwil alleen
die nuwe gedig sal nooit slot hê nie
bard wat leer luister (Krog 1989b: 100).
in the beginning was the WORD
my next poem will say:
singular obscure word
that will carry in it   no pasts only prophecies
                    no guides only mercy
                    everything too
                    that is blind exultant blood

in this destructive southeaster in Upper Meul Street
the poet wants to write a poem
beyond the clothed skeletons
of everyone who is crippled and Afrikaans
but the tongue will have to settle differently
free the quintessential word through verse
that will flap in succession
and show the poem anew how
word becomes true in this landscape
for the sake of word alone
the new poem will have no conclusion
bard who learns to listen (translated by Neil Sonnekus).

Krog is looking for a biblical, God-breathed word that not only captures an essence perfectly but also is spirit-inspired to have the power to create something different. She makes the connections in this volume and binds together the literary preoccupations that are to remain her fixations for many years to come – word, tongue (literally and metaphorically as in mother tongue), bard and land. While she lays bare the naive, impossible, most extreme desire of seizing hold of the 'wordest' word (the word that is so itself that it *is* the thing it describes) she also shows the awareness that this word is beyond her reach, unattainable, mysteriously obscure and unknown and might in fact not come from the mouth of the poet but might have to be found through a position of listening, maybe even in silence and maybe not at all (if there can actually be no conclusion to poem-making).[47]

tranparant van die tongvis
die lig oor my lessenaar
vloei uit in die donker
ek wag my besoekers in op papier

my vier kinders
dorsaal en anaal hang hulle in fyn balans
vinnetjies aan die keel roer aanhoudend
oë besonders sag

in die vlak brakkerige water trap Ma klei
met die metafore

kom nader hier oor woordeboeke en leë bladsye
hoe lief het ek nie hierdie tenger skooltjie
hierdie vier vaart visse van my
nadergelok wat voer ek julle?

liefste kind hierdie smal flankie
laat hy meegee na die bedding
oor aan die strekking so ja dit
wring wel maar Ma hou jou vas Ma
is hier

die onderste ogie verwonders blour soos Pa s'n
migreer versigtig met 'n kmplekse bondeling
van senuwee en spiere
tot bo langs die ander
die parmantige mondjie trek byna afwykend
met tyd sal die tongetjie sy le kry
die boonste flank begin donkerder pigmenteer

onopvallend le julle tussen sand en klip
deel van die bodem en nooit
weer roofsugtic of op vlug nie
ek druk my mond teen elke verwronge gesig Ma weet

julle sal die gety oorleef (Krog 1989b: 92)

transparency of the sole
the light over my desk
streams into darkness
I await my visitors on paper

my four children
finely balanced between anal and dorsal

tiny fins at the throat constantly stirring
eyes uncommonly soft

in the shallow brackish water your mother treads clay
with metaphors

come here across dictionaries and blank pages
how I love this delicate little school
these fish of mine in their four-strong flotilla
lure so close now what should I feed you?

dear child of the lean flank
yield to the seabed
yes the stretching makes you
ache but mother holds you to her mother
is here

the lower eye like father's wondrous blue
migrates cautiously with a complex bunching
of nerve and muscle
till it's up beside the other
pert little mouth almost pulled out of shape
with time the tongue will settle in its groove
pigment of the upper flank beginning to darken

unobtrusive between sand and stone you lie
meshed with bedrock never
again to prey or take flight
I press my mouth against each distended face mother knows

you will survive the tide (Krog 2000a: 40; translated by
    Denis Hirson).

Lady Anne is the text into which Krog introduces for the first time the
metaphor of the sole (*solea solea*) or flatfish, or to use its Afrikaans name
and the word that allows Krog to burden it with language, the *tongvis*.

This word and the life of the fish it evokes will become the vehicle for Krog to negotiate terrible, overwhelming change through language and to wrestle with Afrikaner identity (the 'skeletons' and 'crippled' of the first poem quoted above), which at this point (1989) is indistinguishable from Afrikaans as a mother tongue. She explained to Rina Thom on radio: '*Die tongvis is 'n belangrike motief vir verandering om te kan oorlewe*' (The tongue fish [sole] is an important motif about change in order to survive).[48] And to Joan Hambidge in 1994, Krog gave a fuller description of how the fish is born upright but as it matures it turns on its side, its mouth and eye migrate to the top of its now flattened body and it moves down to the bottom of the sea where it lies flat and undetectable.[49] (A beautiful, evocative picture of this fish is to be found on the cover of the first editions of *A Change of Tongue*.) This metaphor of painful rearrangement of the physical fish body is intertwined with the poet's self-given task to make her own 'tongue lie differently' so that she issues forth not only the people of the future who will survive the change (literally and physically) but, literarily, the wordest words that do not *lie* the land (and here the double meaning in English is useful).

Krog: The Other in South Africa

If my contention is correct, that Lady Anne is being used by Krog as a guide, primarily to negotiate a new kind of subjectivity in response to South Africa's 'era of horror' – which I am calling, after Driver, 'self-othering' – where can the evidence be found for this? And is it possible to see Krog the writer using the self-othering techniques Driver has outlined in Lady Anne's letters, the interlocutionary and intralocutionary techniques? The most evocative use of multiple positions in Krog's volume *Lady Anne* is to be found in a lengthy poem, which but for a few details, Krog has based almost entirely on an actual experience of Lady Anne's, recorded in great detail in her letters from her 'tour into the interior'.[50]

Lady Anne at Genadendal
10 May 1798
The three Moravian brothers housed us.
Late that afternoon the bell rings

through the valley
(to be heard as far as Stellenbosch).
Biduur.
We sit shyly
face to face with a hundred and fifty others.

My coat is wrinkled, I realise, they are clothed in skin,
the clay floor of the small church lies
languidly cut under reed carpets in afternoon sunlight.
My coat stays with me. I can smell them. They also me.
                              The missionary
lifts his voice and says simply: mijn lieve vrienden.

But suddenly in this simplicity I notice Him –
quiet like a shiny bubble in my brain. Before Him
we are all naked but I see, as always, He sides with them:
the hungry, the poor, the crowds without hope,
the silent stubble, those without rights.
He becomes human in this building and turns to look at me.

It is good that I am here, it is good.
I remember my own church – the velvet matrix
with stones and corrupt chattering and I feel
God, how far away from You am I? How narrowly I know
still only myself – tired of white coinage
and they? The brushers of wigs,
the polishers of silver, the whitewashers of walls –
they know apart from themselves also my innermost bed.
God what do I do? How do I get rid
of this exclusive stain? Unexpectedly a song
swells into a garish passionate grief
supreme in pain (for the past or what is still to come?).

I sit surrendered in liturgical darkness,
my wrists frayed, my lips bleeding densely,
my head hangs in the softest sweat.

Before the closing prayer the missionary folds his hands
relentlessly into the eye of a needle.

I cut the ham into thin fragrant bundles
which the missionaries eat greedily,
swiping their forks through mustard.
'This you have to taste my brother!'
Our Madeira wine runs festively into cups.
I don't hear it. I don't see it.
Outside the moon grates herself insanely on the mountains.

More than millions tonight are huddling close to fires, crude
                                        bread and beer,
songs, stories drifting from the coals.
How do I give up this snug cavity into which I was born?
Turn. Give. And my overstuffed soul? Isn't it simply looking
for something new to thrill about? Shouldn't every settler
carry his bundle of gold and decompose in regret and guilt –

even the choice stinks of privilege.
While the night is still lying in the valley
blood bursts on the peaks. I get up. Brushes, inks,
water. I drink some coffee, bread, cold meat,
my fingers clumsy with my coat. Along the footpath
my eyes scout for heights. Quickly stretch pages, mix greens, yes

green is the colour of balance, green endures
all colours, green is constantly broken
to absorb closer and further.
Black is only a shade of the deepest green.
In water-colour white is forbidden; dimension
comes from exclusion.

I have to find a framework for the complete landscape
if I want to survive my emotion. Try. Pitch the valley
into perspective, the rest will follow by itself.

But the missionary moves between me and the sun,
Gaspar the slave holds the umbrella.
I wave him impatiently out of the way,
but it's too late –
the fixed sun bursts brutally from above
and drums Genadendal into mirage.

I don't get it on paper. It doesn't fit,
the scale is wrong. I aim. I start afresh.
I stare until it dawns on me:
my pages will always spell window, spell distance,
the angle of incidence is always passive
and this is the way Madame wants to live
in this country: safely through glass,
wrapped in pretty pictures and rhymes
but I could
do
differently.
I could slowly pull back my hand and pick up a stone.

> I could throw it,
> shatter the glass
> to gasp, to thaw retchingly in this hip-high landscape
> at last (Krog 2000a: 68).

By injecting the *gaze* as a textual vehicle, Krog takes an experience of Lady Anne's in which she remarks how little attention she was paid by the indigenous people – 'I was even surprised to observe so few vacant eyes, and so little curiosity directed to ourselves' (Robinson 1973: 122) – and makes this the means for the poet to shift position via her guide and observe from multiple places. In Krog's text Lady Anne is seeing and is seen (by 150 pairs of eyes), she smells and is smelt (a pertinent injection of the sense often evoked by apartheid racial prejudice). She pays attention to bodily dressing, conscious of the differences but again, looking at herself and aware that her own clothes are dirty from travelling. The Moravian missionary draws everyone present together in a 'we' by his words of inclusion, 'My dear friends', but Lady Anne has a moment of powerful exclusion. She sees God (seeing her, seeing them) and she sees God making a choice with them against her. This choice (which she observes imaginatively) is made perfectly in line with Christian theology: the poor against the rich, those who have not against those who have ('before the closing prayer the missionary folds his hands / relentlessly into the eye of the needle'). Krog then uses Anne to make the leap into the colonial/apartheid intimate space of knowing and being known differentially. Deftly she parses the types of knowledge that slaves/servants acquire from their tasks of doing everything menial and tedious in the lives of the oppressors. It is the slave who ultimately knows the master more, insidiously and intimately, even into his/her bed. Lady Anne suddenly knows this. She is the one without knowledge of those hundreds of individuals. The one against the many, 'the more than millions'. The apartheid-induced anxieties and evocations are inescapable in the words Krog has chosen.

Krog then shifts from Lady Anne the recorder/writer/diarist to Lady Anne the artist. Lady Anne is framing a valley (typically the land, traditional view of the controlling colonial gaze) in preparation for painting. Her artistic frustration leads to self-consciousness. What she sees is always through a glass, through a frame, via the page/paper. There is no direct, unmediated experience. And hence the shocking desire (certainly if this was read in the context of the burning townships of 1989 with rocks as the weapons of necessity for young activists) to recklessly and destructively remove the intermediary constraint that prevents knowing, seeing, experiencing.

This poem shows quite clearly that Krog uses Lady Anne as an alter ego to self-other through her own text. Krog adopts different discursive positions as Lady Anne Barnard; she shows Lady Anne as conscious of being the Other in relation to others and their watching or non-watching of her and she (through Lady Anne and by the injection of a religious debate prevalent in the late 1980s in South Africa's churches about their complicity with apartheid's denigration of 'the poor') inhabits the position of the Other and in fact judges herself in relation to her Other by invoking biblical categories of rich and poor.[51]

But Krog also self-reflects on the limits of text and use of language and the obscurity and inability of words to deliver not only self-knowledge and knowledge of the Other but also the ungraspable miracle power to transcend, create anew, think another reality.

'Woman' as Othering position

> *Waarom praat ons oor 'vroue' skrywers? Ek was behoorlik woedend toe ek die onderwerp ontvang het.*
>
> *Maar hoekom praat jy oor 'vroue' skyrwers? Hoekom word vroulike skrywers in 'n aparte kompartementjie gepas asof daar dingetjies sou wees wat net vrouens-skrywers sou lus wees om oor te praat? Waar is die manlike stem op die paneel? Waarom is daar nie 'n man teenwoordig om aan ons te verduidelik waar hierdie stupid onderwerp vandaan kom nie? . . . Impliseer die woord skrywer vanselfsprekend 'n man* (Krog 1989d: 41)?
>
> Why do we talk about 'women' writers? I was absolutely furious when I received this subject.
>
> But why do *you* talk about 'women' writers? Why are female writers allotted a separate little category as if there were certain little things only women writers would would want to write about? Where is the male voice on this panel? Why is there no man present to explain to us where this stupid subject comes from? . . . Does the word 'writer' automatically imply a man?

It is in Krog's speech delivered to the ANC writers' conference in July of 1989 at Victoria Falls that we find her engaging with the category of 'woman writer' with a high degree of anger and annoyance. But it is notable that while she questions the category and its theoretical basis, she also puts forward for discussion three critical points that cannot be escaped in dealing with writing that comes from the subject position 'woman'.

The first point is that to eschew the category entirely is to continue to perpetuate the disappearance of many women's voices from collected bodies of literature. In the speech Krog paid a great deal of attention to the external circumstances of support and the internal conditions of self-belief that enable writing and she speculated that it was the lack of these vital elements that has kept black women from being part of the literature of South Africa, particularly poetry (Krog 1989a: 5). She is also alert to the fact that anthologisers perpetuate the invisibility of women (3) and that male writers write on behalf of women, citing Zuluboy Molefe's *To Paint a Black Woman* and the male writer who put on paper the experience of women and children in the South African War concentration camps (4). Krog also shows a keen awareness that the racial dynamics in South Africa of the time had allowed a fairly prolific output of poetry from white Afrikaans women, which then obscured the fact that the majority of women who are black produced very little considered literary.[52]

The second point she makes is that the experience, knowledge and particularities of being female in the world give women a position that is different from that of men from which to write. In the discussion that followed the delivery of Krog's speech, poet and ANC member Jeremy Cronin introduced a thought for debate that bound this particularity of experience directly to language itself: 'It's women who experience language already as opaque, as problematic, as difficult. It's dominated, as we've already been reminded several times by interventions, by male categories. We keep talking about "he" the writer and so forth' (Coetzee and Polley 1990: 145). If we turn back to the text of *Lady Anne*, we find Krog using female physicality, experiences of motherhood and being a wife as part of the poem-making. For example, the inclusion of her tracking sixteen months of her menstruation and her assertion that her body's rhythms and flows have a profound effect on her ability to write. She was quoted in *Beeld* in 1989, explaining: '*Dit is my 'private voice'. Dit dui hoe ek sukkel met 'n gedig. Menstruasie het 'n groot invloed op my*' (It is my 'private voice'. It indicates how I struggle with a poem. Menstruation has a great influence on me).[53] In the public furore that surrounded the printing of this chart, there is an interesting comment from her mother that shows the powerful association with language by the inclusion of this chart: '*Menstruasie is deel van jou – net soos digwerk, wat ook ontboeseming is*' (Menstruation is part of you – just like writing poetry, which is also an outpouring).[54] The word Dot Serfontein uses is '*ontboeseming*', which is also an unburdening or a confession. There is no doubt that while she fights with the category 'woman writer', Krog holds powerfully to the unique experiences that being female give to the poet as material and techniques to deal with the body and the visceral. There is also the suggestion, incipient in the *Lady Anne* work, which found fruition in *Country of My Skull*, that unlike the slipperiness of words, the truth of a situation (political/social) is often to be found in the embodied experience, especially as encapsulated and experienced in a woman's body. An interesting insight on this point comes from Marius Crous (2003: 1), who remarks that while a central theme of *Lady Anne* is the body and while Krog uses the body as a writing instrument and as a 'textualised object' (referring here to Hélène Cixous's work) she also has a deep interest in the actual bodies of the Other(s).[55] Crous says: 'In *Lady Anne* the focus is in particular on the body of the Other(s) encountered at the Cape by the historical subject, Lady Anne Barnard.' But he also points out that Krog transcends the boundaries of the female body-female writer link, 'conveying her intentions' by also using 'phallic metaphors'. Krog does not allow her own experience of being in a female body or speaking with a female voice to be a limit.

The third point made by Krog is that this particularity of experience does not mean that both men and women writers do not have the imaginative and sympathetic capacity to embody the other sex successfully and convincingly in writing. In response to a question posed by Vernon February about whether 'Etienne van Heerden could have done justice to *Fiela se Kind* as Dalene Matthee did', Krog answers: 'I can only answer the answer that I need: that I need to think he could have done that' (Coetzee and Polley 1990: 147).

* * *

Lady Anne is the key text in Krog's literary trajectory in which she experiments with a writer subjectivity that is responsive and responsible to the situation of 'horror' she was living through at the time, a fine-tuning of her aesthetics to speak to a particular politics. Because this volume of work won a very prestigious prize and was reviewed and written about – mostly by literary critics and other poets – this information was widely disseminated to the general public via newspapers. So Krog came to be known by the South African public (Afrikaans-speakers first, then English, as a result of the media coverage of her encounters with Kathrada and the ANC in exile) as a certain kind of poet and public figure. Her specific literary symbolic capital was greatly enhanced via the awards and the acclaim (much of it by already established literary experts) expressed in the reviews. She had reached the pinnacle of achievement in the section of the South African literary field that was Afrikaans writing. But the news about her was to spill over into the English-language news media when her opposition to apartheid was widely reported on, through the news of various events and activities, some shocking, such as the murder in Kroonstad she was connected to. In this period of her life she entrenched her politics and via three important, mutually reinforcing consecrations, established for herself alternative political credentials. Her trajectory into the alternative political field involved the accumulation of political credibility and capital but we can also see her accumulation of symbolic capital as a writer and her increasing salience as a newsmaker for the media and beyond the boundaries of the Afrikaans press.

More importantly, through her engagement with Lady Anne, Krog began a great experiment in subject position, which she has continued as she has grown in stature as a poet and writer. This adoption of self-othering shows a subjectivity seeking to relate to South African Others, those othered by apartheid and now making fierce claims for recognition and citizenship in the post-apartheid era. But also, very importantly, this experimentation with subjectivity continues to be fixated on language and the body.

Notes

1. I was informed by the secretary of Krog's former high school that, after a merger of three high schools in the area, documents from as far back as 1970 had been destroyed, so there is no official record of this school magazine.

2. Two journalists documented this poem's title as 'Jammer'. It is very difficult to establish why the confusion arose. This title does not appear in either of Kathrada's books from his time on Robben Island or attached to the poem when it was published in newspapers in 1970. The only possibility seems to be an association with a poem that appeared in her first volume *Dogter van Jefta* called 'Ma', which contains the lines '*ek is so jammer mamma / dat ek nie is / wat ek graag vir jou wil wees nie*' (I am so sorry mamma / that I am not / what I so much want to be for you) (1970: 12).

3. This version is from the photocopy of the actual page written by Kathrada, given to

me by Sahm Venter, editor of *Ahmed Kathrada's Notebook from Robben Island*. Two slightly different versions appear in the *Notebook* (Venter 2005: 45) and in *Memoirs* (Kathrada 2004: 231).

4. I have transposed the order in which these excerpts appear in Kathrada's book. He must be mistaken about discovering the Krog poem in 1967 or 1968 as it was only written in 1969. His transcription of the translated poem bears no date, only '(Huisgenoot)', which Kathrada said in personal communication may have been a way of referencing an allowed publication in case the notebook was discovered by the guards. The poem may have reached Robben Island either (as Hans Pienaar suggests) through the school magazine, which had somehow found its way there, or through Nelson Mandela's access to outside materials in 1970 when he was studying Afrikaans and so was allowed to read *Huisgenoot*. My attempts to establish whether the poem indeed appeared in this magazine have been unsuccessful, despite searches in several libraries.

5. A wave of meetings outside South Africa's borders had been taking place with the ANC, among them: in 1985 Gavin Reilly, chair of Anglo American, led a delegation of business people to meet with the ANC in Mfuwe, Zambia, and the executive of the Progressive Federal Party did the same in Lusaka. In June 1986, the chair of the Broederbond met the ANC at the Ford Foundation offices in New York.

6. 'Sê Jou Sê', *Volksblad*, 19 July 1989: 10. Krog says ''n mens verkies a boikot bo geweld' (one chooses a boycott over violence). See also Slabber (1989: 34) and 'Debat oor Boikot Was Nodig', *Vrye Weekblad*, 19 October 1989.

7. '*Dot Serfontein het mos verwoestend ingevlieg onder die Afrikaanse skrywers wat die beraad met die ANC bygewoon het*' (Dot Serfontein charged destructively into the debate over Afrikaans writers that attended the meetings with the ANC). 'Moeders en Dogters', *Beeld*, 27 July 1989. Coenie Slabber (1989: 34), reporting on the Afrikaanse Skrywersgilde meeting in Broederstroom, quotes Hein Willemse as being for the boycott and Wilma Stockenström against.

8. 'Woman's World', 16 May 1994, SABC Sound Archives, T94/725 (Marinda Claassen in conversation with Antjie Krog).

9. 'The Poet Speaks', 24 July 1994, SABC Sound Archives, E94/233 (Antjie Krog talking to Joan Hambidge about her poetry and her life).

10. In *Begging to Be Black* (2009b: 7), Krog says it was 'AWB'. But the newspapers of the time say: 'the word ANC' (*Volksblad*, 7 September 1990: 1); 'painted with ANC slogans' (*Saturday Star*, 8 September 1990: 3); the 'letters ANC' (*Beeld*, 8 September 1990: 3) and 'ANC letters' (*The Citizen*, 8 September 1990: 15). It could be that the first newspaper to print this got it wrong at the time and the others followed suit.

11. 'Geterroriseerde Antjie se Motor 'n Vandale-Teiken', *Beeld*, 8 September 1990.

12. 'Antjie Krog na *Die Suid-Afrikaan*', *Beeld*, 22 April 1993: 5.

13. *Account of a Murder* was published in English by Heinemann in 1997, translated by Karen Press.

14. Extract from the Akademie vir Wetenskap en Kuns's written procedural instructions to Krog prior to the prizegiving.

15. 'Antjie Krog se Toespraak', *Beeld*, 26 June 1990: 1.

16. Translator's note: '*pol*' = tuft of grass or hair.

17. Translator's note: '*baas*' = master , '*outa*' = old man. The word '*outas*' refers very specifically to old Coloured or black men. A white man is *never* called '*outa*'. Therefore, within the context of Krog's speech, both the Academy and academe in general are upholding the master (*baas*)/slave (*outa*) relationship.

18. Lines 12–16 are a parody of an old Afrikaans folk song about disowning an immoral cover-up.

19. In other words, the Academy must practise what it preaches. Translator's note: (*l*)*eerbaar*: *eerbaar* = honourable; *leerbaar* = receptive to knowledge/teachable. This has a sarcastic tone. *Demokra(k)ties* involves an obvious wordplay on shit/crap.

20. Translator's note: in line 30 she refers to her husband John as being 'demokra(g)ties'. I take that to mean that he is a powerfully democratic partner; powerfully supportive of her as his equal; powerfully supportive of letting her be to do her own thing.

21. Translator's note: the word *vry* also means free/liberated. The line could allude to her and John being free/liberated in and by their love for each other.

22. Translator's note: Despite her insults Krog accepts the prize. Why? The answer lies in the last three lines of the poem: '*die taal wat my die wintersnag / moersverdaan beethet*' – 'the language that locks me this winter's night / in her fucking exhausting grip'. She does it for the language Afrikaans (her beloved mother tongue) that locks (holds her prisoner) this winter's night (it is literally the winter month June and she is receiving a prize from a 'cold' elitist institution/world that figuratively leaves her cold). '*Moersverdaan*' is a neologism combining uterus + mother + fuck you + exhausted + touched. Such powerfully mixed feelings at being awarded – and accepting – the Hertzog Prize!

23. Translator's note: By using '*u*' – the respectful form of address in Afrikaans – she perhaps mocks the self-importance of her hosts and assembled guests.

24. 'Woman's World', 16 May 1994, SABC Sound Archives, T94/725 (Marinda Claassen in conversation with Antjie Krog).

25. 'The Poet Speaks', 24 July 1994, SABC Sound Archives, E94/233 (Antjie Krog talking to Joan Hambidge about her poetry and life).

26. Unless otherwise indicated, the poems that appear in English in *Down to My Last Skin* (Krog 2000a) are Krog's own translations from Afrikaans.

27. In *Lady Anne* the poem on page 13 begins: '*twee jaar aankomende maand / sedert Jerusalemgangers / twee jaar sonder 'n enkele reël donker // sonder 'n gedagte selfs wat sou kon tot dig // so wil ek my lewe hê so / skryfloos van hierdie huis / die bindmiddel*' (two years this coming month / since *Jerusalemgangers* / two years without a single dark line // without a thinking self that could make poetry // I want my life to be so / without writing of this house / the glue).

28. 'True to the form she had been taught by D.J. Opperman': I owe this insight to Tim Huisamen from Rhodes University's Department of Afrikaans and Nederlands.

29. Julie Augusta Uitenhage de Mist was the eighteen-year-old daughter of Advocate Jacob Abraham Uitenhage de Mist, who was sent by the Batavian Republic to the Cape as commissioner-general in 1803. She travelled the colony with him, going as far as the Fish River in the east and writing a diary in French, subsequently

translated into Dutch and published as 'Dagverhaal van une Reis naar die Kaap de Goede Hoop en in de Binnenlanden van Afrika', which appeared in a magazine called *Penelope* published in Holland (Mills 19–). Marie Koopmans de Wet was the daughter of Hendrik J. de Wet, president of the Burgher Council during the first British occupation of the Cape. She was highly educated for the time, spoke several languages, painted, played music and travelled. She became known as the hostess of the Salon of Strand Street where she received and entertained presidents, governors, politicians, travellers, scientists and academics. Her intervention saved the Castle from partial demolition, prevented unsympathetic alterations to the Groot Constantia homestead, and stopped the removal of old trees in the Company Garden and the closure of a Malay cemetery at the foot of Signal Hill.

30. 'Skrywers en Boeke', 3 August 1989, SABC Sound Archives, T89/843 (Rina Thom in conversation with Antjie Krog about *Lady Anne*).

31. Resulting in the 1849 three-volume *The Lives of the Lindsays or a Memoir of the Houses of Crawford and Balcarres* (Crawford 1849).

32. Krog told Rina Thom that she said in a lecture to the Wits Winter Forum in 1993 that *Lady Anne* was 'not a mirror' but a 'vessel'. 'Skrywers en Boeke', 3 August 1989, SABC Sound Archives, T89/843 (Rina Thom in conversation with Antjie Krog about *Lady Anne*).

33. Nautical imagery is a powerful poetic vehicle in *Lady Anne*, but the transparent sea/ transparency (the pun works well in English) is also being used in the sense of a *tracing* from which another drawing can be made.

34. Barnard left her writings to her nephew, son of her eldest brother. The writings are now the property of the Earl of Crawford and on loan to the National Library of Scotland.

35. Edinburgh was a centre of Enlightenment activity in the late eighteenth century, with its own salons and circulation of powerful people – see Hannay (2005).

36. J.H. Anderson calls Henry Dundas the Secretary of State for War, Treasurer of the Navy and President of the Board of Control in Pitt's first administration (1924: ii, v). He later acquired the title Lord Melville.

37. In her letters gathered together as *Journal of a Tour into the Interior*, Lady Anne claims that they covered 'seven hundred miles of Africa' by ox wagon; see Robinson (1973: 158).

38. 'Bluestockings' were women who gathered for artistic, literary intellectual and witty exchanges. Critics have used the term to refer to learned and thus, in their minds, unfeminine and pretentious women. The term was evidently first used in the 1750s to refer to women and men in London who gathered for conversation. This definition is from Kramerae and Treichler (1992).

39. Her letters to Dundas stayed in his family until acquired by the South African National Society in 1948.

40. See '"I think I am the first" – Lady Anne on Table Mountain' (Krog 2000a: 66) and 'All I asked as a reward . . . was that he should accompany me to the top of the Table Mountain . . . where no white woman had ever been but Lady Anne Monson who

had a little of my own turn for *seeing*, which is *seldom seen*' (Robinson, Lenta and Driver 1994: 217–18).

41. I base this comment on my readings of Lady Anne Barnard's letters from the Cape.

42. A.M. Lewin Robinson (1973: 2) says that the poem dates from after 1771 when her sister Margaret married and 'being left much to her own devices, Lady Anne developed her literary bent'; see also Wilkins (1913: iv).

43. Another irony: *Lady Anne* contains several poems about writer's block – writing about not writing: '*weer eens / voor 'n leë bladsy lynloos A4*' (yet again / facing a blank A4 page) (Krog 1989b: 14).

44. The political text and the book on feminism Krog refers to are James Leatt, Theo Kneifel and Klaus Nürnberger's edited volume *Contending Ideologies in South Africa* (published in 1986) and *'n Vlugskrif oor Feminisme* by Marlene van Niekerk, published under a pen name 'Mieke Krik' in 1987.

45. 'Skrywers en Boeke', 3 August 1989, SABC Sound Archives, T89/843 (Rina Thom in conversation with Antjie Krog about *Lady Anne*).

46. Hutcheon says of this kind of writing that it is 'textually self-aware . . . self-reflective, self-informing, self-reflexive, auto-referential, auto-representational' (1980: 1).

47. This awareness is embodied in the structure of the poem, which begins with the fiat-type declaration (of the WORD in capitals) but unravels into multiple descriptions and many words that chase after, 'flap' around, but do not capture what that quintessential word could be and eventually leave the poet waiting in silence.

48. 'Skrywers en Boeke', 3 August 1989, SABC Sound Archives, T89/843 (Rina Thom in conversation with Antjie Krog about *Lady Anne*).

49. 'The Poet Speaks', 24 July 1994, SABC Sound Archives, E94/233 (Antjie Krog talking to Joan Hambidge about her poetry and life). Krog told Hambidge she wrote the poem in *Lady Anne* 'transparant van die tongvis' for her children, 'for them to become part of this country and not to be frightened and flee'.

50. See Krog (1989b: 55–7) for the Afrikaans version of this poem from *Lady Anne* and Lady Anne Barnard's letters of 5 and 10 May 1798 on this event in Robinson (1973: 106ff.).

51. See, for example, 'The Kairos Document', published in 1985 as a theological challenge to apartheid. http://www.sahistory.org.za/archive/challenge-church-theological-comment-political-crisis-south-africa-kairos-document-1985.

52. Krog makes the point that 'seventy percent of poets making their debut this year were women, the three finalists for the Old Mutual Prize were women' (1989a: 5).

53. 'Antjie Krog Kaart Totale Menswees in Bundel', *Beeld*, 8 November 1989: 3.

54. 'Antjie Kaart die Totale Menswees', *Die Volksblad*, 4 November 1989: 3.

55. 'By writing the self, woman will return to the body which has been more than confiscated from her . . . Censor the body and you censor breath and speech at the same time. Your body must be heard (Cixous 1997: 351)' (Crous 2003: 3). The quote is from Hélene Cixous, 1997, 'The Laugh of Medusa', in *Feminisms: An Anthology*, ed. Robyn Warhol and Diane Herndl, 347–62. London: MacMillan.

5

Second-Person Performances

In May of 1993 Antjie Krog became a working journalist when she moved to Cape Town to become the editor of the relaunched Afrikaans alternative magazine *Die Suid-Afrikaan*. While the motive for the move seemed to be a response to an opportunity – she was asked by the founders to be the new editor – Kroonstad had become a difficult place for her to continue living because of the aggressive attention of right-wing Afrikaner organisations. Editor and academic André du Toit had, with Krog, been one of those Afrikaner intellectuals who met with the ANC in exile in 1989. He had founded *Die Suid-Afrikaan* with fellow academics Hermann Giliomee and Johan Degenaar as a vehicle for Afrikaans intellectual debate in 1984 when they felt that it was impossible to comment on the political and social situation via the Afrikaans press without their views being distorted.[1] He had been co-editing the magazine with Chris Louw (who was moving to work at the *Weekly Mail*) when it was decided the publication needed a new editor, a new design and a new purpose in the volatile years leading up to formal political transition. His choosing Krog as the perfect candidate for the editorship of an Afrikaans, issues-based magazine aimed at educated Afrikaans-speakers of all races was important as an act of attention and transition in Krog's trajectory because it caused her to move to a major urban centre and to relocate to journalism as a field of production. This location and the accumulation of journalistic expertise was to make it more possible for her to then move into the mainstream news media more decisively. It also acted as reinforcement of Krog's alignment with anti-apartheid Afrikaners and again with the intellectuals in that grouping (as when she was invited to make the two visits to the ANC in exile).

Within a year, the editorship with its demands and limits had begun to take a toll on Krog, who experienced difficulty dealing with technical problems, deadlines, political rhetoric and the constant financial struggles to keep the magazine afloat.[2] In an interview in 1994 she reflected on the differences between journalism and poetry: 'Journalism? You have to be a jackal, manipulative, shrewd, there is the tyranny of space, there is the so-called reader to have to capture, influence and manipulate . . . part of me absolutely resents it.'[3]

But this grappling with reporting, editing and managing a magazine was a very important step for Krog into the media field as a recognised practitioner of journalism. At this point in her life Krog had decisively entered the Afrikaans literary field, distinguished herself as a poet with a well-defined idiolect, won the field's prizes and received accolades from its consecrators. She had also authoritatively seized the territory as the poet of the body, the female voice and the transgressive. In the alternative political field, Krog was hailed and now known for her associations with the ANC leadership – both in exile and in prison – and with the local comrades in Kroonstad. Her joining the ANC placed her firmly on the side of the democratic project to make South Africa a nation for all its people. But until this point, her forays into journalism were often based on her literary capital and her political newsworthiness. Her capital in the media field was not yet based on her skills and knowledge of the cultural terrain of journalism as a practice in its own right. In this chapter I pay attention to Krog's transition into the media field and her accumulation of capital in this field. I start by looking at the consecrations that were to facilitate her entry into journalism, this time not as a newsmaker, but as a practitioner.

Trajectory: Into news journalism proper
Afrikaans radio reporting

In 1995 Krog made a far more significant trajectory move in the media field than her editorship of *Die Suid-Afrikaan*. When SABC radio, under the leadership of Pippa Green, approached Krog to join the post-election, reconstituted parliamentary team in January of 1995, she took the job as the journalist responsible for Afrikaans reports. Green and Krog had established a friendship after the interview for Leadership SA magazine in August 1990. When the SABC was placed under new direction during the transition to democracy, Green was in charge of putting together a parliamentary team that could cover the workings of the new democracy in as many South African languages as possible. Krog was her choice for the Afrikaans member of this team.[4] In the newly constituted democratic South Africa it was an important mission to place the public broadcaster under the control of a board, remove its tainted association with the apartheid government and ensure that reporting in the Afrikaans language was in line with journalistic principles of objective information dissemination, rather than in the service of the apartheid regime. Krog was seen as having the right political credentials to help fulfil this mission.

During this year, as developments got underway to set up a truth and reconciliation commission for South Africa, Krog was involved – through her connections with IDASA – in participating in and reporting on various discussions about the necessity of such a commission for South Africa.[5] In the same year Green made Krog head of the radio team to cover the TRC, the only news media outlet in South Africa that would track the entire process and every public hearing over the course of the Commission's life. Green facilitated this transition by recognising Krog's symbolic status as both political actor and writer, rather than focusing on her field capital as a journalist (she had no previous radio reporting experience) thereby enabling her shift into political journalism proper and making possible the conversion of her, by now, very significant literary and alternative political field capital into media field capital. Even though Krog had spent a year as editor of Die Suid-Afrikaan, it was her work on the TRC with the SABC that took her out of the confines of being a writer-commentator and into the daily processes of hard-news journalism, which was to give her access to a very significant political process gaining attention and currency all over the world. But more than that, the TRC was a process ambitiously set up to engage all South Africans in major political and social transition via the media. Krog and other journalists were therefore 'installed as proxy witnesses of trauma on behalf of their readers' (and listeners, in this case) as Gillian Whitlock says (2007: 140). Whitlock, an Australian literary theorist (whose research interest has been in the hearings about the 'stolen children' in her country) points out that such commission processes taking place worldwide have resulted in an altered status for the journalist who is required to become 'conveyer, translator, mediator and meaning maker of trauma on our behalf'.

Krog heartily embraced the role of mediator of the TRC for radio listeners. In Gerrit Olivier's review of *Country of My Skull*, her book account of the TRC, he remarks that 'she and her fellow reporters tried to capture the headlines in order to force the narratives told at the Commission into the public consciousness' (1998: 222).

> In her characteristic Free State Afrikaans accent Samuel combined factual reportage with strong involvement in the process . . . despite her many doubts Samuel has been an advocate of the process . . . not surprisingly some listeners objected to what they perceived to be the moral and ethical pressures emanating from Samuel's journalism (Olivier 1998: 221).

Later, in an interview with Gillian Anstey, Krog explained why she was using her married name 'Samuel' for her TRC work:

> As a reporter I am supposed to speak in correct Afrikaans. But I don't. I speak a lekker Anglicised Afrikaans and I can't report in that. So my reporting is un-me, un-Krog, un-poetic. I see Samuel as the surname that obeys the codes of the SABC and of language, the rules of the game. Krog is the disobedient surname (Anstey 1999: 11).

Here we see Krog making a clear distinction between the practices of the poet and the journalist and, because she recognises the constraints of the journalistic mode, setting aside the name 'Krog', synonomous with poetry and the distinctive voice of transgression. But Krog's crafting of her voice and her experimentations with subjectivity infected her journalism with the very hallmarks she was trying to restrain: Anglicisations, slang, graphic descriptions, a sympathetic tone of voice and insistence that listeners face the horrors being unearthed were so evident in her reports that national radio editor Franz Krüger had to deal with complaints that Afrikaans-language stations did not want to use them.[6]

On the announcement of Krog's appointment to the SABC, an exasperated radio listener, Hannes de Beer of 15 Kommandant Street in Welgemoed, wrote to *Die Burger*, acknowledging: 'Now we all know that this woman can make magic with the language' and commenting that while Krog had a track record as a poet with multiple publications, she also found ways to create 'bastard products'. Using a piece she had written for *Die Suid-Afrikaan* as an example of her 'mix is cool' style, he then went on to say: '*Radio is 'n praat- en luister-medium. Dit het ook heelwat invloed in sekere kringe*' (Radio is a talking and listening medium. It also has a great influence in certain circles) and concluded that if Krog was going to behave at the SABC as she did at her magazine, then '*hemel behoede Afrikaans*' (Heaven protect Afrikaans) (De Beer 1995: 8)!

Another interesting insight comes from a piece for *Rapport* written by journalist Hanlie Retief in a column called 'Hanlie Se Mense' (Hanlie's People). Headlined 'Waarheidskomissie het haar ingesluk en alles hou heeldag net aan' (The Truth Commission sucked her in and everything just goes on the whole day), Retief comments that some people turn off the radio when they hear Krog's 'Avbob-stem' (funereal voice), while others continue to listen fascinated.[7] She is not afraid of graphic detail, Retief says, and comments:

> *sy't 'n onthutsende gewete geword, 'n naelstring tussen die WVK en Afrikaanssprekendes. Sy't soos net 'n digter kan, die dikwels makabere getuienisse soms laat weeklaag, soms laat sing.*
> She's become a disturbing conscience, an umbilical cord between the TRC and Afrikaans-speakers. She has, as only a poet can, let the often macabre testimonies sometimes wail, sometimes sing (Retief 1998: 15).

Retief continues that Krog's doctor had sent her home for six weeks to recover because she was suffering from the effects of reporting the TRC hearings. While other journalists around the country, working mainly for newspapers, covered the TRC processes when they came to town, or when major newsworthy atrocities and historic events were being aired, the radio team travelled with the TRC commissioners and attended almost every single hearing, with the financial help of a grant from the Norwegian government.[8] Krog was direct about her own lack of experience and journalistic knowledge when coming to the SABC, later admitting in *Country of My Skull*:

> A bulletin usually consists of three audio segments: ordinary reporting read out by a newsreader, 20-second sound bites of other people's voices, and 40-second voice reports sent through by a journalist. How can these elements be moulded to our aims? An expert needs to come help me, I plead. And they send me Angie [Kapelianis – an award-winning radio journalist] (Krog 1998: 31–2).[9]

Nevertheless, in addition to the sound bites for the bulletins, by the end of the process Krog had filed 92 more substantial reports, in which (to give an indication) she interviewed and reported on: TRC commissioners (Desmond Tutu, Alex Boraine, Dumisa Ntsebeza, Mapule Ramashala); Vlakplaas killing farm perpetrators (Jack Cronje, Dirk Coetzee, Wouter Mentz, Roelf Venter, Paul van Vuuren, Jacques Hechter); army generals (Constand Viljoen); victims (Tony Yengeni); the 'Trojan Horse' killings in Athlone; the special hearings into business and labour, the medical profession and the media; the special hearing on women; the resignation of the head of the investigation unit Glen Goosen; the National Party submission and the ANC submission. She also spoke to commissioner Wendy Orr about reparations for victims; interviewed commissioner Richard Lister about exhumations of those killed by apartheid forces and interviewed Ntsiki Biko about hers family's anger at the possibility that Steve Biko's killers might get amnesty.

While Krog's brand of journalism was tempered by the other members of her team who were socialised as objective reporters, the fourteen-member radio team, which she headed, was honoured for the 'intensity, quality and consistency' of their coverage by the South African Union of Journalists, which awarded them the Pringle Award for 1997.[10] Krog had achieved her first consecration by the media field itself, thus proving her worth and accumulation of media field capital. But she had also proved that her bringing to journalism a poetic subjectivity, and relating it to a major ongoing news event of high emotion and affect, had enormous value to journalism itself and also to the fragile process of encounter with the past that all South Africans were facing.

Writing in English for the Mail & Guardian

In 1996 Krog was approached by Anton Harber, editor of the *Mail & Guardian*, who decided to mark the second anniversary of the country's transition to democracy by asking writers to produce reflective pieces on the political change for his publication. In Pierre Bourdieu's explication of field theory, symbolic capital and power attach not only to individuals but also to publications and productions. In the South Africa of the 1980s and 1990s, the *Mail & Guardian* (formerly the *Weekly Mail*) had acquired a status as a hard-hitting, investigative newspaper with distinct advocacy stances on the political situation (anti-apartheid, pro non-racism) and many social issues not embraced by mainstream English-language newspapers (it was also pro gay and women's rights). During the 1980s the *Weekly Mail* bravely printed what other papers would not because of the fear of being shut down by the apartheid regime and won for itself the attention of those in the anti-apartheid political movements, as well as the admiration of fellow journalists in South Africa and internationally. Harber and Irwin Manoim were its founders and co-editors. They and a group of journalists started the paper when the *Rand Daily Mail*, the anti-government paper they had all been working for, was shut down by its owners in 1985. After the transition to democracy, many other publications of the alternative press lost their funding bases and began to close.[11] But Harber organised a financial relationship with *The Guardian* publishers in the United Kingdom to keep his newspaper alive. So for Krog to have been given the space in this publication at this time to write what became five extensive features (each one highly personalised), was attention of a rare sort by an editor with particular symbolic capital and a newspaper of powerful symbolic worth within the media field (see Krog 1996a, 1996b, 1996c, 1997b, 1997c). In the first feature, 'Pockets of Humanity', Krog (writing as 'Krog' rather than 'Samuel', her radio name) was given a double-page spread to write about the effects and affects of reporting on the TRC on herself as a journalist. This she did by focusing on the testifiers and her response to them:

> 'And I was only 20 . . .' The words splintered into the harrowing wail of Fort Calata's wife as she threw herself back into her chair – this cry of distress and uncontained grief ushered in an experience which changed my life.
>
> Voice after voice; account after account – the four weeks of the truth commission hearings across the country were like travelling on a rainy night behind a huge truck – images of devastation breaking wave upon wave on the window. And one can't overtake, because one can't see; and one can't lessen speed or stop, because then one will never progress (Krog 1996b: 30).

By the time Krog wrote the third piece for the *Mail & Guardian*, the TRC reporting was beginning to take a heavy toll on her. Again Krog was given a double-page spread to speak to *Mail & Guardian* readers:

> I am not made to report on the Truth and Reconciliation Commission. When told to head the five-person radio team covering the truth commission, I inexplicably began to cry on the plane back from Johannesburg. Someone tripped over my bag in the passage. Mumbling excuses, fumbling with tissues, I looked up into the face of Dirk Coetzee.[12] There was no escape.
>
> After three days a nervous breakdown was diagnosed and within two weeks the first human rights violation hearings began in East London. The months that have passed proved my premonition right – reporting on the truth commission has indeed left most of us physically exhausted and mentally frayed.
>
> Because of language.

Week after week, from one faceless building to the other, from one dusty godforsaken town to the other, the arteries of our past bleed their own peculiar rhythm, tone and image. One cannot get rid of it. Ever.

It was crucial for me to have the voices of the victims on the news bulletin. To have the sound of ordinary people dominate the news. No South African should escape the process (Krog 1996c: 10).

In giving Krog this substantial amount of space in a newspaper to write in English and to bring to his readers her particular experience of the hearings, Harber was enabling Krog to consolidate her media field capital as a practitioner. In the media field (and particularly in South Africa) while radio has reach and facility (being easily affordable by millions) and television has economic power, political value and reach, serious newspapers, the original news mass medium, still have the cultural capital of being the pre-eminent vehicle for journalists. To prove one can write, at length, knowledgeably and with authority, remains a high mark of media field cultural capital. Harber also gave Krog the entrée to a new public, in the English language and to a newspaper readership with very high media field capital in South Africa at the time. In doing so, Harber acted as an important consecrator in Krog's media field trajectory. And the accolades followed: Krog received an award from the Foreign Correspondents' Association for her features, showing that her media field capital had also been acclaimed by international journalists working in South Africa.

International non-fiction publishing

The series of *Mail & Guardian* features attracted the attention of Stephen Johnson, managing director of Random House in South Africa.[13] Johnson was to also act as a consecrator in Krog's trajectory, enabling her to take her hard-earned journalistic capital and affix to it her value and distinctiveness as a poet and to use both to produce a book of non-fiction that would be distributed internationally, setting Krog on a journey to become a representative of South Africa, taking this country's unique political transition to the world. As books page editor for the *Sunday Independent*

Maureen Isaacson commented on the imminent publication of of *Country of My Skull*: 'The publication is part of Random House South Africa's drive to bring to its rich international list what MD Stephen Johnson calls "the South African flavour"' (Isaacson 1998: 20). As a result of reading the *Mail & Guardian* articles, which showed Krog's direct engagement with the process as an implicated, white Afrikaans-speaking South African and as a beneficiary of apartheid, Johnson approached Krog and persuaded her to work these writings and the reporting materials into a book. Krog was reluctant to write a book and reluctant to work in English.[14] As a result Johnson hired author Ivan Vladislavić to edit Krog's reportage, filtered empathically through her personal account and in 1998 *Country of My Skull*, a hybrid blend of reportage, memoir, fiction and poetry, was published to enormous acclaim.[15] Its initial print run was 15 000, which indicates the confidence Random House placed in its reception.[16] *Country of My Skull* had an immediate and powerful impact. It was widely reviewed by English and Afrikaans newspapers and magazines and it drew substantial attention internationally.

The authority to write

Despite the fact that thousands of new voices of testimony had entered the public space to be heard for the first time and hundreds of other journalists had also reported on the TRC, it was Krog's voice that was seized on by the publisher to speak on behalf of this experience and for all South Africans involved in this process. What is the political economy of such a decision? Whitlock remarks that a commission's granting of authority for the previously silenced to speak is not a carte blanche opening up of the public space nor can it be an assumption for them of a hearing in public that is now assured. These voices are carefully orchestrated by such commissions, as are the texts that issue from them:

Access to the public is provisional, carefully negotiated, and strategic. The circulation of these narratives is almost always tied to larger imperatives of interracial debates and campaigns, not just at the time of origin, but also in the context of when and where they re-emerge with renewed force, as they tend to do. The narrative structure, and most specifically, the narrator and the editor, write with a sense of the production of truth and authority in autobiography. Let's be clear about that: these texts must authorise the narrator, and must offer clear signals on how the narrative is to be read and what constitutes its truth to be witnessed by a believing reader in an appropriate way – what I have earlier called an appropriate ethical responsiveness. These texts maneuver for their public, and the story they tell needs to be read in terms of a particular culture and particular readerships. What must be told to, and what will be heard by these readerships is limited, and negotiated with care. The occasion requires 'truth', a culturally specific and appropriate presentation of subjectivity and experience (Whitlock 2001: 208).

In her book *Soft Weapons* Whitlock distinguishes between memoir and testimony:

> The memoir is a genre for those who are authorised and who have acquired cultural legitimacy and influence . . . memoir is the prerogative of those who possess cultural capital, and it follows that the place of the memoirist in culture is quite 'other' to that of those who testify (2007: 20).

Krog had been made head of the TRC team without serving a traditional apprenticeship in the genre of hard-news journalism and she had been seized on by the publisher to frame an autobiographical response to the stories coming out of the Commission. These choices were made on the basis of her already existing cultural capital and this Krog had in abundance – as an award-winning and high-selling poet and as a dissident Afrikaner who had attained the status in the South African media of an important newsmaker and agenda-setter. In addition, her new status in the media field as a news journalist had been acclaimed for her important and distinctive production. Krog's work in the literary field allowed her to accumulate significant *cultural* capital (as an excellent and acclaimed poet) and *economic* capital (as a high-selling poet and valuable asset for publishers) and therefore *symbolic* capital as a literary figure in South Africa. And because of her forays into the political field (some informal and personal, some more overtly on the public stage) she also had political credentials and the acclaim of political actors who were now extremely important as leaders in the shift to democracy. Her work in the news media had given her the media field's cultural capital and its economic capital, given the reach of the SABC radio stations and the significance of the public broadcaster to the politial change in the country. But also Krog the newsmaker, the agenda-setter, became even more newsworthy because of her witnessing and making public her own experiences of the TRC. This translated into *symbolic* capital as an expert witness of one of South Africa's signature transitional events. This accumulated capital on three fronts made Krog an ideal choice for a publisher as the representative writer for this project.

As Whitlock says, 'memoir is traditionally the prerogative of the literate elite; alternatively, the testimony is the means by which the disempowered experience enters the record, although not necessarily under conditions of their choosing' (2007: 132). In a case such as this – even as the memoir was serving the function of allowing the testimony of the disenfranchised into public for the first time officially – Krog was the authorised author. Whitlock points out that very seldom do the actual people who appear before commissions get to speak directly for themselves through vehicles other than the live hearings. If they do, because they have no cultural capital, they are framed, narrated and 'surrounded by authenticating documentation' (2001: 208). They can attain status as narrators only through those with authority who mediate them to us: 'Indigenous/ First Nations/Black testimony almost always circulates in networks that are beyond the control of their narrators and minority communities. In marginalia – of editors, collaborators, and writers of prefaces and appendices – the circulation of testimony is carefully controlled in the public domain' (2004: 23).

It is interesting that having chosen Krog with her symbolic capital to be the representative voice of the South African TRC, Johnson then positioned her for an international public, whose attention he wanted to attract, as a very ordinary South African. This was done using the same kind of marginalia usually employed for the unknown testimony givers. In the peritexts – the framing devices within the book (see Genette 1997 for this terminology) – in the 1998 edition publisher's note, Johnson commended Krog to an international audience by situating her not as a poet with the highest literary capital but as a very ordinary 'living South African', struggling, suffering and forging a future with other South Africans. But in the epitexts (those on the outside of the book) Krog's cultural capital is foregrounded in her published volumes and the prizes she has won. So the first edition of the book was being used as an important test of whether Krog – positioned both as an author of substantial but South African-based cultural capital *and* as an ordinary South African – would be read locally and taken up internationally. Johnson's gamble on the 'South African flavour' of *Country of My Skull* and the positioning of Krog as simultaneously authorised *and* ordinary, proved to be a shrewd assessment of the trends in international publishing and of the desire worldwide for a life narrative based in a major event garnering publicity and interest.

The reaction to *Country of My Skull*

Krog's harnessing of her poetic and journalistic skills to produce an unusual hybrid-genre book was remarked upon as not only having served the subject matter through its literary treatment but also Krog was commended as a witness both in South Africa and internationally. Nadine Gordimer said of her willingness to go to extremes to make an account of the hearings:

> Here is the extraordinary reportage of one who, eyes staring into the filthiest places of atrocity, poet's searing tongue speaking of them, is not afraid to go too far. Antjie Krog breaks all the rules of dispassionate recounts, the restraints of 'decent' prose, because this is where the truth might be reached and reconciliation with it is posited like a bewildered angel thrust down into hell.[17]

Despite Krog's insistence that she could not adequately report under her name as a poet for the SABC, she gave free rein to a mixture of both Krog and Samuel in this book, as noted by Archbishop Desmond Tutu who said: 'Antjie Krog writes with the sensitivity of a poet and the clarity of a journalist . . . it is a beautiful and powerful book'.[18] Her act of hosting both the victims and perpetrators between the covers of the book was also picked up for comment, notably by *Publishers Weekly*, which commented that the book 'gave voice to the anguished, often eloquent stories of numerous victims of apartheid . . . [and] it put faces on stealthy killers and torturers seeking amnesty'.[19] Anthony Sampson, former *Drum* editor and biographer of Nelson Mandela, said of the book in *Literary Review*:

> Antjie Krog gives us a vivid answer in this strange and haunting account of the hearings . . . the power of this passionate and original book comes from its ability to describe universal human horrors which are not distinctively Afrikaner or African: to throw light on the nightmare world in which quite ordinary and boring people are transformed into practitioners of terror and counter-terror.[20]

As well as the book being reviewed in South Africa, Krog as a writer was recognised for having endured and reported truthfully on the ordeal. Barbara Trapido writing in the London *Sunday Times* said: 'The book . . . is wonderful. Few could have done Krog's job without resorting to nervous breakdown and to have written the book is heroic.'[21]

As a result of the publication of *Country of My Skull* and her extraordinary literary enactment of bearing witness and of confession, Krog became internationally known as a writer profoundly engaged with the events and human drama uncovered by the TRC and her voice was read as that of an expert witness of trauma, forgiveness and the means by which the horrors of the past may be ameliorated.[22] In addition to being called upon as a journalist in South Africa with specialist knowledge to write press articles about situations arising from the TRC – see, for example, Krog's piece in the *Sunday Times* on Gideon Niewoudt, implicated in the murders of Steve Biko and Siphiwo Mtimkulu (2004b: 21) – Krog's TRC expert status was given further international exposure by journalists who invited her to talk on BBC current affairs programmes, for Radio

Hilversum in the Netherlands and media programmes in Belgium, Australia, New Zealand and Canada. Several American documentaries on the TRC and South Africa interviewed Krog. Despite the fact that Krog had not served a traditional apprenticeship within the journalistic field, she nevertheless converted her literary and political symbolic capital into currency that carried over into this field. Using her distinctive poet subjectivity, she inflected her journalism with a particular dimension of implicated and affected reporting.[23] The acclaim demonstrated by journalists themselves with the South African Union of Journalists' Pringle Award for the TRC radio reports and the Foreign Correspondents' Award for the newspaper features showed decisively that Krog had successfully negotiated the field, accumulating symbolic capital. This media field capital, as well as an increase of symbolic capital attached to her public persona (as an affected witness to the process of the TRC, which was remarked on and became a notable feature of her reportage), was then converted back into the literary world with the facilitation of the publisher. But this time, as a book author with international exposure, Krog was no longer operating at the avant-garde pole of the field of cultural production or at the heteronomous pole of journalism but in the section of the field in which both cultural and economic capital came together powerfully with the production of a non-fiction book. And the international exposure and new public amplified Krog's status as a public figure in South Africa.

The enabling global context

There are four factors that enabled Krog's account of the TRC to find an international audience of not only sympathetic readers, scholars of trauma and the writing of atrocity, but also those influential internationally in politics and in dealing with such events and their impacts.

'Truth' commissions worldwide

Within the last four decades 'truth' commissions have sprung up all over the world as the preferred mechanism to effect political change in situations of political impasse and to deal with pasts characterised by atrocity, injustice and exclusion.[24] While these commissions vary greatly in the degree and types of 'truth' being elicited, their openness to public scrutiny, their terms of reference and their intent, there is no doubt that this international trend is evidence of what Priscilla B. Hayner calls 'an expanding universe of official truth-seeking' (2002: 255). These inquiries have been provoked by the dissolution of states, the conclusion of wars and the (re)integration into citizenship of dispossessed peoples. They have multiple purposes: resolution, justice and reconciliation, as well as the creation of new political and social entities. Globalisation is often characterised as the 'flow of goods' across the world but it is interesting that the *idea* of the 'truth commission' has taken such a hold internationally as a solution to political problems of a fraught and complex nature.

Focusing on this spate of commissions, hearings and public engagements around the world, Whitlock says:

> Testimonial forms of autobiographical expression elicited by Commissions of Inquiry are at the forefront of debates about race and identity, most particularly in thinking about the role of the State in the politics of race and reconciliation. The meaning of reconciliation as a strategy, policy, and ethics, is being shaped as a global politics, albeit one which finds quite different local formations and expressions. Testimony is at the heart of this struggle (2001: 201).

The South African TRC was following an already established trend but is nonetheless still hailed as remarkable for its significant differences from other such commissions. Calling it 'illustrative', Hayner remarks:

> The commission's empowering act provided the most complex and sophisticated mandate for any truth commission to date, with carefully balanced powers and an extensive investigatory reach. Written in precise legal language and running to over twenty single-spaced pages, the act gave the commission power to grant individualised amnesty, search premises and seize evidence, subpoena witnesses, and run a sophisticated witness-protection

programme. With a staff of three hundred, a budget of some $18 million each year for two-and-a-half years, and four large offices around the country, the commission dwarfed previous truth commissions in its size and reach (2002: 41).

As Hayner (2002), Kay Schaffer and Sidonie Smith (2004a, 2004b) and Michael Ignatieff (2001) show, the use of truth commissions worldwide is embedded in a human rights 'regime of truth' (Foucault 1980: 131).[25] Ignatieff says the idea of human rights is evidence of a 'juridical revolution' in thinking, coming out of the 'reordering' of the world politically since the end of the Second World War. This idea has undergone 'global diffusion' (Ignatieff 2001: 4), giving impetus – as Schaffer and Smith (2004a, 2004b) point out – to struggles of many kinds not intended or even conceived of at the time by the Allied powers who drafted the Universal Declaration of Human Rights in 1948.

The rise of confession

One of the most insightful contributions made by Michel Foucault towards an understanding of the Western subject is his investigation into the extent to which confessional practices have long permeated the fabric of Western societies and their writings. In the introduction to *The History of Sexuality Vol. 1* in particular, he points out that confession has, since the Greco-Roman period, been used to shape a particular type of self-disclosing, self-knowing human subject, while at the same time used to compile bodies of scientific knowledge about the human subject. 'We have become,' says Foucault, 'a singularly confessing society' (1998: 59).

> The confession has spread its effects far and wide. It plays a part in justice, medicine, education, family relationships, and love relations. In the most ordinary affairs of everyday life, and in the most solemn rites; one confesses one's crimes, one's sins, one's thoughts and desires, one's illnesses and troubles; one goes about telling, with the greatest precision, whatever is most difficult to tell. One confesses in public and in private, to one's parents, one's educators, one's doctor, to those one loves; one admits to oneself,

in pleasure and in pain, things it would be impossible to tell anyone else, the things people write books about. One confesses or is forced to confess (Foucault 1998: 59).

The rise of truth commissions worldwide has given new life to confession as a discourse, which is now being harnessed not only in the personal sphere, where Foucault demonstrates that it has long been one of the West's most distinctive technologies of self but, perhaps most vividly, now surfacing in the political and judicial spheres in order to elicit details about gross violations of human rights. Confession has become one of the public modalities used to establish and maintain the modern, human rights-informed democratic enterprise by providing a way to deal with many forms of political and social injustice.

A second reason for the ascendancy of confession in relation to the rise of truth commissions is that it allows the exercise of voice and expression to those previously denied them. In an interview, Homi Bhabha said he sees this as a worldwide phenomenon coming out of the 'great social movements of our times – diasporic, refugee, migrant' and calls it the 'right to narrate' (Chance 2001). And, he says, this is not only an 'expressive right' but also an 'enunciatory right' (not only a right to speak but also a right to proclaim and therefore make claims), happening in a situation of 'jurisdictional unsettlement', in a world in which settled ideas of nation and nationality are being recognised as flawed in their tendency to oversimplify.

In the case of South Africa, the constitutional and legislative procedures underpinning the TRC enshrined as the new South African citizen the human subject entirely recognisable in the confessional mode of self-construction. According to Deborah Posel (2005): 'A particular kind of faith in the production of selfhood is at the heart of the South African Constitution.' Posel's argument is that the TRC became the 'first vector' of the project to reconstitute the South African self through the constitutional provision that every single South African has the right to speak: 'The mutuality of damage and the shared need to be healed gives access to a shared community and a shared humanity predicated on the shared experience of pain.'

The confessional mode also has the potential to recreate social entities. Dealing decisively with its shameful past via a commission has not only allowed South Africa to rejoin an international community politically but also to enter the 'global community of suffering . . . which leads to mutual humanity' (Posel 2005). Posel remarks that the usual notion of the person that underlies liberal democracy is the rational, deliberative subject. But the TRC and many processes like it around the world have consolidated the 'emotional, affective, damaged' subject of the confessional as another important type not only nationally, but globally.

In South Africa, the confessional form, as Susan van Zanten Gallagher points out, has both a long history and a new dimension:

> . . . the confessional mode is a prevalent form . . . appearing in texts from both the apartheid age (1948–1990) and the post-apartheid period. In the 1990s, with the unfolding drama of the Truth and Reconciliation hearings, confessions and confessional literature proved a particularly appropriate mode for a society struggling to carve out a new national identity based not on race but on geography . . . confessional discourse provides a way of articulating these moral claims (Gallagher 2002: xx).

Returning to the roots of confession in the Christian church, Gallagher points to the fact that traditionally confession involved not only the admission of sin, error and guilt but also the acknowledgement or declaration 'that something is so' (2002: 3), as expressed in the 'confessing of the faith'. In church tradition confession is also, very importantly, used as a means of returning the one who confesses to the community of the faithful:

> Confession – both admission and testimony – provides both the act of signature and the necessary witness that contributes to the formation of the communal yet individual self. In theological terms, what confession entails is less a renunciation of the self than a decentering and subsequent recentering of the self with the community of faith (Gallagher 2002: 29).

Thus the power of the confessional mode in situations where the reconstruction of a social entity is critical for the resolution of a fractured past. And while the reconstruction of social and political bodies as a result of commissions of inquiry usually takes place within national boundaries, these new bodies – as Posel has alerted us – bear the marks of suffering and so have characteristics in common with all those Others across the world caught in similar processes.

The 'transnationalising' of the public sphere

In her more recent work Nancy Fraser has turned her attention to the phenomenon that the public sphere (as the national arena where ordinary citizens hold political power accountable via shared information and the formation of opinions) actually operates beyond state boundaries. Fraser's recognition of the salience of 'transnational phenomena' (2007: 8), 'cultural hybridity' (18) and 'the visual' (19) within globalisation has led her to examine whether the idea of the public sphere is now 'overflow[ing] the bounds of both nations and states' (7). Detecting that there is burgeoning and commonplace talk of a multiplicity of public spheres, Fraser considers the notion of a transnational public sphere 'indispensable' for understanding and reconstructing democratic theory for the present state of the world. For my purposes, it is key to note that 'globalisation', as evidenced in communication flows and circulations of texts and their publics – as in Michael Warner's *Publics and Counterpublics* (2002) – means that the three components I have discussed so far ('truth' commissons worldwide, the rise of confession and the transnationalising of the public sphere) are all taking place in an arena that transcends the nation-state. In this arena the movement of information and the cohesion in relation to issues has the facility to bind people all over the world together as transnational citizens concerned about global issues affecting all human beings. The rise of what are now being called 'new social movements' across the globe in response to the factors pointed out by Bhabha above is an indication that 'a broader grammar of governance has thus emerged, one that has extended the vocabulary of citizenship both within the nation-state and outside it' (Randeria 2007: 39).

To give an example that points to the functioning of a transnational public sphere and a wider sense of implicated citizenship: in his study about television as a medium that conveys evidence of human suffering across borders, Luc Boltanski (1999) shows that 'reflexive modern subjects are both immediately morally obliged and emotionally bound to act to relieve suffering that we witness' – in the words of Kate Nash (2007: 54). These 'reflexive modern subjects' are those people who identify as fellow humans across national boundaries and who use transnational public spheres to crystallise the salience of events and issues with which to become involved.

> According to Boltanski, the modern subject who witnesses (mediated) suffering is reflexive and therefore both capable of, and required to, justify their understanding of what they have seen, how they feel about it and how they intend to respond to it . . . Boltanski's understanding of the possibilities of entering into social dialogue is very similar to Habermas' in this respect. Modern subjects attribute reflexivity to each other, so creating a communicative space for potential partners in dialogue who are able to justify their beliefs, values and actions to each other, and to reach consensus on how to proceed (Nash 2007: 55).

The burgeoning market for life narratives

Numerous literary theorists point to a coincidental, detectable shift in the publishing industry worldwide: the rise of non-fiction as a category and the noticeable eagerness for autobiographical works, especially of the confessional or testimonial kind. Schaffer and Smith say:

> The last decades of the twentieth century witnessed the unprecedented rise in genres of life writing, narratives published primarily in the West but circulated widely around the globe. This 'memoir boom' has certainly occurred in English-speaking countries, from Australia to Jamaica, from England to South Africa, in European countries, especially France and Germany (2004a: 1).

Schaffer and Smith quote Leigh Gilmore (2001) as noting that the number of books published in English and labelled as 'autobiography or memoir' tripled from the 1940s to the 1990s (2004a: 21).

It is important also to note that vast markets now exist that support the global commodification of non-fiction and autobiographical narratives. Life narratives are 'salable properties in today's markets', Schaffer and Smith remark, pointing to 'increasing education, disposable income, and leisure time of the post-World War II generations in Western democratic nations and pockets of modernities elsewhere around the globe' (2004a: 11). And alongside the voraciousness of the market and the proliferation of the belief in the 'individual and the individual's unique story', there is also the fact that many of these stories, told by the West's Others, make visible the claims of the disenfranchised and 'enable victims to speak truth to power' (19).

* * *

These four globalised situations corresponded with an exemplary local situation and context (as in the form of the South African TRC); a publisher/publishing house connected to global flows of information and global markets, seeking out a local publication to make the fit and an individual who had the facility to experience, embody, speak and write about trauma and transition. These four factors (the rise of 'truth' commissions, the increased use of confessional, the expanding market for life narratives and the transnationalising of the public sphere) are completely interwoven as causes and effects of each other. As Schaffer and Smith point out:

> The rise in the popularity of published life narratives has taken place in the midst of global transformations, both cataclysmic and gradual, that have occurred in the decades since the end of World War II . . . these geopolitical and temporal transformations form not so much a backdrop, but rather a fractured web of intersecting geographic, historical, and cultural contingencies

out of which personal narratives have emerged and within which they are produced, received and circulated. These global transformations have spurred developments in the field of human rights as well, developments that demand, for their recognition in the international community, multiple forms of remembrance of and witnessing to abuse (2004a: 1).

However powerful these four global factors and the intervention of a canny publisher might have been in facilitating Krog's entry onto an international stage and however much the 'field' might have authored the 'author' (in Bourdieu's words), the other important factor is that Krog produced a highly unusual and extraordinary account of the TRC process, which was not simply reportage and not simply non-fiction. My contention is that Krog took very seriously the responsibility to craft a position from which to speak in relation to South Africa's Others that did not obliterate or claim a position of silencing those Others. I have shown in Chapter 3 how she worked to craft a distinctiveness of voice, which in the literary field could be singled out as her idiolect, and in Chapter 4 how she modified that voice (both through her poetry and her political practice) to 'self-other', to shift the writerly self into different positions from which to see and engage with South Africa at that time. Now, I argue, she takes her experimentation in the TRC reporting and the book account even further in relation to the new voices of testimony she witnessed for the first time. This position I am going to call, after Whitlock (2001), the 'second-person performance' since it is not only a shift of position that is noticeably pronounced but also, importantly, it is a performance and it is in public.

Subjectivity: The second-person performance

> Beloved, do not die. Do not dare die! I, the survivor, I wrap you in words so that the future inherits you. I snatch you from the death of forgetfulness. I tell your story, complete your ending – you who once whispered beside me in the dark (Krog 1998: 27).

The encounter with 'amazing otherness'

In an interview she did with me in 1998 for *Rhodes Journalism Review* shortly after the publication of *Country of My Skull*, Krog said she was intrigued in her TRC reporting by the 'amazing otherness of where they [the testifiers at the TRC] have been and how they've dealt with it' (Garman 1998: 27). Writing, in the face of atrocity, is a complex decision and writing the experiences of others, even more complicated. To make beautiful in words the atrocities of experience is a travesty, as Theodor Adorno points out in his statement made famous by overuse (and often misinterpretation).[26] Paul Celan, the poet and Holocaust survivor, asked that his 'Fugue of Death' not be published anymore because the writing was 'too lyrical' and 'too beautiful' (Sanders 2000: 13; see also Krog 1998: 237). But as Mark Sanders points out, Krog's decision to commit her experiences and the words of the TRC testifiers to paper is a decision based on 'being host to their words' (2000: 14), of not allowing those already silenced to be further lost to record because of their lack of facility and vehicles for representation. Sanders considers this aspect of both *Country of My Skull* and the official TRC report:

> As formulated by Krog, the question of poetry, or literature, after apartheid concerns less an excess of lyricism or beauty, from which its creator stands back, than a writer's facilitation of the utterance of others. If the question of literature after apartheid is a question of advocacy, of its dynamics and ethics, then the Commission shares a set of concerns and conditions of possibility with literary works. In interpreting its public hearings as occasions for advocacy, the Commission reveals that the structures of identification and substitution, on which it relies when it solicits the testimony of victims, are as integral to its own operations as they are to a literary work. Krog's book makes itself host to testimony in ways that allow us to understand how this is the case, and how even lyric poetry, in a sense ignored by the Adornian principle, is able to display this joint partaking (2000: 14).

Sanders calls *Country of My Skull* a 'hybrid work, written at the edges of reportage, memoir, and metafiction' (2000: 16). He sees it as a supplement to the Commission's official report:

> In the testimony of witnesses at the public hearings, truths are interlaced with acts of telling and questioning, which are, in turn, implicated in the intricate dynamics between questioner and teller. *Country of My Skull* mimes such elements by relating its author's own attempts to find an interlocutor, an addressee, an other for whom her story will cohere. Written from a position of acknowledged and troubling historical complicity – its dedication reads 'For every victim who had an Afrikaner surname on her lips' – Krog's book does not claim any facile identification with victims who testify (Sanders 2000: 16).

In this book, one sees Krog again in search of an interlocutor, again to negotiate an 'era of horror' (this time the evocation of the past of atrocity). But in choosing to not only report (and therefore stand procedurally outside the process) but also witness the TRC testimonies, Krog is positioned (and positioning herself) as a white Afrikaans-speaking South African, as implicated, as complicit and as a beneficiary of apartheid. She is also dealing with thousands of voices who have been given the official platform by the Commission and its backing legislation to legitimately speak for themselves, saying 'I' in public for the first time, recognised as having the right to make claims that were once denied. She is crafting a subjectivity in order to respond ethically to 'amazing otherness'. As Sanders points out, her relationship to these testifiers is not a facile one of claiming and using their testimony. In order to explain this relationship I turn now to Whitlock for insight.

The first-person, second-person transaction

Whitlock says that the silenced people who speak at these hearings take on the authority and position of the 'first person' (using a grammatical metaphor) and force the hearer (and very often the enfranchised, empowered and usually complicit) into the listening position of the 'second person' who must respond ethically and satisfactorily: 'The presence of the first and the second person, the narrator and the witness, is vital to the narrative exchange established through testimonial speaking and writing' (2001: 199).

Whitlock's interest is in the person who is placed 'in this textual economy as the second person', the addressee, the recipient (2001: 199–200). The burden now placed on this second person is to become a witness who 'affirms the experience and trauma of the first person', who 'reflect(s) upon the self, upon his/her own responsibility and implication in the events being narrated by a traumatised subject' (200).[27] She comments that in this transaction the burden of shame shifts to the listener and by extension to the dominant culture. In response 'the politics of reconciliation comes into play . . . as a quite specific discursive framework, as a personal and collective strategy which recognises the complex dynamics of this shaming as a catharsis'. Furthermore, Whitlock notes: 'The politics of reconciliation as it is currently emerging in Africa, Australia and North America requires in the second person a subjective identification, contrition, introspection, and finally a change of heart' (210).

While Krog's brand of reportage for SABC radio was remarkable in its breaching of the constraints of news journalism (for example, the strong prohibition on saying 'I' as a journalist), it becomes evident why the book she subsequently wrote is the better textual vehicle for such an important transaction. Calling Krog's *Country of My Skull* 'a brilliant autobiography of the second person', Whitlock says:

> The fragments of traumatic memory spoken by victims to the South African Truth and Reconciliation Commission are braided together with Krog's autobiographical narrative. Krog struggles to get the relationship between these narratives right. Like Carmel Bird, Krog too produces her book as an apology and as a recognition of complicity (2001: 210).[28]

But, says Whitlock, 'these testimonies are profoundly disturbing to dominant ways of thinking about history, identity and race' (2001: 198).

She goes on: 'What they can tell in the first person, and what we will hear as the second person, are always sharply circumscribed, one by the other. Both telling and listening are performative' (209).

While asserting with Whitlock that in *Country of My Skull* we can see Krog adopting a further modification of her subject position as responsive to the Others of South Africa, the second-person listening position, there is also evidence that this positionality has facets and allows Krog also to manoeuvre from one facet to another, as seen in Dorothy Driver's analysis of Lady Anne Barnard's writing subjectivity in Chapter 4. This position also allows Krog as a writer, someone who works powerfully and consciously with language as a meaning-making mechanism, to explore through factual material sourced in journalism some of literature's major preoccupations.

Saying 'I', hearing 'I'

> At Tzaneen a young Tswana interpreter is interviewed. He holds on to the table top, his other hand moves restlessly in his lap. 'It is difficult to interpret victim hearings,' he says, 'because you use the first person all the time. I have no distance when I say 'I' . . . it runs through me with I (Krog 1998: 129).

> Consciousness of self is only possible if it is experienced by contrast. I use I only when I am speaking to someone who will be a *you* in my address. It is this condition of dialogue that is constitutive of *person*, for it implies that reciprocally *I* becomes *you* in the address of the one who in his turn designates himself as *I*. Here we see a principle, whose consequences are to spread out in all directions. Language is possible only because each speaker sets himself up as a *subject* by referring to himself as *I* in his discourse. Because of this, *I* posits another person, the one who, being, as he is, completely exterior to 'me', becomes my echo to whom I say *you* and who says *you* to me. This polarity of persons is the fundamental condition of language, of which the process of communication,

in which we share, is only a mere pragmatic consequence. It is a polarity, moreover, very peculiar in itself, as it offers a type of opposition whose equivalent is encountered nowhere else outside of language. This polarity does not mean either equality or symmetry: 'ego' always has a position of transcendence with regard to *you*. Nevertheless, neither of the terms can be conceived of without the other; they are complementary, although according to an 'interior/exterior' opposition, and, at the same time, they are reversible. If we seek a parallel to this, we will not find it. The condition of man in language is unique.

And so the old antinomies of 'I' and 'the other', of the individual and society, fall (Benveniste 2000: 40-1).

Émile Benveniste's rooting of subjectivity and agency in language and his insight that our use of the simple pronominal words to designate ourselves are always dialogical, relational and shifting, is a useful place to start unpicking the Krog text. In *Country of My Skull* Krog not only explicitly performs the responses of the second-person listener, she also engages in the debates surrounding the seeking and telling of truth and the connections between language and extremities of experience and their implications for forgiveness, setting the past aside, the possibility of a new nation and belonging. Krog's implicit understanding that the ability to speak for oneself is of utmost importance as a technique of recovery, when violence has been used to obliterate that self, can be seen clearly in the book. She refers to those whose work she has drawn on and among the names is Elaine Scarry, author of *The Body in Pain* (1985) (Krog 1998: 47). Scarry's contention is that experiences of extreme pain and trauma render the sufferer wordless and so literally, pain takes away the language to speak itself. If language is the means humans use to grasp the world, the world too is unmade for the sufferer, or to put it in the reverse of Benveniste's terms: if 'it is in and through language that man constitutes himself as a *subject*' (Benveniste 2000: 40; emphasis added), the loss of language to speak one's experience of pain is the terrible loss of oneself as a subject, as the 'I' of one's own story, experience and life.

For me, this crying is the beginning of the Truth Commission – the signature tune, the definitive moment, the ultimate sound of what the process is about. She was wearing this vivid orange-red dress, and she threw herself backwards and that sound . . . that sound . . . it will haunt me for ever and ever . . . and to witness that cry was to witness the destruction of language . . . was to realise that to remember the past of this country is to be thrown back into a time before language. And to get that memory, to fix it in words, to capture it with the precise image, is to be present at the birth of language itself (Krog 1998: 42).

Krog shows this unmaking in her interlocutors and in herself. But she also shows a making, the emergence of a book full of words, full of experience, of dialogue and interlocution as the TRC unfolds its hearings across the entire landscape of the country. To return to Sanders's idea about a 'joint partaking', Krog has produced this book as record, testimony and confession but also advocacy and recognition that from this point onwards, white South Africans can no longer speak for the Others who now occupy first-person position; they will have to negotiate their speaking to and with (and for) those now legislated into citizenship and into rights-making claims.

The beneficiary position

Taking up the second-person listening position in relation to South Africa's apartheid history also means, with absolute logic, that if the second-person is white, one's race makes one also a beneficiary of apartheid and therefore implicated in the atrocities being given words. In Country of My Skull Krog does not shrink from this implication and positioning.[29] The concern with the millions of normal South Africans, both black and white, also affected by apartheid permeates Country of My Skull:

Just before midnight, six black youths walk into the Truth Commission's office in Cape Town. They insist on filling out the forms and taking the oath. Their application simply says: Amnesty for Apathy. They had been having a normal Saturday evening jol in a shebeen when they started talking about the amnesty deadline and how millions of people had simply turned a blind eye to what was happening. It had been left to a few individuals to make the sacrifice for the freedom everyone enjoys today. 'And that's when we decided to ask for amnesty because we had done nothing' (Krog 1998: 121-2).

Critics of the TRC have pointed out that one of its major failings was to focus almost to the exclusion of all others on certain acts of extraordinary atrocity (torture, murder) and to divide those appearing before it into the victim-perpetrator binary.[30] The hearings were divided into human rights violations hearings, at which victims testified, and amnesty hearings, at which the perpetrators came forward with what was required to be a full disclosure of their politically motivated crimes. Tens of thousands of submissions were reduced to thousands in order to make the public appearances manageable. But in the process, the all-pervasiveness of the apartheid system that made non-citizens of millions, robbed them of rights, condemned them to substandard housing, education and opportunities, while privileging an entire stratum of people because of the colour of their skin, received little formal attention.[31] The beneficiaries of apartheid, mostly white South Africans, were treated as a ghostly cloud of witnesses vicariously participating through the media. The fact is, in reality, that those suffering from human rights abuses numbered in the millions, not thousands. Mahmood Mamdani (2000) points out that an investigation into how the system impoverished millions by enriching millions should have been the focus of such a commission. While most commissions worldwide have confined themselves to dealing with extreme abuses of human rights, they have also opened up the possibility that these abuses had structural roots and that entire societies are constructed in unjust and oppressive ways but the avoidance of investigating the underpinnings of societies is kept in political check by those in power in case entire social and political systems unravel.

Schaffer and Smith (2006) point out that in *Country of My Skull* Krog 'enacts an ethics of reconciliation through claiming the position of beneficiary'. This positioning puts Krog the observer, listener and witness into a position of complicity and while she does at certain points identify with the perpetrators because of shared language and culture – 'they are as familiar as my brothers' (1998: 96) – the beneficiary position is a complex and uncomfortable place because it cannot be identified with one moment of human rights abuse that can be claimed, confessed and forgiven. It suggests that one's entire life as a white South African is built upon the denigration and oppression of others, which has been centuries in the making. From the beneficiary position, Krog speaks to other beneficiaries and implicates them – her readers – in the discomfort of hearing and then having to respond to the testimonies by weighing up their own lives in these terms. Schaffer and Smith comment on this position but also observe that Krog uses a multiplicity of positions to craft her book:

> Throughout *Country of My Skull*, Krog is tenuously, and often multiply positioned: as a professional observer reporting on the historical event of the TRC; an interlocutor interpellated in the TRC's spectacle of witnessing and its reconciliation process; an advocate for the witnesses; a guilt-ridden Afrikaner prompting other Afrikaners to recognise their complicity in the violence of apartheid; and a white South African desirous of finding a home for herself and, by implication, other beneficiaries of the past in a post-apartheid future (Schaffer and Smith 2006).

As a journalist Krog (Samuel) could have chosen to operate solely from the 'objective' position of reportage mandated by professional practice, which would have put her at a remove from the personal implications of the testimonies. By clearly adopting the beneficiary position, Krog makes complex and even undermines the TRC's binary of victim-perpetrator as the primary relation underpinning abuse of power, damage and forgiveness. This position also calls into question the one-to-one personal relationship demanded by confession in order for forgiveness to be sought and given. If millions are guilty and millions hold the power of forgiveness, how is this to be effected successfully except via holding to a belief in the hermeneutic value of vicarious participation, which turns on feeling affect? But, as Krog the author demonstrates through her literary enactment of confession, producing a work that not only documents a process faithfully but seeks also to allow others to understand and participate in the larger project of national renewal and reconciliation is a difficult and complex task. As Whitlock points out, in responding to testimonies of atrocity a writer witness has to modulate her performance of culpability so as to be seen to act ethically and sincerely in response to the seriousness of the testimonies aired. The emphasis in such narratives, says Whitlock, is on the 'making of the ethical respondent' (2001: 205).

The credibility of Krog's performance of beneficiary culpability in *Country of My Skull* has also been subject to intense debate in some academic reviews of the book. An example of one of the extremely critical reactions to Krog's methods of writing and positionality is the critique by Meira Cook, who comments that *Country of My Skull* is a 'radically overdetermined narrative' and says:

> Her protestations of unworthiness, self-indulgent guilt, and a frequently expressed ambivalence about the project that she has undertaken undermines our reliance on her objectivity as a witness . . . her pain is represented in the fractured voice of her narrator, the jaggedness and angularity of her address, and the ambivalence with which she insists on her contingent position as interlocutor. At times forceful, even strident, at other times diffident, alternately addressing the reader directly and mediating her position through the reported speech of others, Krog's narrator seems pathologically uncertain of her place in this text (2001: 77).

Cook focuses on the 'postmodern' writing techniques that Krog uses and on her fluctuating narrator positions and judges them to be interesting experiments, which, in her estimation, are inadequate to the task of properly conveying the horror of apartheid atrocities. There is no doubt that Krog's task in writing into her book the voices of the testimony-givers and her own responses to them is to ensure that her own reaction is not read as overwhelming or more important than the witnesses. Obviously, readers will make their own judgements as to how effectively Krog has achieved this task but most often this has been the fault line in critical reactions to the book. It seems that *Country of My Skull* has either convinced completely or persuaded certain critics that Krog has failed in the writing task and therefore also failed ethically.

The assertion of the body

'This inside me . . . fights my tongue. It is . . . unshareable. It destroys . . . words. Before he was blown up, they cut off his hands so he could not be fingerprinted . . . So how do I say this? – this terrible . . . I want his hands back' (Krog 1998: 27).

'When I opened the door . . . there was my closest friend and comrade . . . She was standing on the doorstep and she screamed: "My child, my little Nomzamo is still in the house!" . . . I stared at her . . . my most beautiful friend . . . her hair flaming and her chest like a furnace . . . she died a day later. I pulled out her baby from the burning house . . . I put her on the grass . . . only to find that her skin stayed behind on my hands. She is with me here today' (28).

'They held me . . . they said, "Please don't go in there . . ." I just skipped through their legs and went in . . . I found Bheki . . . he was in pieces . . . he was hanging in pieces . . . he was all over . . . pieces of him and brain was scattered all around . . . that was the end of Bheki.'

We also learn quickly. Bulletin-writers and newsreaders squirm away from whatever is not fashionable or harmlessly clinical. For words like 'menstruation' or 'penis' there is no place on the news; a phrase such as 'they braaied my child on a fire' is out of the question. We are told that the writer Rian Malan has complained that he doesn't want to mix 'breakfast and blood' in the morning . . . (How quickly our own language changes – fantastic testimony, sexy subject, nice audible crying) (32).

As we have seen already in Krog's working with writer subjectivity and positioning, she has never shied away from engagement with the body and its messy situatedness. In *Country of My Skull* she is well placed to take on what is, at times, the overwhelming and overtly graphic testimony of the victims. But again the modulating of her reaction to this material is very important. Any hint that she is lapsing into overly graphic and salacious uses as a writer would undermine her credibility as a second-person witness. Krog uses her multiple writer positions to deal with this very tricky area, sometimes adopting an objective reporter position and putting the testimony in direct quotes, sometimes speaking as implicated beneficiary and reacting with powerful emotion directly to the hurt and ruin she sees. Asserting the value of writing and recording of such testimonial details, Ashleigh Harris remarks:

> It is precisely this transferring of the traumatic past from the individual's body, to his/her speech, and finally to national discourse, that creates the cathartic potential of a nationally validated process such as the TRC. Within the discourses of the TRC, individuals' narratives and bodies become traces to the broader national and historical trauma inflicted by the apartheid regime (2006).

Harris calls the work that Krog does in *Country of My Skull* a 'shifting of trauma from the body of the victim to the realm of nationally validated speech' (2006). It is important here to remember that in Warner's study of public and mass subjectivity, he argues that it is often the cataclysmic and dreadful that happens to the body that is the vehicle for others to imagine themselves as part of the 'non-corporeal mass witness' in the public domain (2002: 177). There is no doubt that this was a distinct possibility for those participating in the TRC hearings via the media but through the pages of Krog's book the vicarious participant has more than only the details of the atrocities; they also have Krog's performance, listening, relaying, shifting position, giving voice and responding ethically and with respect for the depth of pain and destruction. As a writer Krog is also containing the atrocities, giving words, shaping the flow of the experiences and ultimately asserting the meaning and value of the testimonies for the goal of reconciliation, healing and new nationhood. She is also enacting her own bodily affectedness, mirroring the witnesses' bodily distress but within the pages of the book finding resolution in her belonging to a newly constructed land.

The assertion of a woman's body as the bearer of truth

> She is sitting behind a microphone, dressed in beret or *kopdoek* and her Sunday best. Everybody recognises her. Truth has become Woman. Her voice distorted behind her rough hand, has undermined Man as the source of truth. And yet. Nobody knows her (Krog 1998: 56).
>
> We pick out a sequence. We remove some pauses and edit it into a 20-minute sound bite. We feed it to Johannesburg. We switch on a small transistor. The news comes through: 'I was making tea in the police station. I heard a noise, I looked up . . . There he fell . . . Someone fell from the upper floor past the window . . . I ran down . . . It was my child . . . my grandchild, but I raised him.'
>
> We lift our fists triumphantly. We've done it!
>
> The voice of an ordinary cleaning woman is the headline on the one o'clock news (32).

In Krog's earlier poetic work she asserts the passion and depth of her capacity as a feeling, thinking woman writer. She is not constrained by a feminist politics but gives this female voice what is often considered a male power to register strength of emotion and especially anger. We have also seen Krog's experimentation with female interlocutors in her previous work where she used their experiences (often written by themselves) and her responses to them as a way of engaging in listening and hosting their embodied and situated knowledge of being in South Africa. In *Country of My Skull* she takes this engagement much further by making the startling assertion: 'Truth is a woman' – the title of Chapter 16 (Krog 1998: 177). By dedicating the book to 'every victim who had an Afrikaner surname on her lips', Krog is emphasising that the situated suffering female body has a great deal to say about the truth of South African apartheid experience.

When this assertion is laid alongside Krog's stated discomfort with the truth, as propounded through facts, an interesting new insight into how to grasp and understand the extremes of experience is made possible: 'The word "Truth" makes me uncomfortable. The word "truth" still trips the tongue. "Your voice tightens up when you approach the word 'truth'," the technical assistant says, irritated. "Repeat it twenty times so that you become familiar with it. *Truth is mos jou job!*"' (Krog 1998: 36). In Chapter 16 when she focuses closely on the testimony at the special hearings into women, she names each one and allows each one space to speak in the book without comment. Krog seems to be saying that the truth is to be found in the female experience, in the body of experience, in the words that each woman uses to give voice to her experience and that official, recorded and sanitised truth in documents is to be treated warily. This places Krog's account of the TRC in an interesting relation to the official TRC reports and, as commentators such as Sanders suggest, for readers to understand the TRC process they should read Krog alongside the official TRC report.

A new public for Antjie Krog

While Stephen Johnson certainly intended *Country of My Skull* to have an international audience (see Krog 1999a), Krog was adamant that she wrote with only South African readers in mind. According to Gillian Anstey:

> Antjie Krog has the most unusual reaction to the success of her book on the truth commission, *Country of My Skull*, an entrant in the *Sunday Times* Alan Paton Award for non-fiction writing – anger. Besides the 15 000 copies sold in South Africa – an extraordinary figure for a non-fiction work of this type – the book has also been published in London and New York. The Italian rights have been sold and the German, Spanish, Danish and Dutch rights are being negotiated. Chartoff Productions, a Californian film company responsible for blockbusters such as *The Right Stuff* and *Raging Bull*, has bought a two-year option for the film rights. Yet chat to Krog about overseas readers and, instead of expressing pride, she becomes aggressive and agitated. 'How can they understand

a single word?' she says. 'It is so South African, so Afrikaans, so white. I don't know what it is doing there' (Anstey 1999: 10).

Carli Coetzee, conscious of the fact that Krog had a previous and devoted poetry-reading audience of primarily Afrikaans-speakers, analyses her attempts to find another audience for *Country of My Skull*. Coetzee claims that the primary addressee of the book is two-fold: 'Krog directs her work at both her traditional Afrikaans-speaking audience and at a new audience by whom she wishes to be accepted' (2001: 685). Coetzee finds significance in the use of the poet's name 'Krog' as author of the book but points out that the resource material for the book was gathered as the journalist 'Samuel':

> This divided identity, this double signature, is more than a case of a married woman making a choice to publish under her maiden name . . . The nature of the signature in this text points to a series of displacements and sometimes uncomfortable divisions: Krog uses the word written by Antjie Samuel, publishing it here under her own name, her other name, but in English, which is not the language associated with the signature 'Krog'. The signature of the text is significant, in terms of the audience it evokes: Antjie Krog is the name under which the author is known as the adored woman poet of the Afrikaans tradition . . . The signature thus captures the attention of her Afrikaans-speaking readers, who are called on to take notice, and are forced to read this book alongside, or on top of, the other work produced by that signature (Coetzee 2001: 686–7).

In the text Krog seems to calculate in certain ways calling into being another readership alongside her already existing Afrikaans readership. Coetzee calls this a 'self-conscious desire to address an audience that includes black South Africans' (2001: 686) – see, for example, the book's dedication. Coetzee remarks that Krog is calling her 'historic reading public' to 'witness her addressing a black woman' (688).

The other interesting device is the performance of alienation by the author from her Afrikaner history, heritage and language.[32] Coetzee comments that the text shows the same concern and crisis many other South African authors evidence about audience.

> It is a crisis about the name of the fathers, the legacy of the past and of the Afrikaans language; and a crisis around who the addressee of the text produced by a white South African could be. In texts such as this one, the author is at pains to distinguish herself from the men of her race (as she calls them), and the voice becomes one in search of a new ear, a new genealogy into which she can write herself (Coetzee 2001: 688).

But added to this reaching across the race and language barrier to attain a new public in South Africa is also the evidence that the book found an international public immediately on its publication. While I have enumerated the factors that prepared the reception of the book and gave it salience internationally, I want to make a further point here that is more about the subjectivity enacted in the book and its echoes internationally.

Australian literary theorist David Carter (2001), who has an interest in burgeoning book clubs and the non-fiction material they often consume, talks about there being 'a developing audience for certain modes of interiority and of aesthetic experience' and he defines aesthetic as 'what happens when style, voice or authorial persona is invested with ethical value'. Carter detects a

> new 'specialist' function for literary reading among the array of mediated lifestyle and entertainment choices, a specific kind of *ethical training* which the process of reading and talking about books enables in distinctive ways . . . My point, though, is to see this kind of literary reading as a distinct 'technology'; to emphasise, for example, the different temporality involved in reading and how this might be suited to certain forms of ethical exercise or the different ways books circulate as commodities . . .

> I don't think we should say that the new tastes are 'merely' tastes or, for that matter, 'merely' products of smart marketing, as if there were a pure form of attachment to culture. We can instead conceive of lifestyle and consumption in terms of *self-fashioning* which extends to a whole range of ethical and political commitments (Carter 2001).

Carter says that reading groups that are consuming memoir and non-fiction are acting as 'occasions for *ethical reflection* . . . They address, as they constitute, readers who want "history", moral and intellectual sophistication, cultural context, authenticity, and structures for self-reflection' (2001). Carter concludes this argument by saying that in this type of book, history, ethics and aethestics come together in one package that allows a reader to use the book for engagement with and understanding of the world – in Warner's (2002) terms, the book is a vehicle for mass subjectivity, for being a public. If this is the case internationally, it is no surprise that *Country of My Skull* found an international readership so readily.

*   *   *

Krog's ongoing experimentations with subjectivity, which started in her early career as a poet, continued in her TRC reporting and subsequent book and, as is evident in the volume *Lady Anne*, are driven by her desire to relate ethically to the Others of South Africa. In response to the TRC testimonies this necessitated the adoption of the second-person position so that Krog was able to make the creative space to allow these Others into her writing. This position still contains elements of Krog's distinctive idiolect and her self-othering, particularly when she activates the experience of being female and being situated in the body.

That this desire to fashion an ethical response found an echo in the experience of readers internationally as well as in South Africa is because, in Carter's terms, a confluence of history, aesthetics and ethics created the right environment for the reception of this experimentation with subjectivity (2001). A global issue with great currency and impetus (dealing with the past through the now powerfully pervasive framework of human rights) found an exemplary local situation in the South African TRC and a market-driven, international, publishing industry, attuned to the desire for real-life stories operating in the mode of the confessional, found an author with significant literary capital and the factual journalistic material to fashion into a book.

These impetuses came together in the representative South African author Antjie Krog and the book *Country of My Skull*. An investigation of her trajectory through three fields, as well as an examination of Krog's adaptive capacity to mould a writer subjectivity responsive to those with the right to narrate (but not necessarily to be published) illuminates why Krog has become not only internationally known but also the kind of public figure who continues to have a voice and the power to speak in a political context where many white voices and especially Afrikaans-speaking white voices have now lost this automatic power.

Notes

1. In an interview in 1993 with Daniel Hugo, Krog talked about the founding of *Die Suid-Afrikaan*. 'Skrywers en Boeke', 30 September 1993, SABC Sound Archives, T93/1164 (Daniel Hugo in conversation with Antjie Krog).

2. Afrikaans audio (no programme name given), 20 April 1995, SABC Sound Archives, T95/230-1 (Charmaine Gallon in conversation with poet, Antjie Krog).

3. 'Woman's World', 16 May 1994, SABC Sound Archives, T94/725 (Marinda Claassen in conversation with Antjie Krog).

4. Personal communication from Pippa Green, 22 April 2005, and from Franz Krüger, 5 May 2005. Krüger was SABC radio's national editor at the time.

5. For example, in 1995 Krog (as Antjie Samuel) interviewed Dr Alex Boraine (director of IDASA) about 'justice in transition' for the SABC. 'Monitor', 17 January 1995, SABC Sound Archives, T94/1235 (Antjie Samuel interviews Dr Alex Boraine).

6. Personal communication from Franz Krüger, 5 May 2005.

7. Avbob is a chain of funeral parlours in South Africa.

8. See *Truth and Reconciliation Commission of South Africa Report*, Vol. 1 (318, 356). http://www.justice.gov.za/trc/report/finalreport/Volume%201.pdf.

9. Angie Kapelianis confirmed this in personal communication, October 2000.

10. http://vcmstatic.sabc.co.za/VCMStaticProdStage/CORPORATE/SABC Corporate/Document/About SABC/The SABC In Detail/tenyears.doc. The Pringle Award carried no cash prize but it was the highest award bestowed by the community of journalists on their peers. The South African Union of Journalists no longer exists and the prize is no longer awarded.

11. The stridently anti-apartheid press that sprang up in the 1980s to print the news the mainstream press would not was supported financially by churches, non-governmental organisations and international donors.

12. Dirk Coetzee was one of the perpetrators of apartheid atrocities. Coetzee made a full confession of hit squad activities. Journalist Jacques Pauw used Coetzee as an informant to expose the apartheid government's third-force destabilisation activities in the early 1990s for *Vrye Weekblad*. See Pauw (1997, 2007).

13. Personal communication from Stephen Johnson, 19 August 2004.

14. See the Acknowledgements at the end of *Country of My Skull* where Krog says: 'How do I thank a publisher who refused to take no for an answer when I said, "No, I don't want to write a book about the Truth Commission", stuck with me when I said, "No, I can't write a book," and also, "I dare not write a book"; and was still there when I came around to saying, "I *have* to write a book, otherwise I'll go crazy"' (1998: 280).

15. Personal communication from Stephen Johnson, 19 August 2004.

16. *The Star Tonight*, 31 August 1998: 6–7.

17. Barnes & Noble website: http://search.barnesandnoble.com/Country-of-My-Skull/Antjie-Krog/e/9780812931297#TABS.

18. Ibid.

19. Ibid.

20. Ibid.

21. Ibid.

22. See Chapter 2 for details of Krog's writing and speaking engagements in this regard, as well as the awards she received after the publication of *Country of My Skull*.

23. For an elaboration of Krog's journalistic methods, see Garman (2014b).

24. Since 1971 'truth' commissions/tribunals/inquiries have been held in Albania (1993), Algeria (2003–5), Argentina (1983–4), Australia (stolen aboriginal children, 1996–7), Bangladesh (1971), Bolivia (1982–4), Brazil (1992), Bulgaria (1992), Burundi (1995–6), Cambodia (2006), Canada (on aboriginal peoples, 1991–6 and 1998), Chad (1991–2), Chile (1990–1), Colombia (several interventions, 1997–), Côte d'Ivoire (2012–14), the Czech Republic (1991), Democratic Republic of Congo (2004–7), East Timor (2002), Ecuador (1996–7 and 2007), El Salvador (1992–3), Ethiopia (1993, ongoing), Fiji (2005), Germany (1992–4), Ghana (1993–4), Guatemala (1997–9), Guinea (2011), Haiti (1995–6), Honduras (1993), Israel (1983), Kenya (2007–8), Kosovo (2000), Liberia (2006–9), Malawi (1994), Mauritius (2009–11), Mexico (1992), Morocco (2004–5), Nepal (1990–1), Nicaragua (1992), Niger (1992–3), Nigeria (1999–2000), Northern Ireland (1997–8), Panama (2001), Paraguay (2004–8), Peru (2002), Poland (1992), Romania (1992), Rwanda (1999), Serbia and Montenegro (2002–3), Sierra Leone (2000–1), Solomon Islands (2009–11), South Africa (1995–2000, two commissions of inquiry were held into ANC activities in military camps in exile [1992 and 1993] before the TRC got underway), South Korea (2005–10), Sri Lanka (1994–7), Sudan (1992–4), Thailand (1992), Togo (1992), Tunisia (2014), Uganda (1974, 1986–95), Ukraine (2006), United States (into wartime relocation and internment of citizens, 1981–2 and into radiation

experiments, 1994–5), Uruguay (1985), Yugoslavia (2001) and Zimbabwe (1985). Groups and individuals in Afghanistan, Angola, Colombia, Croatia, Indonesia, Jamaica, Kenya, Mexico, the Philippines, Uganda, Venezuela and Zimbabwe have since called for new truth commissions. Commissions have also been called for into 'violence against women' internationally (by the Fulbright New Century Scholars on the Global Empowerment of Women Working Group) and into the 'impact of the nuclear cycle' (by the Women's International League for Peace and Freedom). See Hayner (2002); Charles O. Lerche III, 'Truth Commissions And National Reconciliation: Some Reflections On Theory And Practice', http://www.gmu. edu/programs/icar/pcs/LERCHE71PCS.html and the Truth Commission Digital Collection at http://www.usip.org/library/truth.html#tc. Interestingly Michael P. Scharf (1997) has argued 'the case for a permanent international truth commission'.

25. '"Truth" is to be understood as a system of ordered procedures for the production, regulation, distribution, circulation and operation of statements' (Foucault 1980: 133).

26. Adorno's phrase, 'To write a poem after Auschwitz is barbaric', appears in the conclusion to 'An Essay on Cultural Criticism and Society' (Adorno 1967: 34). Adorno originally wrote it in 1949 for a Festschrift.

27. 'Witness' is one of those ambiguous words that can mean, in such a context, either someone giving their own testimony or someone listening to that testimony.

28. Carmel Bird is an Australian writer and has a prize for short stories named after her. She is the author of *The Stolen Children: Their Stories*, published in 1998 by Random House (Australia), which is based on Bringing Them Home, the findings of a government inquiry into the removal of Aboriginal and Torres Strait Islander children from their families.

29. Krog introduced herself decisively as 'a beneficiary of apartheid' at a special reconciliation event at the National Arts Festival in Grahamstown on 4 July 2003.

30. See, for example, Mahmood Mamdani (1996b), a critique cited by Schaffer and Smith (2006) and by Krog (1998: 112). See also Mark Sanders's discussion of the acknowledgement within the TRC report that focusing on the 'exceptional perpetrator led to a "fail[ure] to recognise the 'little perpetrator' in each of us"' (2002: 3).

31. When at some point in the hearings it became clear to the commissioners that such an individualising of atrocity was taking place, institutional hearings were set up into specific social structures, such as the media, the business world, faith communities, the medical sector and the legal sector. See *Truth and Reconciliation Commission of South Africa Report, Vol. 4*. http://www.justice.gov.za/trc/report/finalreport/Volume%204. pdf.

32. It is interesting that it was *Country of My Skull* that gave Krog a significant English-speaking readership and from this point in her writing career, she has deliberately translated her own new work and released further books and poetry in both English and Afrikaans. But this particular book has not been translated into Afrikaans. It seems to show Krog's uncertain position in relation to her heritage, even while she fiercely continues to use (and abuse) her mother tongue.

6

Authority and Authenticity in the New South Africa

If I have to find among Afrikaans thinkers one who I would call an 'African intellectual', it is her. I have been so formed as a 'Western' intellectual; that it is Antjie Krog who, every time I read her, challenges me to acknowledge the restrictions of that formation and to address them. Few other Afrikaans thinkers dig so deeply and insistently about Africa and the moral and intellectual challenges of our continent and land (Gerwel 2007: 20).

Authority

In December 1997, as Krog was putting the finishing touches to *Country of My Skull*, the *Mail & Guardian* declared that she was one of the 'next hot one hundred' South Africans to pay attention to. The article proclaimed:

The next generation: those who will be at the forefront of their fields in the years to come. We have captured a snapshot of 100 people, groups and trends that will be leading the pack as South Africa heads for the next millennium. The people featured here are not necessarily young; rather it is their plans and ideas that are on the ascent. They are the people who are set to influence (and are influenced by) the way we live and the issues which we debate.

M&G reporters have searched and found them across the political terrain, cutting a swathe through each arts discipline, ploughing up land concerns or fashioning a new, homegrown sense of style. From opera stars to soccer heroes, the future could rest in their hands . . . Poet and journalist Antjie Krog is polishing off *Country of My Skull*, her account of the Truth and Reconciliation Commission – which she attended from day one – for Random House, due out in April 1998. Judging by the responses (including a prize) for her coverage of the commission in this newspaper, it could well be the definitive book on the subject.[1]

Ten years later, long after the publication of *Country of My Skull* and after Krog's second book of non-fiction in English (*A Change of Tongue*) as well as a number of new volumes of poetry,[2] Judith Lütge Coullie and Andries Visagie, the editors of a special edition of *Current Writing* entirely devoted to Krog, talked about her as a 'mediator of South African culture', as a translator, journalist, poet and as a person 'on the world stage'.[3]

The *Mail & Guardian* article correctly predicted that Krog's book would be definitive but it was also a portent of Krog's newly altered status in South Africa as a result. It was an indication that she was now entering the realm of those who step out of their fields as the pre-eminent and consecrated and are acclaimed as public figures that span the social landscape, who 'influence the way we live'. But I would like to take this further: Krog is not only considered a very important writer or public figure or representative South African, I believe she also operates as a public intellectual, as claimed by Jakes Gerwel in the chapter epigraph above. But first, I want to look at the indications of Krog's status as a public figure, which extends over fields and operates more generally in the public domain.

In 2004 the SABC was also to lift Krog out of the literary and into the larger public arena when the broadcaster embarked on a quest to discover the '100 greatest South Africans of all time'. The series, hosted by talk show host Noeleen Maholwana Sangqu and journalist-author Denis Beckett, involved a nationwide poll in which South Africans cast their votes by telephone, SMS and on the channel's website, which was broadcasting profiles and documentaries in the weeks leading up to the announcement of the top 100. Predictably Nelson Mandela was number one. But Krog came in at 75, just behind Kaizer Motaung, founder of Kaizer Chiefs Football Club (73) and Basetsana Kumalo, a former Miss South Africa, and ahead of Nobel Literature Laureate Nadine Gordimer at 80.[4] More recently Jonathan Ancer profiled Krog in a podcast for the *Mail & Guardian* as part of a series on 'extraordinary lives'.[5]

While Krog's literary output has always been the topic of attention for literary study, since the publication of *Country of My Skull*, the academy has begun to treat her differently, as not only the author of a literary corpus but also a producer of knowledge in her own right. This has taken the form of acknowledgement via the conferring of honorary doctorates, her inclusion as a keynote speaker among academics at major conferences and more importantly a post created specially for her as an extraordinary professor attached to the Faculty of Arts at the University of the Western Cape. Ironically in 1992, Krog applied for senior lecturer positions at the University of the Western Cape and the University of Cape Town. Both universities turned her down because she did not have a doctorate or (at that time) the necessary symbolic capital to make a doctorate unnecessary.[6] After *Country of My Skull*, she had the capital and the University of the Western Cape approached her. Her *personal status* (rather than only her literary output) is also the serious subject of academic inquiry, as can be seen in the special edition of *Current Writing* devoted to her and her work.

As has become a hallmark in Krog's relationship with the media, she is not only the object of media attention but also continues to be a commentator and opinion writer who weighs in on national debates. In 2006 when former minister of law and order Adriaan Vlok atoned for his role in apartheid repression by symbolically washing the feet of ANC activist Frank Chikane, causing an outraged public reaction, Krog appealed for 'a space for the disgraced' (Krog 2006b). And when popular Afrikaans singer Bok van Blerk wrote a song calling for Boer War hero General de la Rey to come and lead his people and sparked an outcry, Krog entered the debate by writing 'De la Rey: Afrikaner Absolution' (2007a). When Eugene Terre'Blanche was murdered, she wrote 'When It Comes to Dialogue We Don't Have the Words' (2010b). And when

Nelson Mandela died, Krog wrote on his relationship with Afrikaners for both the *Cape Times* (2013a) and *Sunday Argus* (2013d).

To this public recognition is added the attention of politicians who recognise her value for the national reconstruction project. This has been demonstrated by more than simply the quoting of her work publicly. In June of 2003 Krog was selected as part of a panel of 'eminent South Africans' to advise President Mbeki on appointments to the Commission for the Promotion and Protection of the Rights of Cultural, Religious and Linguistic Communities. In 2009 Dr Mamphela Ramphele, chair of the convenors, invited her to be part of the Dinokeng Scenario Team, which aimed to draw South Africa out of its quagmire of white withdrawal from the public domain, inept government and selfish and unethical business leadership.[7]

South Africa has produced many great writers whose work and voices have moved beyond the literary domain and into public and political life, often at crucial moments. But in most cases it is the symbolic capital of the literary field that allows them to be heard, called upon or quoted at certain times. Krog has mobility across several fields and a facility to inject into the public realm her opinions and voice, which is sometimes substantially different from the usual behaviour of authors in public spaces and the media. How did it transpire that what she does and says is received as so important in our public domain?

I would argue that it is because of a systematic accumulation of capital across three fields and also because of a particular relationship of interest and mutual benefit developed over many years with the news media that Krog is treated as more than simply a well-known writer with important thoughts. Over the decades she has maintained a relationship with an Afrikaans-speaking public via the Afrikaans press but she has also acquired an English-speaking public (both national and international, black and white) through the attention of the English-language press, her work at the SABC and the publication of her English-language books *Country of My Skull*, *A Change of Tongue* and *Begging to Be Black*. When compared, for example, with the fraught relationship another dissident poet – Breyten Breytenbach – has had both with the media and the Afrikaner *volk* (see Galloway 2004: 5, 11) Krog's relationship with the news media has worked powerfully to advance her standing within the Afrikaans community and literary establishment and enabled her to transcend this community as her public when she began to work in English and was taken up as a representative voice of post-apartheid South Africa by the English-language media and a publishing house. Krog continues to be able to use her specificity as an Afrikaner (in producing poetry and translations in Afrikaans) but has also acquired the power to speak for the interests of the new South African nation, both locally and abroad. This ability is precisely because of a double-sided relationship with the media: with their particular treatment of her as a newsmaker, their framing of her as valuable and important and of us (even as this 'us' was enlarged into the new nation) and her use of and involvement in the media both as a journalist and an agenda-setter. This sets her apart from other writers who enter the public domain and marks her as a person who has acquired media meta-capital and uses it.

In seeking to understand how heightened attention from both the consecrators in a field and the news media can attach to someone and confer status on them, it is useful to be be reminded of Pierre Bourdieu's 'three competing principles of legitimacy' (1983: 331–2). These are, he says:

1. the recognition by other producers in the autonomous field;
2. the taste of the dominant class and bodies that sanction this taste and
3. popular legitimacy – 'consecration bestowed by the choice of ordinary consumers, the mass audience'.

What we see from the reportage on Krog's life, person and writing output is not only the acclaim of the field consecrators (category 1) and the acclaim of the dominant classes that sanction 'taste' (category 2) but also recognition from a mass audience (category 3). Krog demonstrates Bourdieu's supposition that an individual who accumulates both cultural and economic capital within a field is able to take the resulting symbolic capital and convert it into forms of capital acknowledged as valuable in other fields (Bourdieu 2002: 17). In Krog's case, the news media have been key to such transitions and have often been the reason she has been enabled to convert her capital. This has resulted in Krog acquiring what Randall Johnson calls 'prestige', 'celebrity' and 'honour' (Bourdieu 1993: 7). As a result Krog has the 'almost magical power of mobilisation', the 'power to construct reality' (2002: 170), which has effects on other fields and across the social landscape. Krog has indeed become part of the 'general culture' through a 'process of familiarisation' with the mass audience (Bourdieu and Nice 1980: 290).

Authenticity

Since the final poem that ended *Country of My Skull* with an appeal to those who testified at the TRC (in their multiple mother tongues) to 'take me with you', Krog has returned to the literary field as her scene of action and as a powerful generator of the symbols and meanings that can make new community and in particular to the work of translation. As Stephan Meyer (2002) shows so clearly in his essay on Krog the translator, the persistent symbol of the connection to the land that threads through Krog's poetry and into *Country of My Skull* has found a second, more powerful dimension in Krog's turning to translation as a mechanism for a poet/writer to make the new nation. Since the success of *Country of My Skull*, which was written in Afrikaans by Krog and then translated by her into English, then edited by Ivan Vladislavić, Krog has embarked on numerous translation/transcription projects. Some of these are of her own work,[8] some are reclamations of older work in indigenous languages,[9] some are commissions. Krog's preoccupations with language, tongue, mother tongue and with the metaphor of the *tongvis* (the sole or literally 'tongue fish') as a recurring symbol of change and therefore possibility, underlie many of her recent projects in continuing the TRC's work of transformation in the increasing complexity of South Africa's democracy.[10]

As Meyer points out, there are two traditions of translation operating in South Africa (2002: 3). The first is located historically when the missionaries and colonisers learnt the indigenous languages, reduced them to writing and translated various oral texts for European audiences or for the record (the Bleek-Lloyd archive is one such example). The second tradition is more interesting and it is this one in which Krog participates. Here certain key texts are translated into many South African tongues, thus allowing a choice of the same stories about who we are as a people to be available in most of the official languages. Notable here is Nelson Mandela's *Long Walk to Freedom*, which Krog was commissioned to translate into Afrikaans. Says Meyer:

> The effect, if not already the aim, is to create a single South African text which most of us have read – albeit in different languages. In this case, selected stories held in common (rather than one unifying national language which establishes a common national ground) become the basis of an imagined community. Instead of leaving behind our private languages to communicate in the public sphere of English, these texts help us to establish a community in languages which permeate our own immediate, everyday, linguistically structured life worlds, which are in turn enriched by these texts (2002: 3).

It is clear that Krog has not waited for some official agency to decide what are to be the key texts and has done her own work of reclamation in translating into Afrikaans and English the Bushman texts from the Bleek-Lloyd archive and into Afrikaans a selection of poetry from /Xam, Xhosa, Zulu, Ndebele, Swati, Venda, Tsonga, Northern Sotho, Tswana and Southern Sotho. She is provoked into this translation of indigenous texts into Afrikaans by the insularity she sees in the white Afrikaans-speaking community, which she fears will be increasingly isolated from the circulating discussions and symbolic content other South Africans have access to. The translations into Afrikaans are about ensuring that there is a significant amount of material available in this language that comes from a diversity of South Africans and contributes to a broad conversation being possible also in this language. Krog told me at the launch of *'n Ander Tongval* at Boekehuis in Johannesburg on 2 November 2005 that 'Afrikaans is falling out of the national debate' and is 'losing a foothold'.

This concern for the national conversation and the creation of a talking, new, imagined community is considered a third tradition by Meyer. He sees Krog clearly locating 'translation within a political context in which the power of different languages, as well as the historical moment of liberation are crucial' (2002: 4). Here 'translation/transliteration' is an 'act of transformation'. According to H.P. van Coller and B.J. Odendaal:

> Her concern in the first place is with South African society and her 'rainbow nation' which grows out of the African spirit of *ubuntu*, and a tolerant multi-culturalism which flourishes into an inclusive, collective African identity . . . Krog has repeatedly said she strives for a (South) African cultural and language dispensation in which all the country's languages in all their variety are respected equally, where people cross language boundaries freely, aided where necessary by translation (2007: 114).

The *authority* that her symbolic capital gives her means that Krog has been acclaimed as a public figure who has entered general culture and is recognised by the masses. As Tom Gouws has commented, Krog is a 'contemporary people's poet', a 'forceful and innovative figure' in Afrikaans literature and even a 'cult figure', who 'in each succeeding poetry volume enlarges not only herself and her world, but dedicates herself to enriching her people and her followers' (1998: 562).

But there is another aspect to Krog's ability to perform in public as the literary host to many voices and facilitator of a great, multi-tongue conversation and that is *authenticity*. In order to understand how Krog has become not only a representative South African of the peaceful transition to the world but also recognised as a transformed Afrikaner with a platform to speak in this country, I turn now to some insights on citizenship in democratic states. Both Ivor Chipkin (2007a, 2007b, 2008) and Preben Kaarsholm (2008) point out in their work on states and citizenship that while anyone nominally the citizen of a country can claim citizenship as a politico-legal status, in actual effect, citizenship is a quality of relation to the type of state operating in a country. Chipkin shows that the ANC control of the South African government since 1994, and more particularly between 1999 and 2008 when Thabo Mbeki was president, resulted in a state in which the nationalist project was paramount and nation-building its prime expression. The citizen who shows him/herself to be the ideal *national* subject comes to be associated with *authentic* citizenship. Chipkin argues:

> Nationalism is driven to invoke a distinction between citizenship as a status and citizenship as an authentic national identity. There may be individuals who are granted rights in the political community, but they are not necessarily authentic members of the nation – 'truly' loyal to their country, 'properly' patriotic and so on (2007b: 16–17).

Chipkin reaches into history to find other examples where the practice of democracy has privileged certain classes of people as 'authentic' citizens. He finds that in the early United States Jefferson privileged the land-owning farmer, Marx privileged the urban, working class (1008: 7), and so a similar privileging is going on in South Africa with the ANC in power.

Chipkin continues (and while he centres on the Mbeki government I would argue this is largely true of the Zuma government resting on the direction set by Mbeki): 'What counts is the way that Mbeki's administration has sought to give substance to "the people" of South Africa . . . African values are democratic values, such that the two terms are interchangeable (2008: 8).

This is why in the South African national public sphere we see many assertions of Africanness by way of resort to birth on this continent or the fact of generations of ancestors located here geographically. At the core is the anxiety that simple politico-legal citizenship is not powerful enough to include those not considered Africans by those with the power to chart the course of democracy and nationhood. This kind of assertion is made by public figures such Frederik van Zyl Slabbert who addressed the statement 'I Too Am an African: If Not, Why Not?' at the University of the Witwatersrand on 22 November 2006 (Van Zyl Slabbert 2006) and even by self-described public intellectual Xolela Mangcu, called a 'coconut' by members of the Native Club (Masondo 2008: 4), who performs an impeccable Eastern Cape heritage in his book *To the Brink* (Mangcu 2008) in order to settle the question of his authenticity. The interesting distinction, when it comes to Krog, is that the same anxiety of belonging and identity permeates her poetry and other writing but her reaction is not to assert in public (in rational-critical mode) her Africanness, but to perform it.

This she does in multifaceted ways and primarily by using the methods of the literary field, her accumulated symbolic capital, her voice and her adaptive subjectivity. She also uses her status as a literary consecrator (which includes her powerful relationships with publishers) to enlarge the literary space, to bring to it new, reclaimed and Other voices and to deliberately encourage its overflow into generalised public space via her newsmaker and agenda-setter status with the South African media. This she does through collecting, editing, translating and curating. But for her own self, and presumably this is done in public for the emulation of others, she performs (mostly) through her poetry but also through her recent books, the guilty, complicit, contrite and petitioning subject who knows that authenticity as a South African citizen can only be granted to a white person by the previously damaged and dispossessed. But as Chipkin points out very clearly, while the millions of South African poor are intended to be the recipients and beneficiaries of the new democracy, those with the actual power to define democracy and decide on its delivery are an elite, for whom Africanness as the marker of authenticity is key.

If Krog wants her project of enlarging the conversation about transformation and change to have the ring of authenticity, she cannot only rely on her own symbolic capital; she must perform authenticity in a way that captures the attention of the powers of the new South African democratic project. Hence the high value of the attention paid to her poetry when Mbeki quoted it in his presidential speech in 2002 and the public acclamation by Gerwel's statement in the epigraph at the beginning of this chapter: 'If I have to find among Afrikaans thinkers one who I would call an "African intellectual", it is her' (2007: 20).

In his enormous study *The Civil Sphere*, in the chapter dealing with 'encounters with the Other', in which he discusses the assimilation of disparate peoples and cultures into a single state or nation, Jeffrey C. Alexander remarks: 'The public has never been a dry and arid place composed of abstract arguments about reason. It has always been filled up by expressive images, by narratives, traditions, and symbolic codes' (2006: 409). Studying Krog's position as a public figure in post-apartheid South Africa shows very clearly that it is not because she enters the public domain as a Saidian-type intellectual 'speaking truth to power' that she achieves a public and a hearing. Many commentators in South Africa's public domains (writers, journalists, researchers, political analysts) set themselves up deliberately to 'speak truth to power' and to emulate the rational-critical formulations of a persuasive argument and a faculty for representation – as espoused by Edward Said (1994) and described by Jürgen Habermas (1991). But Krog is not this kind of public figure. Her style is to use the literary and its formulations of public address and the licence that literary styles and devices provide and to bend these to her particular purposes. She continues the TRC work she did as a journalist through her poetry, curations, collections, translations and other writings. She ventures into the performance of Saidian public intellectualism only occasionally via the opinion and comment pages in newspapers. Unlike commentators such as Mangcu, who boldly self-describes as a 'public intellectual', she never does so. Her firm location in the literary – coupled with her reach way beyond the literary field – gives Krog the freedom to continue to use literary tropes and techniques to perform the responsibilities of new South African citizenship in public. She uses the autobiographical and the personal to deftly craft a public persona for herself that shows itself to be *responsive* to national concerns of damage and discrimination, access to voice and the crafting of a democracy that gives rights and benefits to the majority of South Africans.

This public persona not only reacts to the affectedness of Others who have been marginalised but is also affected by these struggles and shows herself to be so. In addition, in retrieving indigenous voices from the past and translating them into South Africa's dominant public languages (English and Afrikaans) and in curating festivals (and editing volumes) in which she brings poets and writers from around the world together with South Africans and mixes the established and the emerging, Krog has taken up a self-defined task to enlarge the public sphere and the number and type of voices in it. She deliberately brings together into conversation, often via translation, those she thinks might be excluded by history and language from public deliberations about the issue most pressing – new South African nationhood – and she does this through literary means and techniques.

If the public sphere is the arena in which the key questions of the day are thrashed out, what – and how – does Krog contribute to the debate? Among the multiple issues and debates taking place in our public sphere, the single most pressing question, which infects all others, is the question of who counts as an authentic citizen. Essentially Krog contributes a performance, in the use of herself and her established poetic voice as the mode of both embodiment and address. By enacting contrition, guilt, culpability and complicity, by bearing the burden of the history of the Afrikaner nation, by showing herself to be affected in the public domain, by using poetic language, by saying the *words* laden with emotion that are not used in rational-critical discourse, she sets the terms of inclusion for white South Africans into authentic citizenship. One can see this performance most clearly in those pieces in *Country of My Skull* that revert to poetic form:

> But I want to put it more simply. I want this hand of mine to write it. For us all; all voices, all victims:
>
>> because of you
>> this country no longer lies
>> between us but within
>>
>> it breathes becalmed
>> after being wounded
>> in its wondrous throat
>>
>> in the cradle of my skull
>> it sings, it ignites
>> my tongue, my inner ear, the cavity of heart
>> shudders towards the outline
>>> new in soft intimate clicks and gutturals

of my soul the retina learns to expand
daily because by a thousand stories
I was scorched

a new skin.

I am changed for ever. I want to say
    forgive me
    forgive me
    forgive me

You whom I have wronged, please
take me

with you (Krog 1998: 278-9).

This then became a further poem in 'Land van Genade en Verdriet' (Krog 2000b: 37) and its English translation 'Country of Grief and Grace' (2000a: 95):

(a)
between you and me
how desperately
how it aches
how desperately it aches between you and me

so much hurt for truth
so much destruction
so little left for survival

where do we go from here

your voice slung
in anger
over the solid cold length of our past

how long does it take
for a voice
to reach another

in this country held bleeding between us . . .

(e)
deepest heart of my heart
heart that can only come from this soil
brave
with its teeth firmly in the jugular of the only truth that matters
and that heart is black
I belong to that blinding black African heart
my throat bloats with tears
my pen falls to the floor
I blubber behind my hand
for one brief shimmering moment this country
this country is also truly mine

and my heart is on its feet

(f)
because of you
this country no longer lies
between us but within

it breathes becalmed
after being wounded
in its wondrous throat

in the cradle of my skull
it sings   it ignites
my tongue   my inner ear   the cavity of heart
shudders towards the outline
new in soft intimate clicks and gutturals

I am changed for ever   I want to say
forgive me
forgive me
forgive me

you whom I have wronged, please
take me

with you

This poem goes on to include the section Mbeki quoted in his state of
the nation address to parliament in 2002. This public conversation, in
which the president of the country responds to the poet, is more than
seizing on a literary fragment to underscore a political point and spice
up a public speech. Krog has enacted here exactly the public statement
required from white South Africans, which can then be considered by
the leader and his government and the people they represent to have met
the terms of inclusion for authentic citizenship. While many other white
South Africans assert their citizenship and identity as South Africans (or
more pointedly as Africans) by invoking their legal or constitutional status,
Krog performatively demonstrates her identity and subject status as an
'authentic member of the nation'. It is precisely the distinction between
'political-legal status' and 'authentic national identity' – as Chipkin
(2007a) points out – that makes the difference here.

The importance in South African public intellectual work of
renegotiating the self into a new community has been explored by Mark
Sanders (2002: 1), who argues that when the national society to which one
belongs has been constructed at every level by apartheid, the intellectual,
even in opposition, is shaped by this social structure. If the intellectual is
white, there must be recognition that one is a 'little perpetrator', if black,
the intellectual is theorising and negotiating 'mental complicity', as in
the case of Biko (15). Sanders argues that the South African intellectual
'identifies [as complicit in apartheid] in order to dis-identify' (3) but this
is only the first step. Sanders activates a second definition of complicity,
which he reads as 'a folded-together-ness – in human-being' (5). He sees

in his exploration of South African public intellectuals an affirmation of this larger complicity – the 'being of being human', which then drives their intellectual projects.

That a figure who operates in this way and with this kind of public subjectivity is so deft and creative and responsive to the undercurrents of change in state and citizenship has been far more interesting to explore than using the traditional markers of intellectual activity to judge whether Krog's is a performance of intellectualism that sits convincingly within the definition of 'speaking truth to power'. Krog by no means fits that category but operates in ways that are captured by Paul Bové's formulation (1994: 222) of the classic idea of an intellectual. Krog has 'perspicacious intelligence' and is a purveyor of 'symbols and values' for this country, par excellence.

Notes

1. 'The Next Hot One Hundred', Mail & Guardian, 23 December 1997.
2. Down to My Last Skin and Kleur Kom Nooit Alleen Nie (both published in 2000); Met Woorde Soos met Kerse (published in 2002); The Stars Say 'Tsau' and Die Sterre Sê 'Tsau' (both published in 2004); Body Bereft and Verweerskrif (both published in 2006) and Fynbos Fairies and Fynbosfeetjies (both published in 2007).
3. Quotations taken from the call for papers by the editors, Judith Lütge Coullie and Andries Visagie. This special edition of Current Writing has now been published as Antjie Krog: An Ethics of Body and Otherness (Coullie and Visagie 2014).
4. This idea was modelled on the 2002 BBC programme in which a vote was held to determine whom the general public considered the '100 greatest Britons of all time'.
5. See http://mg.co.za/multimedia/2014-12-09-extraordinary-life-antjie-krog. 'Extraordinary Lives' is a biographical podcast series that celebrates the contributions that remarkable people have made to South Africa and the world. A well-known guest discusses the life of an extraordinary person who has inspired them. 'Extraordinary Lives' is inspired by the BBC's 'Great Lives' and is presented by Jonathan Ancer. It is produced by Triple World Score Media.
6. See 'Burokratiese Misvat', Vrye Weekblad, 29 May–4 June 1992: 13.
7. See http://www.dinokengscenarios.co.za/sa_conclusion.php.
8. Krog translated a selection of her poetry over the years into English for the first time in one volume (Down to My Last Skin) in 2000. 'n Ander Tongval was translated by Krog into Afrikaans from the English A Change of Tongue for an Afrikaans-speaking readership. More recently Krog has been producing her own new work in both

English and Afrikaans, notably *Body Bereft/Verweerskrif* in 2006 and *Synapse/Mede-Wete* in 2014.

9. *Met Woorde Soos met Kerse* (2002) and *The Stars Say 'Tsau'* and the Afrikaans version *Die Sterre Sê 'Tsau'* (2004).

10. The metaphor of the *tongvis* appears first in *Lady Anne* in poem and picture, then again in Krog's translated poetry *Down to My Last Skin* and then most prominently in the book focused on political and social change in South Africa, *A Change of Tongue*.

7

Speaking Poetry to Power
Krog and the South African Public Sphere

This review of Antjie Krog and her work has been based on the premise that the public intellectual, as an important figure in the public sphere, is a 'structural or institutional effect' and not simply to be investigated 'in terms of individual capacities' (Carter 2001).[1] I have also embraced Eleanor Townsley's position that 'public intellectual' is a 'trope' – an embodied means for societies to 'frame meaning and practice' (2006: 40) about nations and publics, about mass subjectivity and the meanings of citizenship and identity.

My assumption, therefore, is that an underlying discourse propels the purported need for intellectuals to be visible and vocal in the public sphere in South Africa. The proliferation of calls – and names – for various types of intellectuals in South Africa (African, black, native, organic, collective, revolutionary) indicates that 'space, legitimacy and power' are being claimed by differing groups of peoples seeking their proxies in the public domain and all three of these categories are very much under contestation. One cannot speak easily in South Africa of the 'public intellectual' as only a particular type of figure who is a thought-leader driving debate in public (see Memela 2006) or even, to use Edward Said's careful and thoughtful prescriptions in *Representations of the Intellectual* (1994), about what an intellectual performance constitutes.

As in other national public spheres, South African intellectuals differ in their assessments of the state of the present and prescriptions for the future and the various types of performers draw on different sources of legitimacy and lineages of knowledge and wisdom. What this multiplicity of voices, styles and arguments (in particular those sharp disagreements where *ad hominem* attacks surface – 'coconut', 'free-floating liberal') show very clearly is that there is a great deal of suspicion and anxiety about adopting the Western, universalising mode of proclaiming a social vision for a nation that calls on the lineage of Western knowledge practices.

This proliferation of types of public intervention and engagement, together with the questions about who represents what and whose interests, is indicative of a deep anxiety about what constitutes legitimate authority to speak, for whom and about what, in a postcolonial state. As Martin Hollis points out, the question of the role of the intellectual all over the world is driven by 'the threat that Enlightenment assumptions about the universal character of truth and reason are by now so uncompelling that they may be unsustainable' (1997: 289). But to this must be added the exclusion and alienation that the experiences of colonialism and apartheid generated, which live on in an ongoing suspicion of Western-informed knowledge practices. For centuries these practices positioned indigenous peoples as uncivilised natives with no useful knowledge practices of their own and then as objects of a civilising project into Western modes of knowledge acquisition. This suspicion is heightened by contemporary global debates about the spread of human rights, the inclusion of the marginalised peoples of the world into proper nationhood and the struggles in many democratic states for full citizenship and recognition. In South Africa this suspicion was sharpened by the findings of TRC hearings, which opened up the past and the atrocities committed by the apartheid government and allowed the dispossessed to speak for the first time in their thousands. Redress and restitution are high on the agenda in South Africa, not only officially but also unofficially. Powerful doubt is cast over whether public intellectual performances rooted in Western forms of knowledge can help to drive a programme of redress and reclamation of dignity, cultural authenticity and indigenous wisdom.

It is important to note that despite this high degree of suspicion of Western-rooted practices, the discourse motivating the calls for intellectuals of whatever type still holds the desire that these public sphere actors should speak in universalising and socially useful ways. Peter Osborne's insights about the intellectual's 'claims on the present', the 'value of thought and ideas' and the need for a 'totalising social vision', while embedded in classic public sphere ideals, still hold power as mobilising ideas and desires and are still considered useful in a postcolonial public sphere. In surveying the lineage of intellectuals from 1899 to Said, Osborne says that while all sorts of provisions of public sphere and intellectual performance have been contested, what has 'stuck' is the 'distinctive aspiration to universality, making the intellectual the *exemplary* figure for humanity as a whole' (1996: xii). As Helen Small says:

> There is nevertheless an evident desire . . . for a language of political and cultural life that can be in some measure holistic or at least coherently generalising. That desire may, I am suggesting, be one reason for the curious persistence of the old narratives of decline and/or imminent revitalisation of the intellectual – and the difficulty for the critic of that literature in getting beyond the merely diagnostic . . . speaking about intellectuals has, in other words, been a way of posing the perennially troubling question of how much what we say matters (2002: 11).

In surveying the debates on intellectuals in the South African public sphere, it is evident that while the multiplicity of performers and performances being called into action is indicative of an unease about what constitutes legitimacy and authority, there is also a desire for exemplary human beings, who will speak in ways that are universalising and visionary and not merely particular. There is a concomitant anxiety about whether speaking has power or if it even matters at all in spaces filled with government deafness and the proliferation of forms of mass media and social media, many of which seem cacophonous.

The question, given the complexity of the contemporary South African public domain, is how does a public figure acquire the authorisation to step out onto the public stage with contributions that are considered intellectually worthy? Krog, a poet, journalist, book author, a literary figure and newsmaker, who eschews the appellation 'public intellectual', does not occupy the classic or normative position, neither is she one of the new types of South African intellectual being called upon to step into public. She is, nevertheless, acclaimed widely as a voice worth listening to. If she has been able, over nearly five decades, to continue in this fractious and fraught public domain to have presence, voice, platform and public, what is the source of her legitimation as a public figure?

Such a public figure acquires legitimacy and authorisation not through genius and brilliance of performance only but significantly also through a series of consecrations and identifications that act as accumulating symbolic capital across the social landscape. Krog has harnessed the powers of the aesthetic and moved this knowledge, style and capacity through three different fields – literary, political and in the media, each of which she entered, distinguished herself, was consecrated by the significant figures and accumulated each field's capital. This resultant accrued symbolic capital, in Pierre Bourdieu's words, has given her the 'almost magical power of mobilisation', the 'power to construct reality', which has effects across society both locally and internationally (2002: 170).

The sources of Krog's authority

> Literature . . . still constitutes a verbal horizon commanding respect (Barthes 1977: 27).

The literary and its extension, the media

As Jürgen Habermas (1991) points out so meticulously in the early sections of *The Structural Transformation of the Public Sphere*, the burgeoning use of literary materials by ordinary bourgeois people in their homes and the consequent alteration of subjectivity and production of a sense of public (quite unlike the sense of public of the feudal or monarchical systems) was the precursor to the formation of the public sphere. Osborne comments that the bourgeois public sphere as a 'privileged site of intellectual activity, came about historically through a political refunctioning of the space of a pre-existing literary culture' (1996: xii). But even more interesting is Michael Warner's emphasis that the literary is integral to the rise of the sense of 'public' *as a mode of being*. He argues that 'the imaginary reference point of the public was constructed through an understanding of print' (2002: 162). It is in reading printed information that one participates in the awareness that the 'same printed goods are being consumed by an indefinite number of others', says Warner. This awareness comes to be built into the meaning of the printed object and the reader is therefore partaking in mass subjectivity (as part of a public) by reading. As José van Dijck says: 'Material inscriptions mediate between individuality and collectivity as well as between past and present' (2004: 270).

A further step is to recognise, as John B. Thompson does, that this subjectivity-altering power also rests in the all-pervasive media of modern democracies. Thompson calls this attribute of media 'self-formation'. He says: 'The process of self-formation is increasingly nourished by mediated symbolic materials, greatly expanding the range of options available to individuals' (1995: 207). In modern democracies the mass media facilitates not the idealised dialogue or conversation of the classic public sphere but very important social relations which, while they might be '*quasi*-mediated interactions', are nevertheless the quintessential methods used to experience the world and to gather knowledge and to form public senses of selves.

So the literary field's centuries-old, very well-established relationship with the public sphere and its functioning still operates today in our world as a site of power and authority because of this very capacity – the ability to create a public, to generate mass subjectivity and to mediate between past and future. But the mass media, which similarly has these capacities, also operates in this way and takes further the reach of the literary. The literary – and publishing – continues to be a vibrant site of the creation, the assimilation and the diffusion of ideas. And publishing's pre-eminent object – the book – still continues to be a useful and functional technology for the distribution of information and ideas. Despite the quantum shift to electronic and mobile forms of information distribution, widespread circulation of ideas is still greatly facilitated by print.[2] The literary field's creation of publics – boundless, unknowable publics, even publics of millions, is a powerful concomitant strength. The vicariousness of participation created by the sense of being part of a public in the consumption of circulating ideas, the ability generated to position oneself as part of an imaginary community and the taking on of the public dimension of subjectivity are still all facilitated by the literary and the publishing industry in its multiple forms.

But while the literary field holds this power to affect subjectivity and self-formation and to create mass publics, its powers of consecration are usually contained within the field. It is the media, which uses many of the capacities of the literary (subjectivity-formation, creation of publics) that can mobilise these consecrations within the field and make them generally significant across society. The media theory concepts of news values, agenda-setting, framing and priming show how news media work to elevate certain issues, ideas and people as worthy of wide attention. But these theories are usually confined in focus to internal media field operations. It is in Bourdieu's very useful concept of consecration that one can begin to unpick how the media works to mobilise this attention in ways that have wide effects socially.

One sees that news media can reach into other fields and, where consecration takes place, disseminate the news of these consecrations more generally across fields. News media also activates consecrations by drawing ideas and people to the attention of those with specific authority and power, thus elevating those ideas and people and enhancing media power and reach at the same time. And as Bourdieu and the media theorists using field theory point out, those consecrated acquire an accoutrement, a symbolic attachment that they themselves can mobilise in their trajectories. All this is very clearly seen in the mediation of Krog's life and work and the resultant effects.

Krog first entered the literary in her trajectory as a public figure and acquired its capital by distinguishing herself as a writer of embodied, raw, autobiographical poetry, with a tension between the personal and the political. She was acclaimed by the literary field's consecrators and won its awards. But very importantly, she also established for herself a public. It was in this field that Krog learnt the techniques of self-fashioning via writing, of a two-fold working with subjectivity – the production of the subjectivity of the poet evident in the poetry itself and the provision of materials for readers to work on the production of their own self-formation. She also established herself as someone with a clearly political stance, which married her poetry and literary field trajectory to the political events of the time. The media attention marked her as a person consecrated both by the literary field and the political field. The media coverage is quite meticulous in showing all the facets of Krog's trajectory, her growing distinction as a poet and her growing political commitments. It also shows the dissemination of consecrations within fields and drawing Krog to the attention of consecrators, thus enhancing her symbolic capital.

Political dissidence and struggles with subjectivity

Through the years of South Africa's 'horror' (the late 1970s and the states of emergency in the 1980s), Krog's public battle against the National Party government and its tentacles into the cultural arena saw her achieving consecration by those working in the political field to unseat the apartheid regime. The acclamation of the local Kroonstad comrades, the hailing by Ahmed Kathrada at the Soweto rally and the inclusion in the groups of intellectuals visiting the ANC in exile were powerful markers of her value and capital politically. In her writing of this time, and particularly in the 1989 volume *Lady Anne*, one can see the struggle that Krog engaged in with subjectivity as an implicated white South African. This self-othering led directly to Krog's engagements with the TRC hearings. *Country of My Skull* shows that Krog the writer acknowledges the moral claim of the dispossessed of this country to take up a first-person position and to speak for themselves. The writer models for her public the self-fashioning of a listening, self-reflexive and ethical 'second-person position' – following Whitlock (2001) – in relation to the world's marginalised now making claims for recognition and speaking positions.

The *ethical* response to a morally unsettling and inherently complicit political situation is often to be found by engagement with the literary or, more specifically, in the aesthetic. David Carter, who has investigated Australian writing, in which 'style, voice or authorial persona is invested with ethical value', has found that such authors not only supply for readers a means for the ethical encounter that leads to self-fashioning but such works also elevate the authors in the public domain:

> They have become *writers* in the fullest sense of the term, and this in turn has meant them becoming at least one kind of public intellectual. Literariness, as a value, has been transferred from 'everyday' kinds of fiction to these new, rarer 'non-fiction' modes, at once highly aesthetic and highly marketable. That the memoir is often a form of history-writing as well adds seriously to its 'being ethical' (Carter 2001).

With the publication of *Country of My Skull*, the subsequent attention of the world's news media in reviewing the book, the invitations for Krog to speak overseas and the awards attached to the book, came celebrity status. The quality of this celebrity status needs further consideration since it is because of and attached to the second-person performance, which recognises the speaking space owed to those who have been othered and silenced.

Celebrity status and the attention of the mass media are not only a 'refeudalising' return to personal publicity – as Habermas (1991) would have it. Celebrities have important institutional and structural functions in our public domains. As Chris Rojek (2001), P. David Marshall (1997) and Graeme Turner (2004) show, it is simply impossible for all human beings of the millions in a Western-style democracy to exercise their unique voice in the public domain as part of their democratic birthright, but it is possible for them to vicariously enter this domain via those distinctive individuals who achieve the status of public figures. These representative people are consumed by publics in the same self-fashioning ways that are made possible by literature but this consumption is – also, in the case of writers such as Krog – taking place via the media. A public attuned to seeking out an ethical response to the dilemmas posed by encountering the Others of the world can find in Krog's literary writings the exemplary material for self-fashioning and in the media the person of Krog as further material for self-fashioning and action in the public domain.

But also interesting and important is Krog's harnessing of the techniques of journalism in her English-language books, which are categorised as non-fiction or memoir. Krog's use of the techniques of reportage, using the subject matter of the real (real events, real people, real dialogue, real experiences) and the present-tense urgency of journalism is an employment of techniques that are legitimised both politically and socially as valuable and important in public life because they place publics in touch with the real and significant. Krog is not simply a writer of books who has become a celebrity. She has taken her distinctive poetic style, married it to the non-fiction techniques of journalism and produced in *Country of My Skull* a book that is a life narrative dealing with the challenge of recognition of the Other.[3] This weaving together of her aesthetic style with journalistic reportage and the ongoing preoccupation with the ethical performance of self in relation to the changing reality of a political upheaval, as well as the mediation of herself and her writing of this book, is what makes Krog more than a famous writer and enables her to occupy the space of the public intellectual both nationally and internationally.

In Neil Lazarus's assessment of Said's consideration of the figure of the public intellectual in *Representations of the Intellectual* (1994), he remarks (and I now apply this insight to Krog):

> Particularly brilliant in Said's [Krog's] representation of the intellectual, in my view, is his clear-sighted awareness of what might be *specific* to intellectual work, that is, his grasp of what it is that intellectuals do that might be both socially valuable and also not within the remit of any other group of social agents – not because intellectuals are cleverer than other people, still less because they are morally better than other people, but because they have been socially endowed with the resources, the status, the symbolic and social capital, to do this particular kind of work (Lazarus 2005: 117).

It is this social endowment and particularly the media role in its creation that has allowed Krog to make her poetic engagements with subjectivity in relation to the political, hugely socially relevant and useful for publics.

Krog's distinctive work as a South African public intellectual

> The perlocutionary act . . . that which we do in saying – the least inscribable element of discourse . . . discourse as stimulus (Ricœur 1979: 76–7).

> Our time-inflected phenomenology places creating and maintaining meaning at the centre of all human activity (Andrews et al. 2000: 1).

Krog affirms the literary as a cultural repository of useful, universalising wisdom

Despite not operating normatively as a Saidian-type public intellectual, a literary performance such as Krog's is able to generate visions for the future through creativity and imagination, thus giving the literary field ongoing life in the public imagination as a valuable repository of visions for the future. Stephen Johnson, managing director of Krog's publisher Random House, asserted in an interview shortly before he left for the Frankfurt Book Fair that Krog is one of 'the most exciting imaginations working in South Africa today' (Toffoli 2008: 88) and that he was seeking out international publics for her work. But literary performances such as Krog's also demonstrate that the literary has a unique ability to be responsive to the huge, critical issues involved in being human and engaging ethically with the world. And interestingly it is not through poetry alone that Krog has achieved this position as a writer. In the non-fiction work that brought Krog international acclaim she used literary techniques out of the literary field and married them to journalism's preoccupations with the real and in doing so has injected consequence, urgency and a political imperative into her writing.

Krog injects the personal into the political domain

Hannah Arendt has made the point that modern-day states function like giant household bureaucracies feeding, educating and skilling the majority in a levelling and conformist way and that the devalued personal will therefore find its place in the public sphere through the aesthetic

(1998: 39). Krog's poetic style, integrating the fiercely personal with the particularly political, places into the public domain the private, the individual, the personal and the intimate, which validates what is real in the lives of millions but is not given credence in the public sphere of political ideas and economic and social problems. Krog's work on this level has been assisted by the rise in the publishing industry of memoir and non-fiction dealing with political change and by the mass media with their increasing focus on individualising behaviours.

Krog introduces the messy, emotional and passionate into public
It was Said who called for amateurs with emotional loyalties and passions (Hollis 1997: 292) to enter the public sphere. In particular, Krog's frequently stated and fiercely held loyalty to the land of South Africa is put into the public domain as an unwavering passion. As Leon de Kock comments: 'She refuses to give up trying to speak the voices of the land, she risks sentimentality everywhere, and she continues to be both publicly personal . . . and very personally public' (2000: 9). Krog 'houses affect' (as the celebrity theorists point out) on behalf of publics who desire to see this attribute operating in public.

Unlike other public figures (and especially unlike public intellectuals who operate on the Habermasian notions of rational-critical inputs into debate) Krog's public performance validates not only strong feeling about an issue's importance but also the extremes of emotion such as shame, mourning, frustration, helplessness, irrational love, and their public expression. While the performance of such affect has to be finely calibrated for authenticity and is always in danger of overstepping the boundaries of what is considered acceptable in public, the recognition of the experience of the Others now making claims for legitimate social space is incomplete without the acknowledgement of pain and suffering attached to those experiences *and* an adequate response to that pain and suffering.

Krog's performance is finely tuned to reacting to major political shifts taking place globally, a reaction that the usual vehicles of the public sphere (such as the news media) are not accommodating because of the prohibitions on affect that constrain them.

Krog personalises and humanises huge political shifts and events

Krog asserts the value of the body, the subjective, the emotional, the affective, the female and the marginalised within and against upheavals and changes that are on the scale of the national and might better have been thought of as purely political or social. As Gillian Whitlock points out, *Country of My Skull* personalises history and historicises the personal, it places the self in relation to public history and culture and enables ethical self-reflection (2007: 135). In fact, in *Country of My Skull* we see Krog asserting that the experience of the body (and most often the female-gendered body) is perhaps the only truth to be trusted (see, for example, Chapter 16).

Krog enables self-formation by an encounter with the Other as first person

Stephen Greenblatt (1980: 9), in his explanation of 'self-fashioning' via literature, points out that self-formation is often constructed 'in relation to something perceived as alien, strange or hostile'. But what if literature offers an encounter with an Other that recognises humanity and the claim of the Other to speak and requires a response of listening and subsequent ethical action? This is the very interesting possibility that Krog's writings offer, as global shifts have required more ethical treatment and recognition of the Other.

Krog deals with the past and enables her publics to imagine different futures

It was Said who made the preoccupation with both past and future part of the task of the public intellectual: 'The intellectual's role is first to present alternative narratives and other perspectives on history than those provided by combatants on behalf of official memory and national identity' and, 'therefore one invents . . . hypothesising a better situation from the known historical and social facts' (Said 2002: 36). The TRC process is the hinge on which past and future for South Africans rest in the new democracy. Krog's self-reflexive performance in response to the TRC testifiers shows clearly the present imperative of acting ethically so that the future can be imagined as substantially different from the past.

Reading Krog (and consuming Krog's person via media) enables agency
Most importantly, Krog embodies and performs the complexity of being a responsive and self-reflexive white person in South Africa. She presents a repertoire of possibilities for people to take up, modify, debate or even reject. As Molly Andrews et al., editors of *Lines of Narrative*, say in their introduction, life narrative can 'recuperate individual and social agency (2000: 1), 'foreclose more imaginative ways of living' (2) and open up 'new spaces for investigating relations between subjects and structures' (8). Krog uses the mode of the personal-intimate and the performance of embodiment, which she honed in the art form of poetry, to bring into the public sphere subject matter and performances usually disallowed by the ideal of the public sphere, yet insistently present in contemporary politics.

Considering her style, Krog is decidedly not a classic public intellectual. She does not generate a thought or idea and then seek a debate or discussion to enter. Krog takes into herself ideas, thoughts, feelings and fragments of experience, her own and others'. She eats, cannibalises and then uses them as raw material for poetry (which she is always engaged in, regardless of the genre she is actually working in). The resulting product is usually herself, the altered, affected human being and this is represented in her writing. Titles such as *Country of My Skull* and the more recent *Begging to be Black* and remarks such as 'I am busy with the truth, my truth' (Krog 1998: 170) are indications that the site, vehicle and repository of Krog's engagement with the big issues of public importance is Krog herself.

This performance asserts and affirms individual agency and responsibility. But this performance is taking place within an enabling context and meeting the need of a desirous public. What the social situation of post-apartheid South Africa shows is that the political terrain has shifted in unexpected ways that have impacts on the constitution of the public sphere. The constitutional provisions, rooted in the belief that all South Africans have shared humanity ('ubuntu') and are bound by sharing the same country into a 'mutuality as human beings' (Posel 2006: 8), are a significant marker that damage, the personal, concerns of the Other and the recognition of trauma and marginalisation have found a place in public discourse.

When the TRC was set up as a process to exorcise the past by placing into the public sphere not only a research document in which statistics detailed the horrors of the past via scientific methods but also an *experience* in which actual individuals were invited to tell the stories of their lives, the social terrain that animated the public sphere ideals also shifted dramatically into an encounter with actual Others speaking about self, the intimate and the personal as affected by the political.

A further point then to be made about the nature of the post-apartheid public sphere is that it is permeated by performances of affect, which are used to raise issues and experiences that are not able to be captured by the 'logos-centred rationales for deliberative democracy' (Huspek 2007: 330). Those who speak in the post-apartheid public sphere are no longer necessarily public intellectuals in the strict Saidian sense and it is profoundly affected by issues and events beyond its boundaries. Not only is the bounded sense of a national polity and citizenry within a national public sphere being challenged by globalised forces and flows of communication but also the question of what it is to be a responsible, twenty-first-century human subject is extremely pertinent. The crucial difference now obtaining in the transnationalising space Krog speaks into is that a different type of authority sanctions her capacity to speak. In the case of the classic public intellectual (Said), the authority rested largely in his recognised excellence as an author and his facility to represent a particular issue and/or people. In the case of Krog, while recognised excellence as an author and a capacity to represent are still important, to these must be added the requirements of the regimes of truth, confession, human rights and a performance that demonstrates affectedness, implicatedness and connection to other suffering bodies. For a public figure now to have a hearing in a transnationalising space, the person must not only facilitate speech and debate but must also embody pain and empathy.

Krog's is not a classic performance of opposition – not a speaking truth *to* power – it is not the antithesis to the state's thesis in a dialectical public debate. Krog's is a presentation of affect and effect, in which the personal and political are entwined. She shows the public how an individual, in a complex, rapidly altering political situation, negotiates an adaptive subjectivity as the primary means of ethical agency. In a reformulation of the much-used Saidian phrase: Krog speaks poetry to power. In this use, 'poetry' means aestheticised and affected embodied communication inflected by literary techniques and 'power' is not the political entities in formal government but in the most general sense the structures of the world that exclude and alienate.

Notes

1. I am indebted to Alette Schoon for the wonderful formulation of Krog's public performance, 'speaking poetry to power'.
2. Digital and web-based media continue the widespread circulation of ideas in print and multiply its effects, as in the case of bloggers who have written about Krog and convey information about her and her writings and who also talk in very personal ways about how she has affected them.
3. Krog's poetic style is described by literary critic Louise Viljoen as 'transgressive', 'strongly feminist' and autobiographical, with an ongoing preoccupation with 'the conflict between aesthetics and politics' (2006: 39–40).

Afterword

As I write this, eleven years after beginning this study on Krog, students at the University of Cape Town and Rhodes University are battling their institutional leaderships about the very visible legacies and deeply entrenched entanglements with the colonial past on their campuses. My research students are passionately involved in what they see as their own struggle for liberation and for recognition as the leaders of the present and the future. Just recently I took a research group to Cape Town for a colloquium at the exact time the protests against the Cecil John Rhodes statue erupted. As we drove the long journey from Grahamstown to Cape Town, they were on Twitter, following the developments at the University of Cape Town and the subsequent eruptions behind us at Rhodes and every pit stop turned into a heightened discussion over the latest public statements. During the conference my students spent many of their evenings with Cape Town students sitting in, occupying the administration building, arguing and debating. When we returned to Rhodes, things were bubbling here, too, demanding of me – as their teacher – to take a position, make a statement.

What is interesting is that while the issues as these students see them are being put forward in no uncertain terms and with all the skills of logic and argument a university education imparts, this eruption of protest is also marked by an intensely emotional outpouring of suffering. As Sekoetlane Phamodi points out in *The Con*, suffering endured by those who have grown up in the post-apartheid moment, who speak of their frustration and feelings of debilitation on campuses that are overtly committed to 'transformation'.[1] On Facebook and blogs angry reactions smack of an intractable racism and there are people refusing to stay in the conversation because of its tone and content (the robust Eusebius McKaiser exited the subsequent discussion of *The Con* article for this reason).[2] There are people shutting each other up by claiming such a degree of pain that anyone without pain to profess is made mute as a participant (except as a commiserater) and there also are those seeking to silence others through outright rejection of that pain.

The other night, as I was leaving work, one of my students popped in with a Zambian friend to have a chat about the day's events. The Zambian woman was forthright with her own opinion, the gist of which went like this: what is wrong with you South Africans that you have not resolved these problems yet? Did the Truth and Reconciliation Commission achieve nothing?

This is a hard question to answer, especially when I am called upon to speak for a nation but it brings me to these thoughts as a result of the study you have just read: despite our recent past of political transition and attempts at reconciliation, the present is full of irresolution. This is the actually existing situation to be taken account of and not the hoped-for one of our teleological dreams. Those hopes for political and social tranquillity devoid of pain mislead us into normative thinking, which we use to judge the present as being all wrong and having not turned out the way it should have. As a result we do not pose the question of what the present is saying to and asking of us now. The irresolutions in our now are still all about race and dehumanisation. As Mahmood Mamdani (1996a: 8) puts it, we have succeeded in deracialising politics and business and the elite strata of society in South Africa but we have not succeeded in crafting a democracy expansive enough not to have to rest on an underclass of subaltern citizens who have no voice and get no attention unless they use methods guaranteed to secure newspaper headlines,

My work on this book about Antjie Krog taught me to think of the South African public sphere as a particularity full of its own features in peculiar combination and to take seriously the idea that emotion is as legitimate an expression in the public domain as rationalisation – perhaps even more so, given the denial of humanity and intelligence built into our particular forms of rational discourse, which we employ not to listen but to control the direction of debate and to deflect the tough stuff. (At our recent colloquim Steven Robins, a social anthropologist at Stellenbosch University, who has been researching the uprisings of the Western Cape for many years, showed us a photograph of a University of Cape Town academic with a placard facing student protesters that said: 'Don't shout louder, improve your argument'.) The Krog study showed me just how personal the political can and should be. It also showed me that to resort to writing and art is not mere sublimation (as Sigmund Freud would have it) but integral to struggle, agency and being human. This is the *longue durée* and it is an approach we should take not only to the past and our history but also to the very precious present.

Grahamstown
April 2015

Notes
1. Sekoetlane Phamodi, 'Six Years: Why Rhodes Must Fall', *The Con*, 31 March 2015. http://www.theconmag.co.za/2015/03/31/six-years-why-rhodes-must-fall-2/.
2. See https://www.facebook.com/niren.tolsi/posts/10153100385366418?comment_id=10153104719431418&offset=0&total_comments=27.

Select Bibliography

Adorno, Theodor. 1967. 'An Essay on Cultural Criticism and Society'. In *Prisms*, trans. Shierry Weber Nicholsen and Samuel Weber, 17–34. Cambridge: MIT Press.

Alexander, Jeffrey C. 2006. *The Civil Sphere*. Oxford: Oxford University Press.

Anderson, J.H. (ed.). 1924. *South Africa a Century Ago (1797–1801), Part 1: Letters Written from the Cape of Good Hope; Part 2: Extracts from a Journal Addressed to Her Sisters in England by Lady Anne Barnard*. Cape Town: Maskew Miller.

Andrews, Molly, Shelley Day Slater, Corinne Squire and Asmal Treacher (eds). 2000. *Lines of Narrative: Psychosocial Perspectives*. London: Routledge.

Anstey, Gillian. 1999. 'When the Truth Hurts the Heart'. *Sunday Times*, 23 May: 10–11.

Arendt, Hannah. 1998. *The Human Condition*. Chicago: University of Chicago Press.

Barthes, Roland. 1977. *Writing Degree Zero*. New York: Hill and Wang.

Benson, Rodney. 1998. 'Field Theory in Comparative Context: A New Paradigm for Media Studies'. *Theory and Society* 28: 463–98.

Benveniste, Émile. 2000. 'Subjectivity in Language'. In *Identity: A Reader*, ed. Paul du Gay, Jessica Evans and Peter Redman, 39–43. London: Sage.

Bertyn, L.I. 1981. 'Waar Is Dolla Minas?' *Beeld*, 23 September: 18.

Boltanski, Luc. 1999. *Distant Suffering: Morality, Media and Politics*. Cambridge: Cambridge University Press.

Bourdieu, Pierre. 1983. 'The Field of Cultural Production, or: The Economic World Reversed'. *Poetics* 12 (4–5): 311–56.

———. 1993. *The Field of Cultural Production*. Cambridge: Polity Press.

———. 2002. *Language and Symbolic Power*. Cambridge: Polity Press.

———. 2005. 'The Political Field, the Social Science Field, and the Journalistic Field'. In *Bourdieu and the Journalistic Field*, ed. Rodney Benson and Erik Neveu, 29–47. Cambridge: Polity Press.

Bourdieu, Pierre and Richard Nice. 1980. 'The Production of Belief: Contribution to an Economy of Symbolic Goods'. *Media, Culture and Society* 2: 261–93.

Bové, Paul. 1994. 'Intellectuals at War: Michel Foucault and the Analysis of Power'. In *Michel Foucault: Critical Assessments Vol 3*, ed. Barry Smart, 222–41. London: Routledge.

Brink, André P. 1989. 'Antjie Krog Se Lady Anne: 'n Roman van 'n Bundel'. *Vrye Weekblad*, 18 August: 13.

Brown, Duncan and Antjie Krog. 2011. 'Creative Non-Fiction: A Conversation'. *Current Writing* 23 (1): 57–70.

Calhoun, Craig (ed.). 1992. *Habermas and the Public Sphere*. Cambridge: MIT Press.

Carter, David. 2001. 'Public Intellectuals, Book Culture and Civil Society'. *Australian Humanities Review*. http://www.australianhumanitiesreview.org/archive/Issue-November-2001/carter2.html.

Chance, Kerry. 2001. 'The Right to Narrate: Interview with Homi Bhabha'. Human Rights Project Lecture Series, Bard College. http://www.bard.edu/hrp/resource_pdfs/chance.hbhabha.pdf.

Chipkin, Ivor. 2007a. 'Citizen-Subject: Some Ideas about the Character of States in Formerly Colonised Societies'. Unpublished paper.

———. 2007b. *Do South Africans Exist? Nationalism, Democracy and the Identity of 'The People'*. Johannesburg: Wits University Press.

———. 2008. 'Democracy's People'. Paper presented at the Paradoxes of the Post-Colonial Public Sphere: South African Democracy at the Crossroads conference, University of the Witwatersrand, Johannesburg, 28–31 January.

Coetzee, Ampie and James Polley (eds). 1990. *Crossing Borders: Writers Meet the ANC*. Johannesburg: Taurus.

Coetzee, Carli. 2001. '"They Never Wept, the Men of My Race": Antjie Krog's *Country of My Skull* and the White South African Signature'. *Journal of Southern African Studies* 27 (4): 685–96.

Coetzee, J.M. 2007. *Diary of a Bad Year*. London: Harvill Secker.

Collinge, Jo-Anne. 1993. 'It's ANC Facing ANC in This Trial'. *The Star*, 12 April: 6.

Cook, Meira. 2001. 'Metaphors for Suffering: Antjie Krog's *Country of My Skull*'. *Mosaic* 34 (3): 73–89.

Coullie, Judith Lütge and Andries Visagie (eds). 2014. *Antjie Krog: An Ethics of Body and Otherness*. Pietermaritzburg: University of KwaZulu-Natal Press.

Cowling, Lesley and Carolyn Hamilton. 2008. 'Thinking Aloud/Allowed: Pursuing the Public Interest in Radio Debate'. Paper presented at the Paradoxes of the Post-Colonial Public Sphere: South African Democracy at the Crossroads conference, University of the Witwatersrand, Johannesburg, 28–31 January.

Crawford, Alexander Lindsay. 1849. *The Lives of the Lindsays or a Memoir of the Houses of Crawford and Balcarres*. Vols 2 and 3. London: John Murray.

Crous, Marius. 2003. 'Die Tekstualisering van die Liggaam in *Lady Anne*'. *Journal of Literary Studies* 19 (1): 1–17.

Darnton, Robert. 2000. 'An Early Information Society: News and Media in 18th Century Paris'. *American Historical Review* 105 (1): 1–35.

Dearing, James and Everett Rogers. 1996. *Agenda-Setting*. Thousand Oaks: Sage.

De Beer, Hannes. 1995. 'Hemel Behoede Ons Taal as Antjie Dit So "Mix"'. *Die Burger*, 27 January: 8.

De Kock, Leon. 2000. 'Voices of the Earth'. *Mail & Guardian*, 17–23 November: 9.

De Wet, Annelie. 1981. 'Getemperde Antjie Krog Is Terug'. *Beeld*, 8 September.

Draisma, Jitske. 1999. *South Africa Media Report*. http://journ.ru.ac.za/ amd/safrica. htm.

Driver, Dorothy. 1995. 'Lady Anne Barnard's Cape Journals and the Concept of Self-Othering'. *Pretexts* 5 (1–2): 46–65.

Du Preez, Max. 2004. *Pale Native: Memories of a Renegade Reporter*. Cape Town: Zebra.

Eakin, Paul John. 1985. *Fictions in Autobiography: Studies in the Art of Self-Invention*. Princeton: Princeton University Press.

February, Judith. 2011. 'New Way of Seeing May Save Us from the Mire'. *Cape Times*, 24 August: 9.

Foucault, Michel. 1980. *Power/Knowledge: Selected Interviews and Other Writings 1972–1977*, ed. Colin Gordon. New York: Pantheon Books.

———. 1998. *The History of Sexuality Vol. 1: The Will to Knowledge*. London: Penguin.

Fowler, Roger. 1991. *Language in the News*. London: Routledge.

Fraser, Nancy. 1992. 'Rethinking the Public Sphere: A Contribution to the Critique of Actually Existing Democracy'. In *Habermas and the Public Sphere*, ed. Craig Calhoun, 109–42. Cambridge: MIT Press.

———. 2007. 'Transnationalising the Public Sphere: On the Legitimacy and Efficacy of Public Opinion in a Post-Westphalian World'. *Theory, Culture and Society* 24 (4): 7–30.

Gallagher, Susan van Zanten. 2002. *Truth and Reconciliation: The Confessional Mode in South African Literature*. Portsmouth: Heinemann.

Galloway, Francis. 2004. '"Ek Is Nie Meer Een van Ons Nie": Breyten en die Volk'. *Tydskrif vir Letterkunde* 41 (1): 5–38.

Garman, Anthea. 1998. 'Inside Antjie's Head'. *Rhodes Journalism Review* 16: 27.

———. 2014a. 'Antjie Krog and the Accumulation of "Media Meta-Capital"'. In *Antjie Krog: An Ethics of Body and Otherness*, ed. Judith Lütge Coullie and Andries Visagie, 73–97. Pietermaritzburg: University of KwaZulu-Natal Press.

———. 2014b. 'Running with the Jackals: Antjie Krog the Journalist'. In *Antjie Krog: An Ethics of Body and Otherness*, ed. Judith Lütge Coullie and Andries Visagie, 184–214. Pietermaritzburg: University of KwaZulu-Natal Press.

Genette, Gérard. 1997. *Paratexts: Thresholds of Interpretation*. Cambridge: Cambridge University Press.

Gerwel, Jakes. 2007. 'Laat Ons met Mekaar Verskil sonder Om te Skel'. *Rapport*, 11 November: 20.

Gevisser, Mark. 1992. 'The Rebel Poet, the Activist . . . and the Dead Gang Leader'. *Weekly Mail*, 10–16 July: 7.

Giliomee, Hermann. 2003. *The Afrikaners: Biography of a People*. Cape Town: Tafelberg.

Gilmore, Leigh. 2001. *The Limits of Autobiography: Trauma and Testimony*. Ithaca: Cornell University Press.

Gouws, Tom. 1998. 'Antjie Krog (1952-)'. In *Perspektief & Profiel: 'n Afrikaanse Literatuurgeskiedenis*, ed. H.P. van Coller, 550–63. Pretoria: J.L. van Schaik.

Green, Pippa. 1990. 'New Jerusalem'. *Leadership SA* August: 44–54.

Greenblatt, Stephen. 1980. *Renaissance Self-Fashioning: From Moore to Shakespeare*. Chicago: University of Chicago Press.

Habermas, Jürgen. 1991. *The Structural Transformation of the Public Sphere: An Inquiry into a Category of Bourgeois Society*. Cambridge: MIT Press.

Hambidge, Joan. 2011. 'Politieke "Lobola vir die Lewe" Wat Lesers Sal Bekoor'. *Rapport*, 16 January: 3.

Hamilton, Carolyn. 2008. 'Uncertain Citizenship and Contemporary Public Deliberation: Social Inequality, Cultural Diversity and a Compromised Commitment to Complexity in Post-Apartheid South Africa'. Paper presented at the Paradoxes of the Post-Colonial Public Sphere: South African Democracy at the Crossroads conference, University of the Witwatersrand, Johannesburg, 28-31 January.

Hannay, Alistair. 2005. *On the Public*. London: Routledge.

Harber, Anton. 2002. 'Journalism in the Age of the Market'. Fourth Harold Wolpe Memorial Lecture, 26 September. http://ccs.ukzn.ac.za/default.asp?3,28,10,452.

Harris, Ashleigh. 2006. 'Accountability, Acknowledgement and the Ethics of "Quilting" in Antjie Krog's *Country of My Skull*'. http://0-galenet.galegroup. com.wam.seals.ac.za/servlet/IOURL?issn=0256-4718&finalAuth=true&locID =rhodes&title=Journal+of+Literary+Studies&c=41&ste=1&prod=LitRC. First published in *Journal of Literary Studies* 22 (1-2): 27–53.

Hayner, Priscilla B. 2002. *Unspeakable Truths: Facing the Challenge of Truth Commissions*. New York: Routledge.

Hollis, Martin. 1997. 'What Truth? For Whom and Where?' In *Intellectuals in Politics*, ed. Jeremy Jennings and Anthony Kemp-Welch, 289–99. London: Routledge.

Holtzhausen, Evelyn. 1989. 'Antjie's "Lost" Poem Was ANC Man's Ray of Hope'. *Sunday Times*, 5 November: 15.

Huspek, Michael. 2007. 'Symposium: Habermas and Deliberative Democracy – Introductory Remarks'. *Communication Theory* 17 (4): 319–32.

Hutcheon, Linda. 1980. *Narcissistic Narrative: The Metafictional Paradox*. New York: Methuen.

Ignatieff, Michael. 2001. *Human Rights As Politics and Idolatry*. Princeton: Princeton University Press.

Isaacson, Maureen. 1998. 'Sales Show That Money Talks, but You Don't Have to Listen'. *Sunday Independent*, 8 February: 20.

———. 2007. 'Achebe on Darfur, Coetzee on Krog, and Apologies to Jeanne'. *Sunday Independent*, 16 September: 17.

Jacobson, Celean. 2006. 'Top Writers in Plagiarism Row'. *Sunday Times*, 19 February: 5.

Jaffer, Zubeida. 2000. 'Whites Need to Make One Single Fateful Gesture'. *Cape Times*, 8 September: 6.

Kaarsholm, Preben. 2008. 'Public Spheres, Hidden Politics and Struggles over Space: Defining the Boundaries of Public Engagement in Post-Apartheid South Africa'. Paper presented at the Paradoxes of the Postcolonial Public Sphere: South African Democracy at the Crossroads conference, University of the Witwatersrand, Johannesburg, 28–31 January.

Kannemeyer, J.C. 1983. *Geskiedenis van die Afrikaanse Literatuur II*. Pretoria: Academica.

Kathrada, Ahmed. 2004. *Memoirs*. Cape Town: Zebra.

Kemp, Franz. 1970. 'Dorp Gons oor Gedigte in Skoolblad'. *Die Beeld*, 16 August: 5.

Kirby, Robert. 2005. 'Cheats, Loots and Thieves'. *Mail & Guardian*, 24 February: 28.

Koz, Nicola, Mphoentle Mageza and Barry Streek. 1999. 'Women with Attitude: The Top 100 Women Who Shook South Africa'. *Femina* December: 82–6.

Kramerae, Cheris and Paula A. Treichler. 1992. *Amazons, Bluestockings and Crones: A Feminist Dictionary*. London: Pandora Press.

Krog, Antjie. 1970. *Dogter van Jefta*. Cape Town: Human & Rousseau.

———. 1971. 'My Beautiful Land'. *Sechaba* 5 (1): 16.

———. 1972. *Januarie-Suite*. Cape Town: Human & Rousseau.

———. 1975a. *Beminde Antarktika*. Cape Town: Human & Rousseau.

———. 1975b. *Mannin*. Cape Town: Human & Rousseau.

———. 1981. *Otters in Bronslaai*. Cape Town: Human & Rousseau.

———. 1983. 'Familiefigure in die Poësie van D.J. Opperman'. Master's thesis, University of Pretoria.

———. 1984. *Eerste Gedigte*. Cape Town: Human & Rousseau.

———. 1985. *Jerusalemgangers*. Cape Town: Human & Rousseau.

———. 1987. 'Skrywers Gee Rekenskap'. *Die Suid-Afrikaan* January: 43.

———. 1989a. 'A Community As Liberated As Its Women: A Critical Look at Women in South African Poetry'. IDASA Occasional Papers 18. Cape Town: Institute for a Democratic Alternative for South Africa.

———. 1989b. *Lady Anne*. Cape Town: Human & Rousseau.

———. 1989c. 'Niemand Was 'n Skoon Wit Papier Nie'. *Die Suid-Afrikaan* December: 6.

————. 1989d. 'Waarom Praat Ons van "Vroue" Skrywers?' *Die Suid-Afrikaan* August/September: 40–1.

————. 1991. 'Los van die Afrikanerlaer: 'n Gans Ander Wêreld Het vir My Oopgegaan'. *Rapport*, 3 February: 1.

————. 1994a. 'Focus on Healing'. *Sowetan*, 4 October: 8. Reprinted in Afrikaans in *Die Burger*.

————. 1994b. 'Untold Damage of Anglo-Boer War'. *Democracy in Action* August: 19.

————. 1995a. *Gedigte: 1989–1995*. Pretoria: Hond.

————. 1995b. *Relaas van 'n Moord*. Cape Town: Human & Rousseau.

————. 1996a. 'Overwhelming Trauma of the Truth'. *Mail & Guardian*, 24 December 1996–9 January 1997: 10.

————. 1996b. 'Pockets of Humanity'. *Mail & Guardian*, 24–30 May: 30–1.

————. 1996c. 'Truth Trickle Becomes a Flood'. *Mail & Guardian*, 1 November. http://mg.co.za/article/1996-11-01-truth-trickle-becomes-a-flood.

————. 1997a. *Account of a Murder*, translated by Karen Press. Johannesburg: Heinemann.

————. 1997b. 'The Parable of the Bicycle'. *Mail & Guardian*, 13 February: 26.

————. 1997c. 'Unto the Third or Fourth Generation'. *Mail & Guardian* 13–19 June: 13.

————. 1998. *Country of My Skull*. Johannesburg: Random House.

————. 1999a. *Country of My Skull: Guilt, Sorrow, and the Limits of Forgiveness in the New South Africa*. New York: Times Books.

————. 1999b. *Waarom Is Dié Wat Voor Toyi-Toyi Altyd So Vet?* Unpublished.

————. 2000a. *Down to My Last Skin: Poems*. Johannesburg: Random House.

————. 2000b. *Kleur Kom Nooit Alleen Nie*. Cape Town: Kwela Books.

————. 2001. 'Healing Stream Petered out Too Soon'. *Sunday Independent*, 2 December: 6.

————. 2002. *Met Woorde Soos met Kerse: Inheemse Verse Uitgesoek en Vertaal deur Antjie Krog*. Cape Town: Kwela Books.

————. 2003. *A Change of Tongue*. Johannesburg: Random House.

————. 2004a. *Eerste Gedigte: Dogter van Jefta en Januariesuite*. Cape Town: Human & Rousseau.

————. 2004b. 'Embarassed by Forgiveness'. *Sunday Times*, 29 February: 21.

————. 2004c. *The Stars Say 'Tsau': /Xam Poetry of Diä!kwain, Kweiten-ta-//ken, /A!kúnta, /Han≠kass'o and //Kabbo*, selected and adapted by Antjie Krog. Cape Town: Kwela Books.

————. 2004d. *Die Sterre Sê 'Tsau': /Xam Gedigte van Diä!kwain, Kweiten-ta-//ken, /A!kúnta, /Han≠kass'o en //Kabbo*, selected and adapted by Antjie Krog. Cape Town: Kwela Books.

————. 2005a. *'n Ander Tongval*. Cape Town: Human & Rousseau.

————. 2005b. 'I, Me, Me, Mine!' *English Academy Review* 22: 100–7.

———. 2006a. *Body Bereft*. Cape Town: Umuzi.

———. 2006b. 'A Space for the Disgraced'. *Mail & Guardian*, 16 September. http://mg.co.za/article/2006-09-16-a-space-for-the-disgraced.

———. 2006c. 'Stephen Watson in the Annals of Plagiarism'. http://www.oulitnet.co.za/seminarroom/krog_krog.asp.

———. 2006d. *Verweerskrif*. Cape Town: Umuzi.

———. 2007a. 'De la Rey: Afrikaner Absolution'. *Mail & Guardian*, 4 April: 23.

———. 2007b. *Fynbos Fairies*. Cape Town: Umuzi.

———. 2007c. *Fynbosfeetjies*. Cape Town: Umuzi.

———. 2008. 'Marital Psalm'. In *Open: Erotic Stories from South African Women Writers*, ed. Karin Schimke. Johannesburg: Oshun.

———. 2009a. *Begging to Be Black*. Cape Town: Random House Struik.

———. 2009b. 'Manipulator or Human Rights Facilitator?' *Niemann Reports*. http://www.nieman.harvard.edu/reportsitem.aspx?id=101964.

———. 2009c. 'Two "Useless" Recipes from My Mother and an Unsent Letter'. In *uMama: Recollections of South African Mothers and Grandmothers: A Collection of Writing by Famous South Africans Remembering the Women Who Raised Them*, compiled by Marion Keim, 76–80. Cape Town: Umuzi.

———. 2010a. 'This Thing Called Reconciliation: Forgiveness as Part of an Interconnectedness towards Wholeness'. In *In the Balance: South Africans Debate Reconciliation*, ed. Fanie du Toit and Erik Doxtader, 140–7. Johannesburg: Jacana Media.

———. 2010b. 'When It Comes to Dialogue, We Don't Have the Words'. *Sunday Times*, 25 April: 11.

———. 2013a. 'Afrikaners Identified with Nelson Mandela's Struggle against Colonialism'. *Cape Times*, 16 December: 5.

———. 2013b. *Conditional Tense: Memory and Vocabulary after the South African Truth and Reconciliation Commission*, ed. Rosalind Morris. New York: Seagull Books.

———. 2013c. *Skinned*. New York: Seven Stories Press.

———. 2013d. 'To an Afrikaner, Mandela Was an Exception Whose Death Was Feared'. *Sunday Argus*, 15 December: 27.

———. 2014a. *Mede-Wete*. Cape Town: Human & Rousseau.

———. 2014b. *Synapse*. Cape Town: Human & Rousseau.

Krog, Antjie, Sindiwe Magona and Meg van der Merwe (eds). 2012. *This is My Land*. Cape Town: University of the Western Cape.

Krog, Antjie and Nosisi Mpolweni. 2009. 'Archived Voices: Refiguring Three Women's Testimonies Delivered to the South African Truth and Reconciliation Commission'. *Tulsa Studies in Women's Literature* 28 (2): 357–74.

Krog, Antjie, Nosisi Mpolweni and Kopano Ratele. 2009. *There Was This Goat: Investigating the Truth Commission Testimony of Notrose Nobomvu Konile*. Pietermaritzburg: University of KwaZulu-Natal Press.

Krog, Antjie and Alfred Schaffer (eds). 2005. *Nuwe Stemme 3*. Cape Town: Tafelberg.

Kruger, Joan. 1981. 'Antjie Krog: Daar Is Poësie in dié Vrou'. *Die Transvaler*, 2 November: 9.

Lazarus, Neil. 2005. 'Representations of the Intellectual in *Representations of the Intellectual*'. *Research in American Literatures* 36 (3): 112–23.

Le Grange, Corinna. 1990. 'Free State's Controversial Antjie Joins Establishment as Prizewinner'. *The Star*, 26 April: 21.

Legum, Colin. 1971. 'Afrikaans Protest Cry Sparks a Big Row'. *Daily Despatch*, 17 May: 11–12.

Le Roux, André. 1981. ''n Krog-Oplewing . . . met Woede'. *Beeld*, 19 October: 16.

———. 1987. 'Die Minste Skade met My Gedigte'. *Die Burger*, 28 April: 13.

Le Roux, Schalk. 1989. 'Antjie Krog Se Gedig Roer Kathrada'. *Beeld*, 30 October: 1.

Malan, Rian. 1998. 'A Guilt-Stricken Orgy of Self-Flagellation'. *Financial Mail*, 2–8 July: 36.

Malson, Helen. 2000. 'Fictionalising Identity? Ontological Assumptions and Methodological Productions of ("Anorexic") Subjectivities'. In *Lines of Narrative: Psychosocial Perspectives*, ed. Molly Andrews, Shelley Day Sclater, Corinne Squire and Amal Treacher, 150–63. London: Routledge.

Mamdani, Mahmood. 1996a. *Citizen and Subject*. Princeton: Princeton University Press.

———. 1996b. 'Reconciliation without Justice'. *South African Review of Books* 46 (November/December).

———. 2000. 'A Diminished Truth'. In *After the TRC: Reflections on Truth and Reconciliation in South Africa*, ed. W. James and L. van der Vijver, 58–62. Cape Town: David Philip.

Mandela, Nelson. 2001. *Lang Pad na Vryheid*, translated by Antjie Krog. Florida Hills: Vivlia.

Mangcu, Xolela. 2008. *To the Brink: The State of Democracy in South Africa*. Pietermaritzburg: University of KwaZulu-Natal Press.

Marshall, P. David. 1997. *Celebrity and Power: Fame in Contemporary Culture*. Minneapolis: University of Minnesota Press.

Masondo, Sipho. 2008. 'Controversial Mangcu Presents New Book at NMMU and Challenges Intellectuals'. *The Herald*, 26 February: 4.

Masson, Madeleine. 1948. *Lady Anne Barnard: The Court and Colonial Service under George III and the Regency*. London: George Allen and Unwin.

Memela, Sandile. 2006. 'Black Brainpower'. *Mail & Guardian*, 5–11 May: 19.

Meyer, Stephan. 2002. 'The Only Truth Stands Skinned in Sound: Antjie Krog As Translator'. *Scrutiny2* 7 (2): 3–18.

Mills, Gwen M. 19–. *First Ladies of the Cape: 1652–1852*. Cape Town: Maskew Miller.

Mkandawire, Thandika (ed.). 2005. *African Intellectuals: Rethinking Politics, Language, Gender and Development*. Pretoria: UNISA Press.

Morris, Rosalind. 2006. 'On Watson, Krog and Plagiarism'. http://www.oulitnet. co.za/seminarroom/krog_morris.asp.

Nash, Kate. 2007 'Transnationalising the Public Sphere: Critique and Critical Possibilities'. *Theory, Culture and Society* 24 (4): 53–7.

Ndletyana, Mcebisi. 2008. *African Intellectuals in 19th and Early 20th Century South Africa*. Cape Town: HSRC Press.

Olivier, Fanie. 1981. 'Antjie Krog Neem Poëties Wraak'. *Die Burger*, 26 November: 21.

Olivier, Gerrit. 1998. 'The "Fierce Belonging" of Antjie Krog: Review of *Country of My Skull* by Antjie Krog, Random House, Johannesburg, 1998'. *African Studies* 57 (2): 221–8.

Osborne, Peter. 1996. 'Introduction: Philosophy and the Role of Intellectuals'. In *A Critical Sense: Interviews with Intellectuals*, ed. Peter Osborne, vii–xxvii. London: Routledge.

Pauw, Jacques. 1997. *Into the Heart of Darkness: The Story of Apartheid's Killers*. Johannesburg: Jonathan Ball.

———. 2007. *Dances with Devils: A Journalist's Search for Truth*. Cape Town: Struik.

Philp, Rowan. 2010. '"Rude" Word for Whites Sparks Feud'. *Sunday Times*, 18 July: 10.

Pienaar, Hans. 1989. 'Antjie, the Poet from Kroonstad, Takes Up an Angry Pen'. *Weekly Mail*, 14 December: 18.

Posel, Deborah. 2005. 'The Post-Apartheid Confessional: Faith in the Self'. Paper presented at the Reasons of Faith: Religion in Modern Public Life colloquium at the Wits Institute for Social and Economic Research, Johannesburg, 17–20 October.

———. 2006. 'The Post-Apartheid Confessional'. *The Wiser Review* 2: 8. Supplement to *Mail & Guardian*, 8–14 December.

———. 2008. 'The Political Life of Talk'. Lecture at the National Arts Festival Winter School, Grahamstown, 3 July.

Pretorius, Willem. 1981. '"Ek Skryf omdat Ek Woedend Is"'. *Rapport*, 1 November: 40.

Prinsloo, Koos. 1990. 'Krog Herverdeel Hertzogprys'. *Vrye Weekblad*, 29 June: 15.

Randeria, Shalini. 2007. 'De-Politicisation of Democracy and Judicialisation of Politics'. *Theory, Culture and Society* 24 (4): 38–44.

Ratele, Kopano, Nosisi Mpolweni-Zantsi and Antjie Krog. 2007. 'Ndabetha Lilitya: Assumption, Translation and Culture in the Testimony of One Person before the South African Truth and Reconciliation Commission'. *Tydskrif vir Letterkunde* 44 (2): 187–203.

Reese, Stephen D. 2007. 'The Framing Project: A Bridging Model for Media Research Revisited'. *Journal of Communication* 52 (1): 148–54.

Retief, Hanlie. 1998. 'Waarheidskommissie Het Haar Ingesluk en Alles Hou Heeldag Net Aan'. *Rapport*, 4 January: 15.

Ricœur, Paul. 1979. 'The Model of the Text: Meaningful Action Considered as Text'. In *Interpretive Science: A Reader*, ed. Paul Rabinow and William Sullivan, 73–101. Berkeley: University of California Press.

Robinson, A.M. Lewin (ed.). 1973. *The Letters of Lady Anne Barnard to Henry Dundas: From the Cape and Elsewhere 1793–1803 together with her Journal of a Tour into the Interior and Certain Other Letters*. Cape Town: A.A. Balkema.

Robinson, A.M. Lewin, Margaret Lenta and Dorothy Driver (eds). 1994. *The Cape Journals of Lady Anne Barnard 1797 to 1798*. Van Riebeeck Society Second Series No. 24. Cape Town: Van Riebeeck Society.

Rojek, Chris. 2001. *Celebrity*. London: Reaktion Books.

Said, Edward W. 1994. *Representations of the Intellectual: The 1993 Reith Lectures*. London: Vintage.

———. 2002. 'The Public Role of Writers and Intellectuals'. In *The Public Intellectual*, ed. Helen Small, 19–39. Oxford: Blackwell.

Sanders, Mark. 2000. 'Truth, Telling, Questioning: The Truth and Reconciliation Commission, Antjie Krog's *Country of My Skull*, and Literature after Apartheid'. *Modern Fiction Studies* 46 (1): 13–41.

———. 2002. *Complicities: The Intellectual and Apartheid*. Pietermaritzburg: University of Natal Press.

Scarry, Elaine. 1985. *The Body in Pain: The Making and Unmaking of the World*. Oxford: Oxford University Press.

Schaffer, Kay and Sidonie Smith. 2004a. 'Conjunctions: Life Narratives in the Field of Human Rights'. *Biography* 27 (1): 1–24.

———. 2004b. *Human Rights and Narrated Lives: The Ethics of Recognition*. New York: Palgrave.

———. 2006. 'Human Rights, Storytelling and the Position of the Beneficiary: Antjie Krog's *Country of My Skull*'. Paper presented at the Memory, Narrative and Forgiveness conference at the University of Cape Town, Cape Town, 22–26 November.

Scharf, Michael P. 1997. 'The Case for a Permanent International Truth Commission'. *Duke Journal of Comparative and International Law* 7: 375–410.

Scheffer, Ronel. 1989. 'Writers Start Journey to New SA'. *Democracy in Action* July: 1, 4.

———. 1990. 'Signs of Change . . . but Where Is the Action?' *Democracy in Action* October–November: 1, 10, 11.

Sitas, Ari and Sarah Mosoetsa. 2013. 'Networks for Scholarly Excellence'. *Mail & Guardian*, 13 June: 5.

Slabber, Coenie. 1987. 'Antjie Se Mense: Jou Enigste Heldedaad Wat Oorbly, Is vir Jou Gesin'. *Rapport*, 3 May: 15.

———. 1989. 'Groot Digters Verskil Nog oor Boikot'. *Rapport*, 20 November: 34.

———. 1990a. 'Deurbraak met Antjie Se "Anne"'. *Rapport*, 22 April: 6.

————. 1990b. 'Geesdrif vir F.W. van SA Skrywers'. *Rapport*, 4 February: 2.

Small, Helen (ed.). 2002. *The Public Intellectual*. Oxford: Blackwell.

Smuts, Dene. 1975. 'Die Dilemma van Antjie Krog'. *Beeld*, 30 August: 9.

Suttner, Raymond. 2005. 'What Happened to the White Left?' *Mail & Guardian*, 18 January. http://mg.co.za/article/2005-01-18-what-happened-to-the-white-left.

Thamm, Marianne. 2011. 'Please Could We Identify the New Parents of the Nation'. *Sunday Times*, 20 February: 5.

Thompson, John B. 1995. *The Media and Modernity: A Social Theory of the Media*. Cambridge: Polity Press.

Toffoli, Hilary Prendini. 2008. 'No Random Choice'. *Financial Mail*, 17 October: 88.

Townsley, Eleanor. 2006. 'The Public Intellectual Trope in the United States'. *The American Sociologist* 37 (3): 39–66.

Turner, Graeme. 2004. *Understanding Celebrity*. London: Sage.

Van Coller, H.P. and B.J. Odendaal. 2007. 'Antjie Krog's Role as Translator: A Case Study of Strategic Positioning in the Current South Africa Literary Poly-System'. *Current Writing* 19 (2): 94–122.

Van Dijck, José. 2004. 'Mediated Memories: Personal Cultural Memory as Object of Cultural Analysis'. *Continuum* 18 (2): 261–77.

Van Vuuren, Helize. 2011. 'Antjie Krog: Towards a Syncretic Identity'. In *SA Lit: Beyond 2000*, ed. Michael Chapman and Margaret Lenta, 224–42. Pietermaritzburg: University of KwaZulu-Natal Press.

Van Zyl, Anna. 1988. '"Apartheid tussen Skrywer en Leser"'. *Volksblad*, 6 October: 5.

Van Zyl Slabbert, Frederik. 2006. 'I Too Am an African: If Not, Why Not?' Lecture for the Platform for Public Deliberation, University of the Witwatersrand, Johannesburg, 22 November. http://www.public-conversations.org.za/_pdfs/slabbert_lecture.pdf.

Venter, Sahm (ed.). 2005. *Ahmed Kathrada's Notebook from Robben Island*. Johannesburg: Jacana.

Verstraete, Claire. 2006. 'Plagiarism: The Cultural Outbreak'. Master of Philosophy Minor Dissertation, University of Cape Town.

Viljoen, Louise. 1982. 'Digteres in Huis Vrou Voelbaarste Teenwoordig'. *Die Vaderland*, 29 April: 21.

————. 2006. 'Translation and Transformation: Antjie Krog's Translation of Indigenous South African Verse into Afrikaans'. *Scrutiny2* 11 (1): 32–45.

————. 2007. 'The Mother as Pre-Text: (Auto)biographical Writing in Antjie Krog's *A Change of Tongue*'. *Current Writing* 19 (2): 187–209.

Warner, Michael. 2002. *Publics and Counterpublics*. New York: Zone Books.

Watson, Stephen. 2005. 'Annals of Plagiarism: Antjie Krog and the Bleek and Lloyd Collection'. *New Contrast* 33 (2): 48–61.

Whitlock, Gillian. 2001. 'In the Second Person: Narrative Transactions in Stolen Generations Testimony'. *Biography* 24 (1): 197–214.

———. 2004. 'Consuming Passions: Reconciliation in Women's Intellectual Memoir'. *Tulsa Studies in Women's Literature* 23 (1): 13–28.

———. 2007. *Soft Weapons: Autobiography in Transit*. Chicago: University of Chicago Press.

Wilkins, W.H. (ed.). 1913. *South Africa a Century Ago: Letters Written from the Cape of Good Hope (1797–1801) by the Lady Anne Barnard*. Cape Town: Maskew Miller.

Index